THE LIBRARY OF POLITICAL ECONOMY

POLITICAL ECONOMY is the old name for economics. In the hands of the great classical economists, particularly Smith, Ricardo and Marx, economics was the study of the working and development of the economic system in which men and women lived. Its practitioners were driven by a desire to describe, to explain and to evaluate what they saw around them. No sharp distinction was drawn between economic analysis and economic policy nor between economic behaviour and its interaction with the technical, social and political framework.

The Library of Political Economy has been established to provide widely based explanations of economic behaviour in contemporary society.

In examining the way in which new patterns of social organization and behaviour influence the economic system and policies for combating problems associated with growth, inflation, poverty and the distribution of wealth, contributors stress the link between politics and economics and the importance of institutions in policy formulation.

This 'open-ended' approach to economics implies that there are few laws that can be held to with certainty and, by the same token, there is no generally established body of theory to be applied in all circumstances. Instead economics as presented in this library provides a way of ordering events which has constantly to be updated and modified as new situations develop. This, we believe, is its interest and its challenge.

Editorial Board

Lord Balogh, University of Oxford
Andrew Graham, University of Oxford
Keith Griffin, University of Oxford
Geoffrey Harcourt, University of Cambridge
Roger Opie, University of Oxford
Hugh Stretton, University of Adelaide
Lester Thurow, Massachusetts Institute of Technology

Volumes in the Library

Dangerous Currents: The State of Economics—Lester Thurow
The Political Economy of Nationalism—Dudley Seers
Women's Claims: A Study in Political Economy—Lisa Peattie and Martin Rein
Urban Inequalities under State Socialism—Ivan Szelenyi
Social Innovation and the Division of Labour—Jonathan Gershuny

The Political Economy of Nationalism

Dudley Seers

OXFORD UNIVERSITY PRESS
1983

Oxford University Press, Walton Street, Oxford OX2 6DP

London Glasgow New York Toronto
Delhi Bombay Calcutta Madras Karachi
Kuala Lumpur Singapore Hong Kong Tokyo
Nairobi Dar es Salaam Cape Town
Melbourne Auckland

and associated companies in
Beirut Berlin Ibadan Mexico City Nicosia

Oxford is a trade mark of Oxford University Press

Published in the United States
by Oxford University Press, New York

British Library Cataloguing in Publication Data
Seers, Dudley
The political economy of nationalism.—
(The library of political economy).
1. Nationalism—Economic aspects.
I. Title   II. Series.
320.5'4   HB74.N/
ISBN0-19-828456-X
ISBN 0-19-828473-X Pbk

Library of Congress Cataloging in Publication Data
Seers, Dudley.
The political economy of nationalism.
(Library of political economy)
Bibliography: p.
Includes index.
1. Economic development.   2. Nationalism—Economic
aspects.   I. Title.   II. Series.
HD82.S398   1983   338.9'24   83-8312
ISBN 0-19-828456-X (U.S.)
ISBN 0-19-828473-X (U.S.: pbk.)

Typeset by Hope Services, Abingdon,
Printed in Great Britain
at the University Press, Oxford

To members of my family

They have often, because of my professional work, been left by themselves, though I can console myself with the convenient but defensible reflection that this helped them to find their own identities, discover what careers suited them — and become 'self-reliant.'

Dudley Seers

Dudley Seers died in Washington on 21st March 1983 just after completing the manuscript of this book. It was typical of him that despite warnings of ill health he continued an extraordinarily active life of writing, teaching, travel and consulting. He was a distinguished development economist who, perhaps remarkably, succeeded in being both unorthodox and universally respected.

He began his academic career as an economic statistician and always retained an interest in problems of measurement and the use of statistics in policy making. At the same time he was acutely aware of the social and political constraints on policy and of the interaction of economic and political behaviour. His impact on development economics came in a stream of articles and official reports and in the many books that he edited. He was always rethinking, revising and discarding earlier ideas — his own as much as those of others. Yet throughout his work there was a persistent interest in the nation state, in the particular problems of small countries and in the power of government to improve the well being of the poor. Well before it was fashionable, he urged the necessity for widespread support for economic change, though for him popular participation was as much an end as a means. Yet while recognising, and indeed welcoming, the scope for public policy his scepticism of authority led him to list 'teasing bureaucrats' as one of his favourite pastimes.

The present volume on the Political Economy of Nationalism illustrates perfectly the purposes of the Library of Political Economy and is a fitting memorial to the life and work of Dudley Seers.

THE EDITORS

Preface

I started this book with the intention of reprinting a number of papers published in the past few years in a variety of professional journals, conference symposia, etc., that covered many different aspects of my approach to economic and social problems. I expected I would be able to integrate them with only some minor revisions and thus produce a true political economy, linking various fields of both theory and practice.

I was too optimistic. The first problem I faced was that the papers were of very different professional levels. I decided to attempt some uniformity of style, aiming to be understandable to what one might broadly call the sort of person who reads *The Economist*, without subjecting the professional economist to long explanations, or to over-simplifications he or she would find shocking. This was not intrinsically impossible: what I am talking about are ways of perceiving problems, which raises social and political issues, rather than highly technical ones. But it has meant a good deal of work attempting to find formulations that would be neither obscure nor professionally shaming, especially since much of what I originally wrote now appears to be both of these! In places I have added anecdotes — a form of evidence rightly despised by social scientists, but nevertheless sometimes the sharpest, if not the only, way of illustrating a point.

Stylistic revisions were only the beginning. I soon discovered that, although there were some common themes, these papers by no means added up to an integrated whole. There were many inconsistencies, repetitions, passages irrelevant to this purpose, and a number of gaps. Although I could use the original phrasing here and there, I had to do a great deal of revision, taking account of new material (and experiences), and write much additional text. (I list, however, in Appendix A, the basic papers from which each chapter was constructed; these contain further detail on many points and more complete references.) It was only in doing this that I really discovered, with something of a shock, what my political economy had become. (I write therefore I think!) The connecting thread in my work has been nationalism.

Apart from attempting a coherent response to the various dimensions of the current world crisis, appropriate for the closing years of this century, I have also tried to make each chapter 'a thing in itself' — an essay to which the reader can refer if he or she is studying a subject such as economic theory, or demography, or natural resources, or planning, or financial policy, or statistics, or the colonial system, or the European Community.

All this has taken much time. In the ordinary way, I would have found it virtually impossible to set aside whole weeks in which I would be sufficiently free from teaching, research, and administrative obligations, not to speak of casual callers, to make a start on this task. The Rockefeller Foundation generously accommodated me for a month at their Villa Serbelloni. This was crucial. There one benefits not only from luxurious accommodation, a quiet setting, and an efficient Italian staff, but also from the vicissitudes of the Italian post and telephone services, which largely isolate those on the shores of Lake Como from the outside world.

I must above all acknowledge the work of those who really made this book possible. First, my secretaries over the past decade, Barbara Taylor and Madeline Rowe, who coped with the innumerable and illegible, not to say mucky, earlier drafts and redrafts of this book (and indeed most of the original papers on which it is based); they have applied expertise and patience much greater than I deserve and have contributed immensely to this work. (Since I cannot read what is written by my own hand, I rely on them to show me what I think!) Annie Yannopoulos typed the ultimate version with similar care and efficiency. Sian Victory as copy-editor spotted many errors and ambiguities in a manuscript I had hoped was free of them.

Richard Stanton helped me through the final stages, not merely by working on the text, checking the references, and producing the bibliography, but also by making shrewd comments and constructive suggestions (as he has often done in our previous work together). He also prepared the Index. I owe a great deal, too, to many others at the Institute of Development Studies — administrators, librarians, and domestic staff. It is so easy to take for granted the infrastructure without which professional work would be almost impossible.

In addition, all the papers on which this book is based have been discussed here. Indeed, interactions at the Institute, which brings together Fellows, students, and visitors of various nationalities, ideologies, and disciplines, contribute to a continual ferment of ideas.

In a draft of this preface I started to list some of the IDS Fellows, past and present, to whom I am particularly indebted — not only for advice and comment but also for the tolerance they have shown to arguments of which they have profoundly disapproved. The selection was invidious. As soon as I had mentioned half a dozen, further names at once occurred to me, and when I had concluded these, how could I leave out certain others? (The Institute amounts to much more than a handful of star performers.) I eventually decided to mention only one, Richard Jolly. This I have to do: before joining forces at the Institute, we worked together on many enterprises — graduate seminars at Yale, a joint book on the Cuban Revolution, collaboration in Africa and at what was then the Overseas Development Ministry (ODM) — at IDS we continued to co-operate in a number of projects, particularly the ILO Employment Missions, and he succeeded me as the Institute's Director. The names of some of the other colleagues with whom I have worked most closely appear in the notes.

Recognizing the benefits of being at IDS is to acknowledge the financial support it receives from the Overseas Development *Administration* (ODA), as the ODM has (significantly) become, and also the insights into the British establishment I gained from working at the Ministry with Sir Andrew Cohen in the mid-1960s.

I suppose I owe most, however, not to desk work in Britain, or the books I have read, but to the jobs I have done overseas. The world is a great laboratory of social experiments, but to take advantage of this wealth of experience one has to work in a variety of countries: the information available in print is very partial and biased. If I had stayed in an academic post at home, I would now view the world very differently: I would analyse it with much less attention to the social aspects and the practical issues of policy and administration in different environments — thus more 'rigorously' and doubtless with more deference to the sacred cows of 'progressives', especially internationalists. The chapters that follow reflect above all what I learned from the 'missions' I led (for various bodies) to Ghana (1951), Zambia (1964), Colombia (1970), Sri Lanka (1971), and Nigeria (1979), which suggested to the governments concerned development strategies oriented to employment and 'basic needs', and the Commonwealth team I led to Uganda in 1978, to estimate the country's aid requirements after the fall of Idi Amin. Pulling together the contributions of team members, who were mostly economists, into a coherent whole, which links analysis to action, teaches one a great deal, not least the limitations — but also the possibilities — of economics.

Earlier, I had gained practical experience working in the office of the Prime Minister of New Zealand and then in the United Nations Secretariat, in UN Technical Assistance in the Eastern Caribbean (setting up a statistical office in Barbados), and in the Economic Commission for Latin America (ECLA) and its counterpart for Africa (ECA). I was especially fortunate to have worked in Chile, Cuba, and Portugal early in their radical periods. But I have also drawn heavily on the lessons of shorter periods of consultancy or research in Argentina, Brazil, Canada, Czechoslovakia, Fiji, Guyana, Indonesia, Ireland, Jamaica, Japan, Kenya, Kuwait, Malaysia, Malta, Mexico, Poland, Puerto Rica, Singapore, South Africa, Spain, Tanzania, Trinidad, Venezuela, and what is now Zimbabwe.

I list these countries not, I trust, in a boastful spirit, but because my knowledge of the world, which naturally shapes my ideas, is based on meetings and discussions and much travel in particular countries. Indeed, the point of the list is that it reveals where I did *not* work. (The world is inconveniently large to cover in one lifetime.) If I had undertaken research mainly in say, China, India, the United States, and the Soviet Union, my approach would without doubt be very different. I would, for example, be less aware of the special problems of small countries (especially *vis-a-vis* the great powers), and more conscious of the importance of regional differences within countries — and of the economic, political, and social costs of central bureaucracies.

My acknowledgements would be incomplete if I did not

mention those who provided the foundations for the way I have come to view the world's problems. My real introduction to the field of 'development' was working in 1957-61 under Raul Prebisch (in ECLA), and alongside Osvaldo Sunkel, as well as many other Latin American economists, who were evolving the 'structuralist' and 'dependency' approaches. A Visiting Professorship at Yale immediately after leaving ECLA enabled me to take stock of this experience and write a number of papers such as 'The Limitations of the Special Case' — about the dangers of naively transferring analytical models from the 'special case' of developed countries to the rest of the world.

However, I approached all of this with some basic questions I owed to my original mentors — whose influence I still feel, indeed — Joan Robinson (the supervisor at Cambridge who made the greatest impression on me) and Michael Kalecki (in whose section I worked at the United Nations). I also gained a great deal from collaborating with Thomas Balogh and Paul Streeten at Oxford in the first post-war decade (at what became the Institute of Economics and Statistics), and in many joint endeavours since, not least in helping to set up ODM and later the IDS itself.

My education also had another dimension. I learned about political realities through close contact with a number of very shrewd and far-sighted politicians — especially Nye Bevan, Barbara Castle, Dick Crossman, and Dom Mintoff (of Malta).

To acknowledge is not to implicate: many of those I have mentioned would, I am sure, be as horrified as some professional colleagues will be at my present 'hardline' approach on issues such as public finance and aid, not to speak of my emphasis on nationalism.

Finally, as I usually confess at the beginning of any lecture course, I was born more than sixty years ago, a white, English, Christian male: the consequently inevitable biases on almost every serious issue should be discounted accordingly. To have been brought up in the family of an executive of General Motors, educated at a preparatory school and Rugby, then at Cambridge, and to have served as an officer of the Royal Navy and in the civil service at home and abroad, is to be a lifetime captive of these institutions, even (perhaps especially) when one is reacting against the attitudes they attempt to instil. (I was president of a Marxist society at Cambridge.)

Age, however, is not a total liability. I feel fortunate in being old enough to remember the 1930s. This was a decade with which the 1980s is in many ways all too comparable, but they both show one great merit: the current decade, like its forerunner half a century earlier forces one to question all types of conventional ways of thinking.

Institute of Development Studies,
University of Sussex.
November 1982.

Contents

Abbreviations	xiv
Introduction	1
Annexe: A technical note on economic growth	18
A. NATIONALISM AND ECONOMICS	29
Synopsis	29
1. Marxism and other neo-classical models	31
2. Coming to terms with nationalism	46
B. THE CONSTRAINTS ON NATIONALISM	55
Synopsis	55
3. Economic and political realities	59
4. Demographic and social realities	67
5. Resources and technology	77
C. NATIONALIST DEVELOPMENT STRATEGIES	91
Synopsis	91
6. From development 'planning' to development strategy	98
7. Development staff work	111
8. Curbing financial irresponsibility	119
9. Statiscal needs	130
D. EXTENDED NATIONALISM	142
Synopsis	142
10. The colonial system and its successor	148
11. The development of Western Europe	162
12. Europe in a world of regional blocs	176
Notes	186
Appendix A: The papers from which each chapter derives	193
Appendix B: Statistical tables	195
Bibliography	198
Index	205

Abbreviations[1]

CAP	Common Agricultural Policy (EEC)
CEPAL	Comision Economica Para America Latina (Spanish form of ECLA)
CMEA	Council for Mutual Economic Assistance (among Communist countries)
DAC	Development Assistance Committee (of OECD)
ECA	Economic Commission for Africa
ECLA	Economic Commission for Latin America
ECU	European Currency Unit
EMS	European Monetary System
IDS	Institute of Development Studies
IFDA	International Foundation for Development Alternatives
JASPA	Jobs and Skills Programme for Africa (ILO)
JUCEPLAN	Junta Central de Planificacion (National planning office of Cuba)
MPS	Material Product System (Marxist)
NIC	Newly-Industrializing Country
ODA	Overseas Development Administration (Britain)
ODM	Overseas Development Ministry (Britain)[2]
ODEPLAN	Oficina de Planificacion Nacional (National planning office of Chile)
OEEC	Organization for European Economic Cooperation[3]
SASOL	South African Coal, Oil, and Gas Corporation
SELA	Sistema Economico Latino Americano
SNA	System of National Accounts (UN)
TNC	Trans-national corporation

1. Excluding the UN and various agencies (FAO, ILO, etc.) and other bodies too well-known internationally to be worth listing.
2. Precursor of ODA
3. Precursor of OECD

Introduction

WE are entering a period in which resource limits can no longer be ignored, nor can the interests of different sections of the world be assumed compatible: to solve one country's problems may well be to aggravate those of another. So the income of anyone, even in the industrial countries, now depends in large measure on the bargaining power of his or her government: the world is not any more such a benign place. A major crisis is aggravating international tensions — or rather, a set of fundamental crises in every part of the world, 'developed' and 'developing' and for that matter 'centrally planned'. (These flattering terms were created to meet diplomatic requirements, but they are inescapable: I shall henceforth use them without inverted commas, to keep the layout cleaner, and — sometimes — without much irony.)

The economic dimensions are most obvious. Almost everywhere, unemployment and/or underemployment (in some sense) have become very severe. (See Table 1[1] for unemployment in the industrial heartland of the world economy, where the growth of industrial output has slowed to virtually zero (Table 2): yet inflation persists (Seers, 1981b).)

It is true that some economic recovery is inevitable in the 1980s, if only because governments devoted to deflationary policy in the United States and Western Europe will in due course be compelled to change their ways. But the upsurge may well prove neither big enough to reduce unemployment substantially, nor lasting. The crisis is not just a cyclical downswing nor even (in my view) the slack phase in a hypothetical Kondratieff cycle. I shall depict it as the culmination of a period of increasing strains on the world's productive structures, natural resources, and political systems. Thus a swift rise in world output would soon reveal shortages in oil, various minerals, and food, and increased international tension, especially since not all economies would benefit equally. The consequences would be renewed inflation and another set of foreign exchange crises. There is a ceiling (even if one that is slightly upward sloping) on world economic activity, and each government — and social group — is being forced to seek its own salvation as best it can. Unpalatable though it may be to ideologists, a universal solution to social problems has now become obviously impossible.

We are thus in quite a new historical era. Although the data on economic growth are extremely poor (see the note at the end of this chapter), it was not unreasonable to believe up to the end of the 1960s, that this was, and would remain, rapid enough for all countries to achieve ultimately, one after another, high material standards and thus democratic systems.

It is now clear that the present international system has been functioning very badly: there were serious flaws, political as well as economic, even in the apparently widespread and fast economic progress of the post-war period. Let me very briefly review these. Take the 'newly-industrializing countries' (or NICs), where the economic performance has been dominated by soaring exports of manufactures — the 'four little tigers' of East Asia (Hong Kong, Singapore, South Korea, and Taiwan) plus some larger ones such as Argentina, Brazil, Mexico, Philippines, and Turkey (Balassa, 1981). Apart from the social costs, to which I shall return, there were economic drawbacks to this route. Their fast growth could no longer be sustained in the decade of the 1970s by increased exports alone, though these continued to rise. Most of their governments borrowed heavily from commercial banks abroad, which (unwisely) saw their policies as 'sound' because of their export performance, their suppression of trade unions, and their commitment to economic liberalism. Many now have had to keep borrowing more even to service these debts, and the total indebtedness of six of them was of the order of $200 billion at the end of 1981 (Table 3). This path cannot be followed indefinitely, especially now that the growth of their exports has proved vulnerable to the recession in the industrial countries.

The petroleum-exporting economies have also grown rapidly. In these countries, however, the growth of the economy as a whole is particularly meaningless as a measure of progress. From any viewpoint, their central task is to use the oil revenues to transform the economic and social structure before the real value of oil exports starts an inexorable decline. While this is not imminent in the main producers of the Middle East, rising domestic oil consumption in the bigger ones elsewhere is starting to eat into their exports, especially in Nigeria, and their rates of economic growth could not be sustained once the world economy weakened. Some had fallen heavily in debt, even by the end of 1981, i.e. while the price of oil was still at record heights, to a total of some $100 billion.Yet none of them, with the partial exception of Venezuela, have had much success in diversification: indeed, in every single case, their imports of food have become massive and chronic.

Industrialization policies have led many other countries to neglect investment in the agricultural sector and, while farmers have had to buy expensive locally-produced substitutes for imported manufactures, the prices of their domestic sales have often been held down. Most countries in the Third World, including many traditional cereal exporters, such as Chile, have become importers, mainly from the United States. A country that cannot meet its own requirements of basic foods is exceptionally vulnerable to a world slump.

Dependence on imports of technology has also greatly increased in almost all countries. The national research base is normally meagre, and weakly linked to the main productive sectors. The clear inappropriateness of many (not all) imported technologies to national requirements raises the question why architects, engineers, working in government or in national firms, so often adopt them. And why are patterns of consumption that are capital-intensive, fuel-intensive, and thus import-intensive, copied so widely?

These questions point to the difficulties raised for most countries by the nature of the world economy. Part of the explanation lies in the rapidly growing influence of the TNCs. They have so much expertise (in advertizing, legal, and tax departments, as well as those containing scientists and engineers), that they can manipulate market forces, especially through patterns of consumption. They can also influence economic decision-makers in governments. Their operations are difficult to tax, let alone control. Relying heavily on *their* capital and technology for economic growth, therefore, means in fact allowing them to shape its pattern, with far-reaching social and political consequences.

These are only some of the factors that are omitted by the conventional economist, though inseparably connected to the 'economic'. Various foreign cultural influences, to be discussed later, also shape the pattern of even material progress, both directly through emulation of production techniques and consumption styles, and, perhaps more importantly, via the mind of the policy-maker — who thus ceases to be an autonomous agent, as he has generally been considered in the past.

This provides an important clue to why the historical models of the social and political development of the 'developed' countries could not be copied abroad as had been widely hoped. During embryonic stages in *their* evolution, these countries had not been exposed to pervasive communication media, disseminating attractive foreign lifestyles, techniques, and theories — in particular a faith in foreign technology in every field. Here lies also the ultimate explanation of the fast-growing imports of many countries, and thus of their indebtedness and their inability to withstand the world recession.

It also helps explain the apparent tendency — in contrast to the history of the industrial countries at comparable stages — for social inequality to increase in the Third World. There is not much usable detail on the incomes of different social classes, races, or regions, and hardly any information at all on the ownership of land or housing. But it is obvious that the distribution of each of these has generally become even more concentrated in the past three decades — especially if one allows for the great spread of administrative corruption, which could not have been as prevalent in the past as it is now. 'Modern' lifestyles — symbolized by cars and colour TV — are not by any means enjoyed by everyone in the industrial countries but elsewhere they can only be afforded by very few, who use every available political and economic means to continue enjoying them. For this reason too, estimates of economic growth, which add together the income of various categories, are of little significance, if not actually misleading — a point elaborated further in the Annexe that follows.

Equality is not just a matter of income, or wealth: these are merely two dimensions of the distribution of economic power. Government bureaucrats in all countries control access to government services, recruitment to official posts, allocation of contracts, etc., which not merely often provide them with much of their income wherever there are possibilities of bribes, but also a degree of domination over the lives of fellow citizens and the benefits of patronage. Officials at lower levels enjoy corresponding though lesser advantages. There is also a parallel power structure in private-sector bureaucracies — those high in the staffs of big corporations often indeed enjoy even greater possibilities of personal enrichment and influence.

Precisely in the fast-growing countries, the concentration of economic power, including income, seems to have increased most rapidly, especially in the NICs (with the possible exceptions of South Korea and Taiwan, where the danger of war must account for the degree of egalitarianism). In the oil-exporting countries, data on income are particularly unreliable because of the vast 'kickbacks' on contracts. But it is a matter of plain observation that the soaring opulence and power of the elite are matched by widespread poverty and helplessness, especially among migrant labourers. In Nigeria, despite having changed from being a big exporter of foods such as groundnuts, to a big importer, nutritional levels appear to be among the lowest in the world,[2] and have almost certainly fallen since 1970, when the oil boom really got under way. Even in Iraq and Saudi Arabia, average nutritional levels are below international norms and death rates relatively very high, despite their published per capita incomes.[3]

It is true that, in general, there has been a fall in death rates since the war, reflected in rising life expectancy, especially in countries which are really poor. This seems to be primarily due not so much to higher real incomes among those in poverty as to the reduction or elimination of mass killers such as smallpox and yellow fever, and to the spread of public health services including vaccination and accessible health care. (Bangladesh, Ghana, Honduras, Mozambique, and Tanzania are among the countries that showed declining mortality in the 1970s, but also falling average food consumption.) Moreover, in many countries, mortality seems recently, from provisional data, to have ceased falling significantly or even started rising.

In any case, there are virtually no statistics anywhere on most of the aspects of life that really matter — the average distance people have to carry water and food; the numbers without shoes; the extent of overcrowding, the prevalence of violence; how many are unable to multiply one number by another, or summarize their own country's history. In many of these respects, progress seems to have been limited or zero, even negative.

This lack of information on poverty is — like the meagre data on distribution mentioned earlier — scarcely surprising. Those who hold power rarely have much interest in such matters, still less in attention being drawn to them. It is preferable to shelter behind the 'growth rates' that are commended in the reports of international agencies. Of course, various 'social indicators' are available, but mostly statistics of state services such as numbers of hospital beds, or school places: these are not measures of actual health or knowledge but of particular 'inputs' which are far from the only influences on people's bodies or their minds. Such data are also difficult to interpret: many such facilities are unavailable to those (e.g. in rural areas) who really need them.

Naturally, there are no official data anywhere on the numbers tortured and killed by the police, or how many are in prison for political reasons or because of personal vendettas. As a broad generalization, indeed, many of the more important social factors are inherently unquantifiable: how safe it is to criticize the government publicly, or the chance of an objective trial, or how corruption affects policy decisions. But to say that these factors cannot be quantified — and are embarrassing subjects for those in power, and thus for the staff in international agencies — does not mean that they are unimportant or can be overlooked by any honest person doing research on a country's development.

In these last and most important aspects, we can, however, detect a clear deterioration in the world. This is not just a matter of common observation. Whereas dictatorships were rare in the mid-1960s, they are now very common. By 1980 there were over fifty governments in the Third World dominated by the military (Table 4), of which the great majority were described as 'repressive' in the source (i.e. using torture, summary execution, etc.) — and these figures do not include the many *civilian* regimes (Egypt, Ghana, Iran, Kenya, etc., etc., and most of the Gulf States) which are hardly democratic on any definition, or those dominated by Communist military regimes (Afghanistan), or those dominated by the military and receiving Soviet assistance but less clear political affiliation (Algeria, Chad, etc.). One might quibble over whether or not one or two particular governments are correctly described in the source as 'military-dominated' (or 'repressive'), but the general picture is unmistakable: the characteristic government in the Third World is no longer social democratic but authoritarian.

The explanation seems to be, in brief, that the bureaucrats, traders, and white-collar (as well as some blue-collar) employees in the modern sector, public and private, have become increasingly determined that they and their children shall continue to enjoy the modern lifestyle, largely imported, whatever the brutality and whatever the inflows of aid and private capital needed to ensure this, (see Table 4 again).

Precisely the NICs most require not merely heavy loans but a repressive regime: wages have to be kept down so as to compete in international markets. Mexico is a partial, and perhaps not permanent, exception (even here 'disappearances' have not been unknown), and there has been some relaxation in recent years in Brazil. But many governments in this group (Argentina, Chile, El Salvador, Guatemala, Philippines, Turkey) have been notoriously cruel in silencing and disposing of opponents by the thousand. (I return to the question of political oppression in Chapter 10.)

These are not the only costs of a dictatorship: it also produces inflexibility. Not having to respond to social discontent in their own societies, nor even knowing its scale — often because their subordinates fear to tell them — political leaders continue along set paths until the day of economic and political catastrophe, viz. the Shah, the Somoza family, Emperor Haile Selassie, President Diem, etc. Attempts to dislodge these leaders were brutally suppressed, with foreign help, though in the end unavailingly.

On the other hand, not even the most fervent Leftist could claim today that the international socialist system has performed much better. Data are even scarcer on the economic privileges of bureaucrats (including free housing and cars, and access to special stores and restaurants). But there is little doubt that they have become considerable, as have bribes and exchanges of favours (e.g. school places or trips abroad). Although attention to basic social services is greater than in most

of the Third World, human rights have been at least as persist-
ently flouted. Criticism can so easily be equated with 'treason
to the revolution'. The Soviet government stands ready to help
suppress opposition wherever it arises. There are occasional
palace coups bringing another Communist clique to power,
but it is unclear how the ruling élites of the Soviet Union,
Eastern Europe, Cuba, China, Vietnam, Mozambique, Ethiopia, etc. can ever be forced to relax their tight grip. The case
of Poland speaks libraries. Indeed in most of them, after some
relaxation in the 1970s, repression seems to be growing more
severe.

Here, again, the cost of political rigidity is considerable.
Economic strains are increasing. Because of the lack of public
debate on alternative development strategies, socialist dictatorships can also continue on disastrous paths. They have been
experiencing, in fact, a very similar combination of chronically
low levels of living for most people, and rising debt (to a total
of about $60 billion at the end of 1981). Even the Soviet
Union has become a chronic importer of wheat, though the
government continues to starve agriculture of capital — and
above all first-class management, technical skills, and incentives.

Thus, for different reasons in different systems, the pattern
of growth has proved economically and socially damaging.
The successful action of OPEC governments at the end of
1973 in raising the price of oil more than threefold taught
the rest of us various lessons. It exposed the vulnerability of
these patterns since they required high energy inputs per unit
of output. (World oil consumption had doubled in the 1950s,
and again in the 1960s.) It reminded us of the finite limits to
reserves of fossil fuels, and it cast a considerable question
mark over a widespread, if tacit assumption that the mass of
the world population would be able to reach a 'modern' standard of living within a few generations: to draw up projections
for this consistent with conceivable levels of energy output is
impossible.[4]

Some of the limitations of these growth patterns had already been stressed by 'environmentalists', notably in Club of
Rome documents, but in a rather sensational way, so that few
professional economists felt the need to take such warnings
seriously. Yet there *has* apparently been a major qualitative

change in the prospects for both international systems, and this has everywhere raised doubts about policies which imply closer integration.

Capitalist and Socialist orthodoxies alike have clearly failed to explain what is happening to us let alone offer a credible solution. It is time to strike a new note. I do not pretend to have fully worked out a 'third way' that would fill this enormous gap. Certainly, I do not espouse any of the varieties of internationalism nor even an environmentalist 'alternative development'. I would argue, in fact, that while most of the ideologies on sale provide certain insights of value, they are all originally based on *ex ante* theory, rather than built up from studies of reality in a variety of countries. Such over-simplifications are dangerous in the current world crisis.

The opening section of this book focuses on the consequent need to let go of much of this theoretical luggage we have been carrying round with us. To do so, we must, as in psycho-analysis, go back to its origins, indeed birth. Then we cannot avoid noticing that Marxism and the economics schools of capitalist countries are all derived from classical political economy, which emerged in Europe nearly two centuries ago. This fitted the European scene at that time. Moreover, what is known as 'neo-classical' economics has continued to be very useful for governments of countries that are clear techno-logical leaders, such as Britain was in the century from 1815 to 1914 (and the US in 1945 to 1970).

Marxism is similarly useful for government leaders in Com-munist countries. Both are in fact close relatives tracing their descent from the same European nineteenth-century ancestors; and they share important common flaws discussed in the first chapter. One is the assumption of progress (towards some ill-defined Utopia), which encourages optimism that continues to mislead, even though it has frequently been dashed.

Another is that they both fail to take due account of non-material motives, especially nationalism — the urge to promote the presumed interests of a group with cultural coherence, probably showing at least a degree of linguistic and ethnic homogeneity, and usually inhabiting a political unit, or nation-state (though sometimes applied to a group of the same kind submerged within one or more nation-states).

Until the 1960s, I too took little account of nationalism. As an economist, I naturally concentrated on material motives: people worked to earn money, and the level of our income determined how we spent it. Moreover, like many of those educated in the Anglo-Saxon cultural tradition, I saw nationalism as fundamentally irrational. Fortunately, with the spread of international contacts, of media such as newspapers and television, and of education there was a growing realization of 'inter-dependence', which would be complete when all foreigners sensibly learned some English.

Nationalism was not merely of little and declining, practical consequence: it was obviously evil. It had lain at the root of war. German chauvinism, in particular, had contributed to two terrible world wars. Moreover, nationalist sentiment was still a menace in the second half of the twentieth century, getting in the way of the creation of a just, peaceful, and prosperous world society, which modern technology had put within our reach — if only population growth could be controlled.

Particularly silly and dangerous were the narrower nationalists who rebelled, often violently, against the state to which they belonged — the Basques, Welsh, Kurds, Matabele, Amerindians, French Canadians, to name a few out of scores of possible examples. They might have economic grievances, but these could be put right by some redistribution of income.

As I worked in different parts of the world, I came — at first reluctantly — to see that nationalism is neither trivial nor in decay. One can easily be deceived by the apparent internationalism of the élites in Africa, Asia, and Latin America and their imported lifestyles that have been mentioned above: if you visit the home of a senior Nigerian official, or a Mexican general, or a Malay businessman (or a Chinese merchant in Kuala Lumpur), you could well be a guest of his counterpart in a modern industrial society — the same type of apartment, the same furniture (including a big colour TV set), the same whisky (even in a Muslim country), perhaps even similar food and clothes. The conversation turns on US presidential politics, or the international debt problem, or the relative merits of Oxford, Harvard, and the Sorbonne.

But these are only small minorities, in some countries tiny. Especially in Africa and Asia, the living conditions of the vast majority of the population are very different indeed. To start with, not even piped fresh water, nor much space. Their preoccupations are not the topics featured in TIME magazine, but how to keep alive. In as far as modern culture impinges on their consciousness, it is as something quite alien, which they may well see not as their own future lifestyle but, on the contrary, quite out of reach, and indeed the main obstacle to their more modest ambition — to escape exploitation and suppression.

Moreover, the allegiance to foreign ways of life and thought of even those apparently assimilated may turn out to be a good deal less firm than it appears to be. A politician in Africa, say, may have been educated at Chicago, employed by a TNC or even a CIA front organization; he may be a devotee of video tapes of 'Dallas' — or *mutatis mutandis* for someone with Communist affiliations — and still respond in a degree, privately, to the call of the hearth. It is a matter of common observation that a parvenu alienated from his own culture may nevertheless not be permanently assimilated into a foreign one: however correct his vocabulary, accent, and clothes, he remains in some degree an 'outsider', especially if he is not white. And I suspect that, deep down, he never forgets this. The present international system is hardly less wounding to his self-esteem than the colonial order.

In any case, the children of the élite are often growing up nowadays with renewed respect for traditional values. This is especially true of Iran and the Arabian peninsula: young women are insisting on separate university classes, and (especially) swimming pools. In Asia there is a renewal of interest in national history and literature. When I lecture or take part in professional discussions in Latin America, I am — in contrast to even one decade ago — expected to do so in Spanish, as best I can. Everywhere there is now widespread, if covert, hatred of the whites.

All this has made me reflect on the strength of nationalism. One does not have to look further than Europe for evidence, especially the trench warfare that persisted on the Western Front for more than a thousand days, from 1915 to 1918, perhaps the most brutal of all the brutal episodes in recent European history. There are now many examples showing that whole populations (*especially* exploited proletariats) can be induced to endure for years the deaths, disablement, and hardship of war by appeals to the national interest.

But if nationalism is so powerful, there is not much point in classifying ideologies or people as merely 'Leftist' or 'Rightist': in Chapter 2 I argue that the nationalist-internationalist dimension increasingly cuts across the traditional political axis that runs from Left to Right.

I will venture further and argue a much more controversial line. Nationalism is not only increasingly important as a factor in world politics: this also seems probably, on balance, a healthy trend. That is in part a gut reaction — I am deeply suspicious of 'modernization', with its drab uniformity which obliterates the rich national and local cultures and thus ultimately threatens our very identities, because these are rooted in them. If the whole world in a century's time is going to be like Westchester County, I am glad I am not going to be there (though I could understand an Indian coolie settling for that).

To internationalists who claim that the world is becoming increasingly 'interdependent', and welcome the idea, I would reply that this interdependence is highly asymmetrical, involving those overseas in accepting not merely the cultural values that the superpowers press on them, but also the arms and other products, and associated political programmes.

Nationalism is, of course, inconvenient for the superpowers, as it once was for Britain. Their ideologists treat it as anathema and their governments try to suppress it — at least in *other* countries. Their leaders, Soviet or United States, have developed the capacity — the experience and the propaganda media — to manipulate those in other countries. Nationalism is the only obstacle to this. Consequently, internationalism is not only naive but also often hypocritical, merely a vehicle for propaganda that suits one of the superpowers.

However, this does not by any means imply that any government, especially of a small country that is not a leader technologically, can now choose to reach out blindly for true independence. The second section of this book argues, on the basis of short case studies, and a proposed new classification of countries, that what a government can do depends very much on the nation's particular characteristics, not only its class structure and its history and culture, but also the size and composition of its population, its resources, its location, etc. A government in Jamaica or Cuba, say, has less room to manoeuvre than one in West or East Germany, which in turn has less than that of the United States or Soviet administrations, which themselves are increasingly constrained by the expectations their own doctrines arouse.

But all this does not rule out, even in a small country, close to a superpower, all economic and social improvements. There is always some room to manoeuvre, if only because of big-power rivalries; how successfully this is exploited evidently depends on the motivation, intelligence, judgement, and skills of individual political leaders, additional factors rather overlooked in the models of social scientists. It also depends on this leadership being willing to welcome suggestions, even criticisms, so that unworkable policies are abandoned before they bring disaster − a rare quality among politicians, perhaps especially nationalists.

If a government is to use what room there is to manoeuvre, however, it will almost certainly need to replace its current administrative machinery with something more appropriate for the crises of the 1980s. The implications are discussed in the third section. National 'plans' have typically been purely economic and covered too few years for any real change to occur, especially a significantly greater degree of economic and political independence. Indeed, they have mostly been little more than public relations exercises.

When I speak of planning I am opening up issues normally suppressed − issues of structural change needing much longer-term national strategies, less quantifiable and more qualitative.

The content of possible strategies will, of course, differ greatly from country to country. Still, a certain checklist is likely to be relevant everywhere, − and I do not exclude developed countries − e.g. food and energy policies, and probably increased equality, if not for ethical reasons then to create a better basis for national unity in the face of outside pressures − the same line of thought that led in Germany to 'Bismarckian socialism'. (Then, incidentally, national income aggregates would not have such limited meaning or operational utility.) But the list would feature demographic and military components as well, mentioned scarcely, if at all, in most 'development plans'. Policies in such areas can only be derived from an analysis of national need, not from internationalist premisses about a 'world community' which does not in fact exist.

This shift in the work programme of a planning office implies a big extension in its functions — from manipulating 'projections' to acting as an economic general staff, analogous in some respects, especially in its position in the administration, to a military general staff. Indeed the two staffs would need to co-operate, because the military strategies, including the sources from which arms are to be obtained, would have to be consistent in scale and pattern with the external implications of the economic.

The firm financial administration needed to back any development strategy especially a radical one has usually been conspicuously and disastrously absent under 'progressive' administrations, as the fate of the Allende administration in Chile, discussed below, tragically demonstrated. (Not the least cost of monetarism is that it has almost totally discredited financial policy as such.) This is all the more necessary now that the world economic boom has petered out.

Finally, although such strategies will be in part qualitative, they need appropriate statistics. This means downgrading the importance of national income aggregates based on Keynesian measures, such as are urged on governments by international agencies. These statistics do not bring out the role of foreign capital or illustrate distributional patterns, especially in geographical or ethnic planes.

In the fourth section, I apply this politico-economic approach, derived from working in other parts of the world, to Europe, in particular Britain; that must be the main concern of a British economist, including one working in the 'development' field — unless he is willing to accept the oft-merited charge of paternalism.

No longer being in the technological vanguard, our first step should be to let go of many international commitments. It is true that the present, or neo-colonial, system has been beneficial to us, almost as beneficial as its forerunner. The word 'neo-colonial' is not used provocatively, it is the only appropriate one: today's system like the colonial one, provides extensive markets for manufacturers and also sources of the primary products our market needs, partly produced with 'our' capital, as well as fields for investing this and spreading our cultural influence (including books on economic policy!). This last has been of fundamental importance, not merely in creating markets but also in shaping the attitudes of overseas political leaders. However, just as the colonial system was undermined by nationalism in its periphery, this is now happening to the system that took its place, reinforced by the main economic expression of nationalism, industrialization – to which we in the developed countries are contributing!

In the end, British governments responded in quite a sophisticated way to the inevitable termination of the colonial system. British history books often imply that this was due to the goodness of our hearts. But this is misleading the young: to draw the right conclusions for today's problems, we need to appreciate that we relaxed our grip reluctantly: the British establishment gradually realized, over several decades, the vulnerability of the system and the cost of trying to maintain it (we owe much to Mahatma Gandhi and the Congress Party of India). We were also fortunate that the British Colonial Empire was so large that to hold on to it would have been obviously no longer within the capacity of a country weakened by two major wars, especially in view of the opportunity these had given to nationalist movements (in Asia above all).

But the same establishment did not seem to realize that there was another equally inescapable consequence of the same economic weakness: Britain would not be able to afford to play a full part in a liberal world economy (with institutions such as GATT and the IMF). Indeed they have still not taken this point.

Moreover, although it was understandable of the post-war Labour government to carry out an enormous expansion of welfare services *at the same time* as conceding independence to the colonies *and* opening up the economy to foreign competition, this combination was an historic error only comparable, in this century, in the damage that was wrought, to the analogous attempt to return to the gold standard after the First World War or the recent abolition of exchange control and consequent necessity for a highly doctrinaire monetarist policy. (The common element in all these colossal misjudgements has been to assume that our technological leadership was still adequate to allow us such ideological luxuries.)

We cannot afford many more blunders on this scale. To avoid them, the first step is to realize that it is time to give up the neo-colonial system in its turn, and in due time. The breakup of this system is becoming increasingly in the interests not merely of the people living under the military dictatorships of the Third World, but also of most of those in Western Europe. The programme of holding on to it (under the guise of promoting 'interdependence') imposes on us the obligation to accept an increasing flood of manufactures from other industrial powers (especially Japan) and the NICs. It involves, in fact, chronic mass unemployment, just as the inter-war attempt to hold on to the colonial system did. It also requires growing exports of capital (corporate investment, bank loans, and aid programmes), and continual political intervention, potentially military action as well. This not merely requires us to divert resources from productive investment to arms; it makes us more dependent on the United States and thus compelled to accept the increasingly onerous terms they impose on their junior partners, reflecting their basically different interests.

This line of argument takes me, of course, to a position directly contradictory to that of well-meaning internationalists such as Willi Brandt who advocate, in effect, according to my analysis, propping up with 'massive' injections of aid and trade concessions a system that is becoming not merely increasingly inhumane but unviable. Their programme is inherited from the liberals of the colonial era, and just as paternalistic, a charge that could be levelled even more appropriately against those who, like the Swedish aid agency, concentrate their help on governments they approve of.

No single West European economy is so large and self-sufficient, however, that its government can afford just to opt out of the Western international system, any more than any in Eastern Europe could, for the present at least, leave the Soviet bloc: the retaliation would be too formidable. In particular, we in Britain cannot afford a programme that would involve strict controls on capitalists, domestic or foreign, especially if social reforms were also attempted simultaneously, and trade unions permitted substantial wage increases. (British governments just do not have any longer *that* much room to manoeuvre: the Labour Party programme assumes we can revive the privileges of a major colonial power.)

A feasible alternative, however, is to hand an extended

nationalism, i.e. a more self-sufficient European Community. To create this would respond to the many voices in the Third World that now speak of 'self-reliance' and 'delinking', i.e. of finally letting go of the apron strings of what used to be called the mother countries. If it were adequately strengthened, the Community would be capable of restricting imports and monitoring US and Japanese investments — in some cases preventing the entry of their capital, and the exit of ours. Only within this framework would substantial economic recovery be possible.

Then, social reforms would not merely be feasible but essential for the Community's international influence, if not survival, especially now that poorer Mediterranean countries are joining. Indeed what is needed in Europe is the sort of development strategy, with demographic and military elements, mentioned earlier.

This section of the book closes by surmising that the logical successor to the neo-colonial system is not merely a stronger European Community but a world of partially self-sufficient regional blocs. These would enjoy the advantages — economic, political, and military — of size, without waiting for population growth. There are questions about the political reality of blocs of this kind, capable of formulating and expressing their own policies, and achieving greater internal integration. This depends ultimately on their cultural foundations (a consideration excluded from materialist philosophies): even in the case of the Community, nobody can be sure that the feeling of being 'European' will overcome a narrower nationalism (over fishing rights, etc.). But it is being strengthened rapidly by economic and political threats from other continents.

If and when nationalism is extended in this way, and a world of regional blocs replaces the neo-colonial system, the governments of the superpowers will feel less compulsion to meddle (whether by financial aid, diplomatic pressure, or military force) in the affairs of other countries, and also be less able to do so: world peace will be more secure.

Undoubtedly in pre-nuclear days there was much truth in the central charge against nationalism, that it caused war, at least in the sense that any government which expected to benefit from a war could whip up support by pointing to supposed national advantage. Now, however, the situation is fundamentally different. The two superpowers cover, together with their allies, almost the whole world, and are between them capable of destroying all human life. Yet the frontiers between the two sides are precarious, and any development that threatened the government of one superpower with humiliation would tempt it to bluff its way out by issuing an ultimatum: should a major war ensue, the countries linked to a superpower would be helpless victims, whereas those whose governments stood apart from both would stand some chance of survival.

But there is a much more telling argument for resisting internationalism (i.e. superpower domination). If a substantial group of governments could detach themselves and form an additional centre of politico-economic strength, they could help prevent such dangerous situations arising at all. The only group that could become strong enough to do all this, in the next few decades, is the European Community, especially if it includes East European governments too in due course. It would also have the motive to play this crucial role. I shall argue that a strong European Community would not merely show less ideological rigidity: it would have a greater interest than the United States government in contributing politically and economically, but also intellectually, to breaking the deadlock in which each of the great powers piles up these weapons of unspeakable horror, and achieving nuclear disarmament.

A full-scale nuclear war would be so colossal an evil that we can really in the end only allow ourselves a single value judgement: developing an independent force for peace should override for the forseeable future any consideration of international equity where these conflict, as they may well do, though the programme of 'delinking' Europe would, I suggest, also create the conditions for the easing of oppression and poverty elsewhere.

Annexe: A technical note on economic growth

In this introduction I have queried the relevance of the *rate* of economic growth and said that the important question is its *pattern*. I want to go into this further than was appropriate there: it is central to much of my argument. (I will take up other aspects of statistics in Chapter 9.)

The main point is that the national income adds together different types of output, or, from another point of view, the incomes of people from different ethnic groups, classes, regions, etc., so that one does not know how to interpret changes in it. Increases in the national income of South Africa may entirely benefit whites (or, much less plausibly, blacks). Where aggregates are treated as yardsticks for welfare (e.g. in setting a target growth rate in a development plan), it is tacitly assumed that a £ of consumption is equally significant whether it benefits town or country, the majority race or a minority, the modern sector or the traditional, rich or poor. This is an assumption that is not widely shared, and it is incompatible with a development strategy designed to unify a country politically and integrate it economically.

I will not dwell here on the use of prices which reflect highly concentrated distributions of income and severe market imperfections, especially in developing countries; or the reliance on actual expenditures on government services, especially the armed forces, as an indication of their value; or the failure to make deductions either for social costs, such as pollution, or for the destruction of assets by war or disaster, or even for the depletion of forests, soil, and non-renewable resources such as oil and metal ores. These would be devastating defects if one were using economic growth as a measure of national welfare.

But it is really useless for this, anyway. For one thing it is not an objective measure. As Simon Kuznets (1941) has written,

For those not intimately acquainted with this type of work it is difficult to realise the degree to which estimates of national income have been and must be affected by implicit or explicit value judgments. . . . The apparent relative unanimity produced by empirical works on national income is due largely to the estimators' unconscious acceptance of one social philosophy and their natural reluctance to face such fundamental issues as would reveal that estimates are conditioned by controversial criteria.

The arbitrary nature of the conventional measure of growth becomes obvious if we remind ourselves that there is another one, the 'material product' used in Communist countries. This reflects a somewhat different view of socio-economic reality, Marxism, which lays down that only goods embody 'value', out of which other activities are financed. Strictly, the output of those services ancillary to goods production, such as rail freight, is also considered 'productive'. This leads to quasi-theological distinctions between, for example, making a film, which is 'productive', and putting on a play, which is not. (Unless someone happens to be recording it on tape.) Kaser (1961:44) argued, following Studenski, that Marx had been misinterpreted and really meant 'capitalistic', rather than 'material', by 'productive'; after all, what he was concerned with was the social generation of a 'surplus', wherever it arose, reflecting the approach of Adam Smith, who wanted an analytical framework for criticizing what he considered the wasteful use of resources by landowners, etc.

The resulting aggregate is not entirely without meaning — especially for those who consider socialist bureaucrats as parasites. In any case, the material product may not really suit the convenience of modern Communist governments. Zoran Popov (1975) has argued that the system reflects the high priority for physical products in the Soviet Union in the 1920s. Ironically in a country like Cuba, where health and education services (and administration) have increased much more rapidly than the output of goods, the growth of the Marxist product has been slower on this approach than on a 'bourgeois' one. (Indeed in economies like Bermuda or Gibraltar, with little production of goods of any kind, the national product on this definition is, and remains, virtually zero). Moreover, the result is a serious neglect of other services in socialist planning, since they do not contribute directly to national product targets — as anyone who has ever tried to use the telephone systems in Eastern Europe can testify.

Other aggregates have also been created — one was developed before the last World War by Kuznets himself, who was then primarily concerned with measuring consumer 'welfare' and quite consistently treated some forms of expenditure, such as police, military, and legislative services, as 'necessary costs' of creating this, i.e. as intermediate products. To include such expenditures in the national product was a 'duplication'. Kuznets has also in places discussed the conceptual desirability of eliminating intermediate consumer products, such as journeys to work and purchases of working-clothes.

It is tempting to try and salvage the concept of economic

'growth': to do so would make the vast quantities of national income figures, and much theoretical literature, of some use. It is not absurd to argue that growth is a necessary, even if not sufficient, condition for development in a more profound sense, i.e. progress towards greater autonomy, as well as the elimination of poverty and increasing respect for human rights. Higher food output is almost certainly an element in development in such a wider sense: if it is not needed in order to reduce imports of foodstuffs or to relieve malnutrition (of both peasants and urban workers), it can be exported to relieve the foreign exchange constraint. The national income, on any of its definitions, will almost certainly rise as well, because food output is virtually everywhere a significant part of it. (Indeed, if the output of food were to rise without any growth in the economy as a whole, this would imply declines in other sectors.)

In addition, a national income aggregate has a technical use as a yardstick against which imports, use of commercial energy, tax revenues, etc., can be judged (especially if income is defined so as to exclude non-monetary output), and appropriate 'elasticities' calculated. But its price weights reflect the distribution of income and the pattern of advertising outlays, so food usually carries a low weight relative to its social and political importance.

Moreover, the pace of economic growth is hardly a guide to the rate of development — indeed, there is some reason for thinking, as indicated above, that really fast growth (e.g. in the NICs) is not merely accompanied by the increased 'output' of military services (which are included in the aggregate) and growing social inequalities and increasing debt: it *requires* them. It may well also raise social and personal tensions (reducing 'welfare' in a more basic sense) by arousing unrealistic expectations.

Apart from all these conceptual problems, the accuracy of estimates of economic growth is much more doubtful than is generally realized. Except in a few industrial countries, estimates of food output are typically assumed to have remained constant per head of the rural population (changes in which have to be estimated very roughly) since some agricultural census a decade or two ago and of doubtful reliability. (One director of an African statistical office — a European actually

— justified to me this assumption, built into his national accounts: 'When I motor through the rural areas, which I do at least once a year, I don't see any change in the consumption of food'!) Moreover, food prices are assumed to have moved parallel with those collected in urban markets; and very crude assumptions indeed are made about movements in the prices and quantitites of inputs.

To assess the imputed rent on owner-occupied houses, another category of 'income' supposed to be covered, figures are needed both for rents and for the stock of houses. These are almost equally impossible to estimate in most countries. Cash rents are rare in rural areas, but they are anyway misleading if paid on houses belonging to the government (or a corporate employer). The stock of houses is usually estimated on the basis of a past population census, employing (since very few countries collect usable statistics on current construction) various arbitrary assumptions, such as that the number of dwellings has increased in proportion to the number of families, which in turn has grown proportionately to the (estimated) total population. Different assumptions on these crucial points can produce very different estimates. Thus for Nigeria, Okigbo estimated that 0.57 million huts were built annually, while the estimate of Prest and Stewart was more than five times as many, 2.94 million, for roughly the same period.[5] In industrial countries, net additions to the housing stock are estimated by making a rough assumption about wastage, which can only be guessed at, even where there are extensive statistical sources. All these guesses can lead to very dubious estimates of changes in the stock of houses, even before we start trying to guess at their rental value.

A particularly important but even weaker area is virtually the whole of capital formation in agriculture — clearing land of trees and stones; digging ditches and contour terraces; construction of storage bins, food troughs, shelters, and windbreaks; making of lanes and paths; planting trees, etc. Although it is unfortunate that most estimators turn a blind eye to these important forms of investment, in many countries the most significant forms, this is not surprising. Even in industry, 'capital formation' depends on what the tax authorities allow to be written off in a single tax year — and 'depreciation' reflects the same set of arbitrary rules.[6]

It is not clear, in fact, which non-marketed production is in principle covered. The UN 'System of National Accounts' (SNA) provides for imputation of — apart from food and housing — processing of primary products into butter, wine, cloth, etc., even when they are not sold, as well as building and construction. The reasons given are twofold: that these products are a 'major source of sustenance', and that it is necessary to 'attain some measures of comparability in national accounting data' since 'a shift takes place from subsistence to market production as development proceeds'.[7]

There are, however, many other such items, especially in a non-industrial society. Religious, military, and medical services are often provided on the basis of customary obligation or barter — monks, warriors and traditional medical practitioners, even if not paid in cash, rarely starve.[8] It seems to be doubted by the authors of the SNA that such activities add to welfare, but this Eurocentric view (implicit also in the popular use of terms like 'medicine men' or 'witch doctors') is highly debatable — especially since the same question could be raised about many activities included in the national income. Furthermore, there are communal entertainments involving preparation and service of food and drink or playing music, as well as a large volume of informal education and training (elders instructing the young in natural history, crafts, etc.). In non-industrial countries, hairdressing, making of clothes, etc. are often unremunerated: even in industrial ones, so is a good deal of 'do-it-yourself' such as carpentry and gardening, not to speak of nearly all domestic service. Even if these are covered in principle, the estimates are highly arbitrary.

The treatment of hunting, firewood collection, fishing, food processing, handicraft output, water supplies, crop storage, and livestock output (including changes in herd size), varies greatly from country to country, but is often the product of guesswork, much of which is heroic.[9] Few of the activities in the 'informal' sector are caught in the statistician's nets — censuses of production or returns of income, employment, or sales. This applies especially to illegal or semi-legal services (e.g. gambling, prostitution, abortion, narcotics trading), but also to legal but small-scale activities in all sectors, from vehicle and TV repair to street trading or laundering or working on construction subcontracts or guarding property or prospecting for diamonds. Even large-scale organizations, such as religious orders, may be very poorly covered. Rarely is proper allowance made in any country for the use of official cars or housing, for expense-account meals or accommodation, for the profits made by being able to purchase foreign exchange at legal rates, or for the many other forms of remuneration that are not taxed — let alone for bribes.

Estimates for what might be expected to be the best-documented sector in a developing country, production of farm products for export, depends very much on what prices are used. These may be quite different from those actually received, because they may be taken from unrepresentative market quotations, or nominal customs valuations, or false invoices (e.g. where companies want to shift their profits to a tax haven, or just to a branch in a country where tax rates are lower). Analogous problems arise for valuing imports, including those that are inputs into the activity of a productive sector, especially manufacturing.

In many countries, less than half the national income estimate is derived from primary data sources.[10] Time series often rest on benchmark estimates brought up-to-date by arbitrary assumptions. The treatment of food output has been mentioned above. It is also usually assumed that the value added in transportation, wholesaling, or retailing (sometimes all three together) moves in proportion to gross sales, despite possible big changes in composition.

In an article sardonically subtitled 'Notes for the regression enthusiast', Shourie (1974) pointed out that about 15 per cent of the estimates of Sri Lanka's GDP (22 per cent in the service sectors) were then derived from assumed trends, e.g. that value added at *current* prices grew at the same rate as the population (p. 22). Thus, 'the time series enthusiast may well find himself regressing a variable on another variable from which the former was estimated in the first place: what appears to be an economic coefficient is no more than a measure of the consistency in statistical procedures' (p. 28).

So there is a degree of fantasy about most published national income estimates. Growth rates are not merely conceptually unclear but also highly inaccurate, especially if one allows for the formidable problems of deflation for price changes, in particular when these are rapid. An estimate of (say) 3 per cent real income growth in a year could best be interpreted in most countries as, 'if one measured the output of a comprehensive bundle of certain goods and services, and weighted them by certain rather arbitrary prices, the total probably neither rose by more than 6 per cent nor fell.' Nobody could be sure that this implied any acceleration over an estimate of 2 per cent growth in the previous year. Such imprecision is dangerous now that many politicians have realized the uncertainty of these estimates and request that growth rates which are awkwardly low be 'looked at again'.

I have occasionally teased official statisticians by offering the following wager for $10,000: that, given the resources, I would produce any growth rate for any country for any period, and that it would pass muster in professional circles, even keeping to the conventions of the SNA (otherwise it would be too easy!); the rate, country, and period would be drawn by random process (though, obviously, it would not be easy to produce, say, negative growth rates for Venezuela or Korea). There have never been any takers.

A second implication is that longer-term estimates of growth are biased upwards, even though the main purpose of imputation is to avoid this: the monetary economy displaces the non-monetary and improvements are made in administrative services which yield additional statistics (such as tax assessments).

Thirdly, the distribution of income is virtually impossible to measure, if only because of the non-taxable expense allowances and bribes received by the rich in particular, mentioned above. Economic growth is typically accompanied by the increased visibility of output at the other end of the social scale (output which had existed previously).

Fourthly, if we allow in addition for the probable inappropriateness of exchange rates, especially when applied to 'non-tradeables' such as rent and services, international inequalities — which are real enough — are also exaggerated severalfold. The statement that, for example, the national income of India is US $240 a head appears to mean that if some 'average' Indian lived in the United States, his current level of living would cost that much, and would amount to about one-fiftieth of the income of an average citizen of the USA. This sort of comparison is often used as a basis for advocating aid. In fact, of course, nobody could survive on less than $5 a week in the United States, even if he slept in the streets (he certainly could not afford a roof over his head). Recent research[11] suggests that about $800 dollars a year would be a more appropriate figure for per capita income in India, i.e. nearly three times as much.

Anyway, there is considerable uncertainty about how to interpret comparisons between countries where there are big ranges around the average — some Indians are vastly richer than the average American (and these might well be the chief beneficiaries of aid).

The ambiguity and inaccuracy of national income estimates would not matter greatly if they had less influence. Economists, as well as journalists, however, use them to show that the growth of one country is faster than another's or faster than it was in some period of its own past, even sometimes claiming that this means a faster rate of 'development', and explaining that this is the result of superior policy.

Students often ask at this point: how then are we to use rates of economic growth? The response can only be a counter-question: for what purpose would you need them? When I led the ILO employment mission to Colombia in 1970, I got the members to agree that though we would cover a wide range of economic and social issues, the problems were basically structural, so we would not discuss the national income or economic growth. This rule was honoured: yet the report (ILO, 1970) seemed to exert a certain influence, and to attract a good deal of academic interest.

It is not hard in fact to see why 'growth rates' continue to be published, despite growing awareness of their weaknesses in both concept and quality. Apart from their obvious political utility, in diverting attention from distributional issues, they have important academic uses. They enable 'national income analysis' to be substituted for research on economic problems. Moreover, it is much easier to teach economics if there is some means of over-simplifying the complexity of economic relations: provided attention can be focused on an apparently quantifiable aggregate, ingenious, even 'elegant', models can be presented to students who are then examined simply on their capacity to manipulate these. The brightest ones, on this sort of criterion, are selected to become teachers and transmit their professional weakness to the following generation.

From the viewpoint of this book, the tables that supplement national income estimates, or 'national accounts' have another major defect: they fail to separate out the sector of the economy under foreign control — I shall deal with this point in Chapter 9.

NATIONALISM AND ECONOMICS

Synopsis

A few years ago, I wrote a conference paper about the basic
similarities between the Chicago and Marxist schools of
economics – the original version of this section. It was in
part a tease, though I had a faint hope it would force some
disciples of each of these doctrines to pause and ask themselves whether there might be a real point here.

It did, indeed, annoy many I hoped it would annoy, and
it amused a number of friends for whom I enjoy providing
entertainment. But there was one common complaint among
some Left-wing associates and friends of mine which does
deserve a comment: what I was summarizing as Marxism was
not true Marxism (which, by coincidence, was precisely the
philosophy of whoever was speaking), but Stalinism. As I said
in the original article, anticipating this criticism, Marxism is
like a duck in a fairground shooting gallery: as soon as you
score a hit, it disappears from view.

There is substance in what my friends say, however. There
are several Marxisms (indeed, disconcertingly for Marxists,
there were several Marxes). In particular, on the crucial point
of 'economism', whether cultural phenomena should be
treated as part of the 'superstructure' (resting on the material
base), Marx's ideas certainly changed as he grew older – some
would say, not for the better.

I was drawing at the time on a paper at that conference
written by the late Bill Warren (1973, 1980). I am quite prepared to accept that he was far from typical of Marxists, even

the British variety — especially in his view that capitalism had decades of constructive life still left, so that egalitarian measures and nationalist policies such as protection, etc., were 'objectively' obstructing progress, i.e. 'reactionary'. On fundamentals, however, Bill's position was surely not far different from that of many other Marxists, not least the Soviet ideologues, as expressed in the official textbook of Marxism, 'Political Economy', translated into many languages and distributed far and wide by the State Publishing House. This in turn is, indeed, not incompatible with a good deal of what Marx had to say himself, and it is surely part of the true faith.

The central point of my paper, and what I think really accounted for the wrath, is that it emphasized the importance of nationalism — and what Marxists and conventional Anglo-Saxon economists have, above all else, in common is first to belittle the influence of nationalism and secondly to treat it as evil. I have responded in Chapter 2 by stressing its importance, following in the footsteps of Raùl Prebisch and other Latin American writers.

CHAPTER 1

Marxism and other neo-classical models

WE all suffer from 'cultural lags', the tendency of attitudes and perceptions to lag behind changing reality, sometimes by years, sometimes by decades, discarded only when their implications threaten disaster. In military affairs, there is the well-known phenomenon of generals fighting the previous war. In academia, cultural lags take the form of reproducing throughout one's teaching career the theories learned as a student, largely through inertia (the understandable wish to limit one's reading and to keep repeating the same lectures), although systems of appointment and promotion, together with criteria for publication, reinforce the reluctance to reconsider basic frames of analysis.

Politicians or administrators (including those in international companies) also, of course, use archaic economic theories, whether they are aware of this or not, in the formulation of policy. 'Practical men,' as Keynes pointed out, in a well-known passage, 'who believe themselves to be quite exempt from any intellectual influence, are usually the slaves of some defunct economists.'[1] Anyway, such a theoretical base might in normal times well serve the purposes of their career. But this lag may be even more of a problem than in the 1930s, now that the pace of change in institutions, power relations, technology, etc., has accelerated, and the crises have deepened.

It may help us to see that we should, in our turn, need to let go of much of our intellectual equipment if we recall how the last fundamental international crisis half a century ago forced on a reluctant profession major changes in ways of thinking and action — including the Keynesian 'revolution'. From my perspective, Keynesian economics is actually a variant of the neo-classical position: nevertheless, it encountered fierce resistance. Orthodox economists, such as Pigou, for example, denied for many years any inherent tendency to unemployment in the capitalist system, and therefore any need for the government to stimulate demand.

In the 'developed' capitalist economies, once this resistance was overcome (with the help of events), Keynesian economics then spread through the universities of Western Europe and North America. This took only a couple of decades — a relatively very short lag indeed.

By the 1950s a strong upward impulse to these economies was still being imparted by the tasks of making good wartime damage and meeting pent-up demand. But another big slump was considered inevitable in the capitalist economies about a decade after the end of the war; this was awaited by the economists of the capitalist and socialist countries alike. With the help of proliferating systems of national accounts, the former were nervously taking the pulse of the industrial economies, and sharpening the counter-cyclical tools which had been implicit in the theories of Keynes. The post-war period would require sophisticated demand 'management' if a repetition of the 1930s were to be avoided.

So economists remained preoccupied with theory which had been developed in answer to earlier needs. The main line of professional 'progress' in the capitalist economies was to models which were increasingly sophisticated. ('Rigour' is now measured by the compiling of the model rather than the relevance of its assumptions or the adequacy and quality of supporting material.)

Bitter memories of the 1930s also shaped perceptions of international policy needs. In the industrial countries, most economists of all schools working in this field saw the post-war task as predominantly one of avoiding the 'beggar my neighbour' policies which had propagated the depression in 1930-3. (Actually, it was only *after* governments left the gold standard and raised protective barriers that recovery got under way.) The establishment of the International Monetary Fund at Bretton Woods set 'rules of the game' designed to prevent competitive devaluation and inhibit recourse to exchange controls, while providing means for short-term foreign exchange support. Under the aegis of GATT, tariffs and preferences were being 'bound' and reduced. Thus the international economy was deliberately integrated. This of course suited the export interests in the industrial countries, especially the

TNCs. A similar integration was planned by Communist leaders for the Soviet Union and Eastern Europe.

To free ourselves from such cultural lags, let us take a brief look at some familiar features of the two main, fully worked-out ideologies which have today to some extent displaced Keynes; Chicago and Marxist. Let me first dispose of the question whether any economic theory is, or can be, 'correct'. Students often ask which theory is right? This is an inappropriate question because there is no objective way of assessing whether any theoretical school is right. As I shall show, the main ones are each self-contained systems, perfectly logical on their own premises, which are in fact very similar, but both the motives and the markets they assume bear only a limited relation to reality. Empirical tests are not very relevant, anyway, because the objectives (e.g. 'economic growth') are derived from the theories, and even predictive experience has been far from encouraging. The crucial questions are: whose interests does a theory serve? How does it serve them?

The purest version of conservative ideology, the 'Chicago school', which underlies official policy in the United States (not to speak of Britain and a number of other countries) suits capitalist interests: the right of the individual is stressed, to make as much money as he can by his own efforts — and to keep it. Moreover, if he is allowed to exercise this right, the whole economy will benefit. Thus state intervention by taxation, subsidies, and social expenditures (even demand management) should be kept to a minimum.

Few of those who believe in this doctrine appear greatly affected by poverty or over-concerned about it. They will talk in terms of a 'national income' that, as explained above, conveniently diverts attention from issues of distribution. But if pressed, they will argue that, were market forces allowed free rein, economic growth would benefit the poor too.

The corollary of this position at the international level is opposition to government restrictions on trade and payments between countries, and distrust of attempts by international bodies to regulate these or to organize transfers of capital from rich countries to poor ones. The way to ease world poverty is through the unfettered expansion of the world economy.

The Marxist doctrine, espoused by the ruling élites of the Soviet Union (and a dozen or so other countries), is that poverty is due to exploitation, especially by big capitalist monopolies. Since capitalism has been abolished in 'socialist' countries, there is no need to discuss exploitation there: attention can be focused on increasing the 'material product', from which the mass of the people must in due course benefit.

But in the rest of the world, on this ideology, political changes (they would formerly have insisted on revolutions) will free the workers and peasants from the tyranny of property owners and the imperialist governments that support them. Once Marxist parties are firmly in power everywhere, states will wither away and international progress will be assured.

Since Marxism is a 'relativist' doctrine in the sense that it describes ideologies as suiting certain class interests, logically, this raises the question, in the interest of which class is Marxism? The answer appears to be the élite in the socialist countries (and those social revolutionaries elsewhere who hope to gain unrestricted political power). The official response, of course, is that the bureaucracy in a socialist country is not a class, if only because it is not hereditary. But social classes do not need to be changeless to be important influences on the way an economy functions or (especially) on political developments. Moreover, there are many mechanisms by which the bureaucrats there can and do help their children inherit in due course privileges similar to their own. In any case, the fact that a particular definition of class suits the material interests of some Marxists is no reason for the rest of us to accept it.

If I were a senior Soviet bureaucrat, of course, Marxism would be a perfectly appropriate doctrine in reconciling my dacha with a realization of the world's social problems. Since there is, by definition, no exploitation in a socialist economy, my personal affluence and power would need no theoretical justification. Indeed — as mentioned in the Introduction — Marxism would enable me to equate criticism of myself, my policies, and my class with treason against socialism. Such advantages apply equally to those in Eastern Europe, Cuba, etc., who maintain similar social systems with Soviet support.

But both economic Conservatism and Marxism appeal to far wider interests than these. They each provide fully worked-out philosophies, intellectually satisfying (up to a point) because they yield consistent answers to a wide range of questions in policy fields not merely economic, but also social. They also both promise Utopia, if not in this century, then the next. Yet they both respond to the needs for a stable social order in which people have defined roles, and for villains to hate.

They provide reasons, therefore, to explain why governments of other countries should enter into military alliances with the United States or the Soviet Union as the case may be, and why they should open up opportunities of investment and cultural 'exchange', concede access to markets, and permit the exploitation of their raw materials. The United States administration expects the international agencies where it has a dominant say, the World Bank and the International Monetary Fund, to apply neo-classical criteria with these effects, when approached for loans. Marxism has rationalized Soviet efforts to expand their sphere of influence and to build an economic bloc of 'people's republics' outside the 'imperialist camp'.

Moreover, both doctrines appeal to malcontents in *the other* system. Many factory workers and miners in Western Europe, looking at the local class structure, especially if unemployed or in danger of becoming so, find Marxist ideology appealing and support a left-wing party in the belief that they would be materially better off in a socialist society – despite all the evidence in the dozen or so such societies that have been set up in this century.

Conversely, some of their counterparts in Eastern Europe, obviously Poland (we do not know how many elsewhere), frustrated by the virtual impossibility of venting grievances against the petty bureaucracy, by the queues, by the boring propaganda, are under the illusion that the 'free society' is a sort of Utopia. (Refugees sometimes get quite a shock.) In each case, dissidents glamorize the conveniently unknown and dismiss local criticism of it as propaganda – which, of course, it is!

The appeal of subversive doctrines is not limited to the proletariats. A university student in a capitalist country, for example, protected by an adequate family income (or student grant) from social reality, may well find that to bury himself in Marxist metaphysics not only makes an intellectual appeal: it enables him with a clear conscience to study rather than relieve human misery. (In many countries he would have the additional satisfaction of shocking his teachers). Somebody with less formal educational qualifications might see in a Marxist movement the hope of a short cut to a position with the sort of personal privileges evidently enjoyed by the faithful in the socialist bloc.

Frustrated politicians in the West find Marxist slogans useful, as do many trade union leaders. Their counterparts in a socialist country use 'laissez-faire' doctrines to bolster the case for the decentralization of decision-making, weakening the concentration of power that excludes them and opening up new channels of advancement. (In both cases, dissidents point to the immorality of their own social order — but without much conviction if they are themselves infected with a materialism that allows little room for moral judgements.)

There are, however, many who are becoming disenchanted with the ideology dominant locally, yet reject the main alternative. Some have good career reasons for this agnosticism. There are business executives, especially outside the USA — those managing motor car firms in Sweden, say — who are clearly not suited by a doctrine that exposes them to foreign competition, but who feel threatened by socialism. There are also many bureaucrats in Eastern Europe who associate Marxism with Soviet hegemony, as is revealed not only in private conversation, but during the periodic political upheavals, yet who do not see much promise in capitalism either.

And while I have said that these two doctrines are suitable for those in the Soviet Union and the United States, and in their satellites, who benefit in the ways I have indicated, this seems to be decreasingly true materially, emotionally, and intellectually, as it becomes increasingly obvious that neither doctrine is of much practical use in the present situation.

Of course, to say that an economic doctrine can serve the interests of some group by no means implies that its leaders need to believe in it themselves. They often, however, do indeed enjoy an ill-founded confidence that 'history is on our side', neglecting the social factors that do not fit the official model but may nevertheless have an important bearing on what actually happens. They tend increasingly to make rash promises of imminent and rapid economic growth, which are soon exposed as foolish (especially in Britain), and to make prophecies about the inevitable and not-distant political collapse of the capitalist or socialist bloc, as the case may be.

Indeed, there is a good deal in common between the leaderships. Both stress material incentives, and show traditionally upper-class indifference to civil liberties and dislike of spontaneous working-class action. Both demonstrate highly bourgeois lifestyles (including suits and large saloon cars); they share a similar technocratic culture (expressed for example in 'brutal modern' architecture). Both of them find the youth culture, with its tolerance of drugs and cohabitation, offensive, and they are particularly horrified by violent threats to *any* establishment, especially kidnapping. They also both espouse the slogans of internationalism and modernization, and show little practical interest in religious values. Neither of them sees much point in research to adapt technology to local needs, or has great patience with ecologists, especially those opposed to nuclear power.

Both also see the potential threat of fast population growth to the *status quo* and use the arguments of Malthus to favour and facilitate the expansion of birth control and abortion services; their own members tend to have small families. Their ideology embraces, in both cases, feminism and racial equality, which is demonstrated by at least token appointments of women and members of ethnic minorities to senior positions.

The missionary fervour of communist bureaucrats has burnt out long ago. On the other hand, the managers of big private corporations do not find government planners or even leaders of organized labour nearly as objectionable as did their more individualistic forebears. In certain situations, even a communist union leader is acceptable — there may be nobody else willing and able to help a company avoid strikes. And nationalization of a subsidiary is not necessarily very outrageous to the TNCs, provided they are left in control of marketing (as for Middle East oil).

There are clearly common elements, too, in the doctrines. The reliance on economic growth in each case is legitimized by the assumption that market prices, which are the implicit weights in a national income index, reflect the (also assumed) competitive interplay of economic forces in both product and factor markets: imperfections being considered not severe enough to deprive prices of meaning, or of their functions in organizing the economy on a national or world scale.

More basically, men and women are assumed to be driven —

at least in their capacities as producers and consumers — by only economic motives. Important economic areas where other influences predominate, such as distribution of consumption within the household and the division of labour there, have been almost completely ignored.

These common characteristics demonstrate their common origin: in classical economics. Though it seems provocative to say so, and always annoys both parties considerably — those who cannot cope should treat it as just leg-pulling — Marxism can be described with accuracy as a neo-classical doctrine.[2] There can be no dispute that, like the Chicago school, its origin can be found in the work of Adam Smith and Ricardo, early in the industrial revolution. And after the mainstream of classical thought split into two, both continued to develop in the same buoyant atmosphere of the nineteenth century, a time when the possibilities opened up by industrialization still seemed limitless.

Place was also important. Both these derivative schools, like their ancestors, were developed in Western Europe, in fact Britain, and reflected its historic experience as well as its cultural values. Marx drew nearly all his illustrative material from this part of the world. While of course less was known then of the history of other continents, sources *were* available (e.g. Spanish documents on Latin America, already being used by Prescott), certainly enough for the colonial systems to be analysed more exhaustively and more critically. (Although Adam Smith had more excuse for being Eurocentric, because he was writing at an earlier date, he was perhaps less so: the explanation may lie in the fact that his upbringing was not in Germany but Britain, a country with much broader connections outside Europe.)

Russell Means, an American Sioux 'indian' (a people who have much reason to criticize European culture as purveyed by their neighbours of European origin, or neo-Europeans) said recently, referring to a Soviet scientist's statement that new energy sources could always be found: 'Science has become the new European religion for both capitalists and Marxists; they are truly inseparable . . . in both theory and practice, Marxism declares that non-European people give up their values, their traditions, their cultural existence altogether. . . . I do not believe that capitalism is really responsible for the situation in which we have been declared a national sacrifice. No, it is the European tradition. European culture itself is responsible. Marxism is just the latest imitator of this tradition, not a solution to it.' (Kaighn Smith, a graduate student at Sussex, drew my attention to this statement — which slightly over-simplifies the position — to the Citizens' Review Commission on Energy, Black Hills, South Dakota, 19 July 1980.)

The temporal and geographical matrices of both neo-classical schools explain the 'economism', which was typical of nineteenth-century Europe: progress is still seen as essentially material, the necessary and — in the end — sufficient condition for progress in the political, social, and cultural spheres (in Marxist terms, the 'superstructure'). Since, as pointed out above, Marxism is historically relativist, it logically demands, of course, that it should itself be considered part of the superstructure, to be discarded as the material base is transformed.

Naturally, few neo-classical economists admit that their doctrines are only applicable, if anywhere, in a particular part of the world. It is characteristic, we must admit, of European social theorists more generally, to believe that propositions derived from their local experience in a particular period can have worldwide and permanent application. (Unfortunately, because of the prestige of the European academic, those in other continents often accept this.) Even today, neo-classical textbooks of all kinds, circulating in many parts of the world, illustrate with purely local European (or US) evidence propositions which are put forward without qualification, as generally applicable. I do not wish to imply that any neo-classical theory is, in fact, appropriate in all West European countries, especially now, though of course, as I suggested above, some form of it is often useful for particular classes — Marxism for workers, Chicago economics for capitalists who want arguments against socialists and bureaucrats. And it may well be less inappropriate as a guide to national policy, i.e. would only damage a small fraction of the population, in a country that is a technological leader such as West Germany, where there is some justification for the basic assumption of high factor mobility. (The same might be said about Japan: about the United States, one can no longer be sure.)

Anyone who draws attention to some feature of neo-classical economics, such as its 'economism', must expect to be charged with over-simplification. In Marxist company, whatever one is criticizing turns out to be 'vulgar' Marxism. Most Chicago economists will also argue that *they* are not 'economistic' either: they are only talking about economic phenomena, not about the social or political aspects, which are the responsibilities of the sociologists and political scientists. They will admit that there are other dimensions to 'welfare'. But, especially when they draw policy conclusions, such qualifications are somehow often lacking.

Many economists in the capitalist world in fact resent being called 'neo-classical', especially Marxists, but even some Keynesians (who differ from the Chicago school principally over the necessary extent of government intervention). One cannot, however, necessarily accept the opinion of the objects of any classification on whether a class is being correctly described or whether they belong to it. A whale might well object to a zoological classification that puts him in the same broad category ('mammals') as a guinea-pig. Although it is difficult for non-Christians to understand, many Catholics and (e.g. in Northern Ireland) Protestants insist that they belong to quite different faiths.

The criterion is surely one of utility. Is it not useful to look at the common elements in dogmas within the classical tradition (including Marxist and Keynesian), especially now that there are many economists who no longer believe in any of them?

The common policy implications are far-reaching. In the post-war period, the economism of the main neo-classical schools has implied treating development as a largely, even purely economic phenomenon. They both take some definition of national income based on neo-classical conventions as its measure. (See the Annexe to the Introduction.) The important test of even a capitalist country's progress is, in Marxist terms, the growth of its 'productive forces': by one route or another, economic growth will — in their view — ultimately force a change in social relationships, to the benefit of the people as a whole. It is, of course, this emphasis on economic growth which largely explains the touching neo-classical faith that there has been development in the last few decades, despite increasing inequalities and political repression discussed above.[3] Since these appear implicit in some high-growth patterns, one could make out a case for arguing that growth is negatively correlated with development.

Parenthetically, it would be interesting to find out whether there has been any increase in per capita income in Britain since the Middle Ages, if we priced cathedral, monastery, castle, and mansion construction at today's replacement cost, allowing of course for the current wages of masons, carpenters, etc., and valuing personal services, such as running royal courts, at today's skilled wage rates (allowing for the long-term decline in hourly productivity in such services and reduction in hours worked per week and weeks worked per year), and artistic products such as the paintings of that period at current market prices. One would have to take into account, of course, all the medieval buildings and works of art which have disappeared in the meantime, and to include all the output which was once domestic (such as bread, clothes, teaching, etc.) but is now commercial. The result might be that the medieval income per head was larger than today's, even without allowing for the great increase in pollution. The main economic change has been, of course, in distribution. (The moralist might well ask why one should attach any value at all to castles when people were hungry — but for a neo-classical economist even to pose that question would bring down the whole house of cards.) There has certainly been development but in non-economic dimensions — in rough order of importance, the greater liberty of the individual *vis-à-vis* those with state power, the elimination of smallpox and other plagues, the availability of medicines that cure many other ailments, and much greater access to education.

The view of history shared by Adam Smith and Marx as essentially a record of material progress still persists in European culture. Progress has occurred, is still taking place, and will moreover continue in the future. There are some simple and obvious explanations such as curiosity, leading to inventions, 'animal spirits', or enterprise. The key to progress is to overcome the political and cultural 'obstacles' that thwart the operation of these. The 'invisible hand', in Adam Smith's graphic metaphor, that shapes economic progress, belongs — on the whole, and in the long run — to a benevolent deity: Marx agreed (see the extraordinary praise of the capitalist system in the 'Communist Manifesto'), though he thought (over 100 years ago) that it was already outrunning its period in human history and was due for replacement.

Their (neo-classical) successors still believe that economic growth will lead to a social and political Utopia some day — despite all evidence to the contrary — justifying sacrifices by the present generation (e.g. thrift, and many political crimes). This would be an integrated world of prosperity and peace (capitalist or socialist as the case may be), at high levels of income, to be achieved if not in the next generation, then two or three generations later. Different branches of the neo-classical tradition have differed profoundly about the mechanisms by which it will be achieved but not about its plausibility or even in outline its social content. The twenty-first century visions of Herman Kahn and those of the Soviet futurologists are in essence the same.

Implicit in all neo-classical schools is a blind belief in the majestic civilizing role of modernization, as the destroyer of archaic superstitions and ethnic loyalties. Urbanization and industrialization are inevitable and progressive — whatever their social and political cost.

The uncritical faith in science, characteristic of European thinkers in the nineteenth century, persists. The latest profitable technology is still considered by most neo-classical economists as a prima facie desirable (even if it has been devised for a completely different socio-economic environment). Oil and other natural resources are tacitly assumed adequate to sustain any rate and pattern of economic growth, with scientists inventing gadgets to relieve scarcities as they arise. Once a problem has been correctly identified, it can be solved.

The resultant policies raise questions not only about the social cost of these ideologies — only too well-founded — but also about their cultural impact and political viability, especially when imposed in a country with its own deep traditions, inconsistent with many of the customs imported alongside economic modernization — atheism, feminism, etc. The classic case is that of Iran.

There is yet another aspect to neo-classical technophilia, also rooted in the nineteenth century. Neo-classical economists of all kinds like to consider *themselves* 'scientific', able to emulate in their own field the accelerating progress in the physical sciences that was made possible by the work of Galton,

Clark Maxwell, etc. Such an approach lies at the root of the systematic elaboration of growth models, which reduce complex social phenomena to quantifiable relationships — for which confirmatory material is then obtained.

But this is 'scientific' in a highly restricted sense, closer to the metaphysical sciences of the Middle Ages. The propositions derived from such models are inherently difficult to verify or refute, and since they are often about matters of great social importance, carrying major policy implications, it is not surprising if neo-classical economists tend to show even greater dogmatism and emotional involvement than is customary among real scientists. More modern scientific traditions would have suggested the patient collection of comparable material by observation of the static and dynamic patterns of large numbers of economies over long periods and their classification — before great theories were built. (A few truly scientific economists such as Simon Kuznets and Colin Clark have in fact tried to do just this.)

Classical economics is also the origin of the belief — and this is what it is — that capital investment ('accumulation' in Marxist jargon) is overwhelmingly the most important determinant of economic growth (e.g. in the Harrod-Domar model and its derivatives, and in the Marxist scheme of 'reproduction'). Consequently, the generation and allocation of savings are seen as the mainsprings of development. This has appealed to Victorian and subsequent puritans (a category which included, of course, atheists such as Marx and Engels). Its ultimate technical expression, the Harrod-Domar model of the 1950s, in which growth depends solely on capital investment, soon began to look too simplistic to provide an adequate basis for analysing or even predicting growth, let alone development in a true sense. Already by the 1960s the range in incremental capital-output ratios (from about 2 to 20 for various countries)[4] assumed stable in Harrod-Domar, implied, as did research on production functions, what is obvious to anyone with practical experience: that capital investment is only one influence on growth.

The definition of investment excludes, on both Western and Marxist definitions, educational services. These are treated in the national income accounts as a form of 'consumption', and the economics of education, which emerged belatedly, is confined to a sort of professional ghetto. This attitude may have been defensible in Western Europe in the past, but is certainly hardly suitable in the rest of the world — or indeed in Europe itself today.

It has considerable practical implications.[5] If education were treated as 'investment' the definition of government *current* expenditure would have to be changed, and savings would have to be redefined. When orthodox economists (Chicago or Marxist) criticize deficits in government current accounts, they overlook the fact that educational expenditure is only a 'consumption' item and appears in this account because of conventions, which are quite artificial. This imparts a bias against education in budgetary policy — though not as much as in the Marxist set of definitions, which leaves education out of the product too.

Another implication is that capital is generally assumed to be the most important form of property and determinant of inequality — educational qualifications, lifelong tenure, bureaucratic positions, etc., being therefore hardly considered (a supposition most convenient for socialists).

Because of this emphasis on capital, geographical influences on growth are also virtually ignored, even the size of a country's population, its area, its location, its climate, its soil, its mineral resources, and so on (see Section B).

Still another corollary is a general disinterest in the ethnic, religious, and linguistic compositions of nations (though Marx and Engels were far from oblivious to these in their practical work in journalism — or in their correspondence). Yet these affect important categories in schemes of economic analysis, such as consumption habits and savings propensities — both assumed in neo-classical economics to be functions of income — and attitudes to work. If referred to at all, cultural influences fall under the heading 'obstacles to growth', as mentioned above.

Naturally, there is no great interest in institutional change — except, of course, for Marxists, in major revolutions.

One could continue for many pages listing the inherited beliefs that neo-classical economists hold in common. But there is one more that cannot be ignored: treating the quantity of money as the determinant of inflation is common ground between economists in, for example, the governments of the

Soviet Union and the United States — and throughout their respective satellites.

Still, I must not fall into the temptation to shock the reader by exaggerating the congruence. To mention very briefly just a few of the important differences, Chicago-school economists are characterized by a much greater belief in quantitative techniques. They are thus more likely to restrict their analysis to variables which are quantifiable, and are particularly inclined to treat statistics as if they were facts. Secondly, a central concept for them is 'equilibrium', which is normative. Marxists, on the other hand, focus attention on social crises, due to class relations, study the 'internal contradictions' in capitalist (but not socialist) 'modes of production', and stress how 'uneven development' is linked to 'imperialism'. They therefore tend to emphasize the historical origins of problems, and long-term dynamics.

Yet one still can talk of a neo-classical tradition spanning virtually the whole range of economists. It is a majestic structure, internally quite consistent — which helps explain its intellectual appeal and its continued influence. One great attraction of any of its varieties to a student with a tidy and logical mind is that the task of mastering it sufficiently to obtain a degree is limited and thus manageable. Intuitive doubts gradually die away. (As Joan Robinson once pointed out to me, the effort needed to understand the algebra diverts the student's attention from the plausibility of its assumptions.)

After graduating, he sees that his career depends upon publishing analyses derived from the models he has absorbed, which he passes on to the next generation, instilling, in them too, long cultural lags. A well-known Cambridge economist told me that after each lecture in his standard course, he stops in the King's Parade to put the notes in a safe deposit, where they remain until he calls at the bank on the way to give the same lecture a year later (thus preserving his intellectual assets intact).

CHAPTER 2

Coming to terms with nationalism

MOST people use a uni-dimensional ideological map running from revolutionaries on the Left to conservatives and fascists on the Right:

	Anarchists	Marxist socialists	Fabians, social democrats	Liberals	Conservatives	Fascists	
EGALITARIAN ←							→ ANTI-EGALITARIAN

This is conveniently simple. Not only political leaders and parties can be given definite places on the spectrum (which even has a colour range, from deep red, via pink, to true blue and black). One's friends and colleagues can be readily classed as less or more Leftist (or Rightist) than oneself. Economists of the central tradition described in the previous chapter can be differentiated according to whether the implications of their theories are more or less egalitarian.

Moreover, predictable packages of views are appropriate at various points in the political dimension. Someone on the far Left can be expected to be more vehemently against racial or sexual discrimination — and against capital punishment, nuclear energy, etc. — than a person closer to the political centre of gravity; a person on the far Right would be strongly against not only high rates of income tax, but also comprehensive schools.

The main touchstone of controversy is increasingly, however, not so much egalitarianism as nationalism. As explained in Chapter 1, this is anathema to neo-classical economists of all kinds, as indeed it was (in the form of mercantilism) to the founding fathers of classical economies. It is incompatible with their assumptions of the overwhelming importance of material motives and therefore a form of 'false consciousness', in Marxist terminology — which requires nationalism to be prefaced by pejorative terms such as 'petit bourgeois'.[1]

The Right used to have almost exclusive rights to nationalism. This, indeed, was one of the reasons for their continued dominance in the political scene for so many decades. The Left were nearly all internationalists and pacifists. But in a tight corner — for example in Russia in 1941 — even Marxist governments base their rallying call on patriotism.

The Marxist concept of 'imperialism' is, in fact, sufficiently elastic to mobilize not merely all exploited classes everywhere against 'monopoly capitalism' (Lenin's original intention), but also country against country. This is particularly clear in the Chinese use of the term 'imperialist' to designate the Soviet government, which by implication restores to the word an older, pre-Leninist, connotation of national territorial ambitions. It has been similarly used in recent frontier wars between various governments calling themselves 'Marxist' or at least 'Socialist'. (Kampuchea and Vietnam, Ethiopia and Somalia, Iraq and Iran — inter-socialist wars have been the main international ones in recent years.)

Many socialists still stress international solidarity, but sections of the movement also draw now on patriotic, even religious traditions, previously considered 'Right-wing'. Conservatives are also divided, some stressing the old nationalist concerns, whereas others, associated with the TNCs and international banks, speak of 'one world' and 'interdependence'. In fact, the old bundles of 'progressive' and 'reactionary' objectives have been burst open and re-assembled in new packages.

These splits have been opened up by the realization of the depth of the economic crises. The fundamental ideological choice now is no longer whether idyllic social conditions are likely on 'Left' or on 'Right' economic programmes. Utopia is no longer even on the horizon. So specific cultural characteristics of nations, which used to be seen as merely transient obstacles to the modern world that technological advance growth had brought almost within our grasp, now appear as basic sources of national and personal identity under increasing attack by the transnational culture — which is now patently inappropriate as well as arrogant.

In that case, the old Left-Right axis, along which various neo-classical ideologies are ranged, is not much use. We all need some ideological map, however, if only to help us assess political information and theoretical developments, and tell friend from foe. An interesting one is obtained if we super-impose a vertical axis, showing the degree of nationalism, on the conventional 'Left-Right' one. We then get the following:

Ideological map, today

ANTI-NATIONALIST

AN

Marxist socialists   Neo-classical liberals

EGALITARIAN E◄————————————►AE ANTI-EGALITARIAN

Dependency theorists   Traditional conservatives,
populists, neo-Marxists   fascists

N

NATIONALIST

The ideology in the top right-hand quadrant (AN, AE) is broadly compatible with the interests of the TNCs. It also suits local capitalists who are associated with them, and a small 'labour aristocracy' which is provided with relatively high wages and fringe benefits by capital-intensive technology. These classes have come to depend on the governments of the United States or Western Europe for military support and technological and cultural inspiration, and also slogans to legitimate their policy. Economic liberalism still serves this purpose.

In the Soviet bloc, Marxism still holds out to Communist parties and their sympathizers the goal of a socialist world order; it can be put in the AN, E quadrant — however strong the current of both nationalism and élitism in socialist countries.

But, despite the strains in capitalism, Marxism no longer has in West European countries the appeal it once possessed for the leaders of the organized working class or for intellec-tuals who need a consistent ideological framework, basically critical of the inequalities they see around them. Nor is it so successful as an ideology of protest in other continents either, although sanctioned by the prestige of European theorists. Peasant movements, in particular, are better suited by some-thing that is not only egalitarian but draws on national roots, like the forms of populism common overseas, especially in

Latin America, which can be put in quadrant N, E. The 'social incentives' which are heavily emphasized by Marxist governments, in non-European countries (such as China and Cuba), can be interpreted as largely national incentives.

Many of the programmes of other non-European governments, especially those of the large countries, are best placed in the quadrant N, AE — whatever its platform, a government may, in fact, not bother much in its day-to-day business about reducing inequality. Landowners and indigenous capitalists naturally prefer an anti-egalitarian ideology, but — as mentioned above — not one that is internationalist. Significant parts of the bureaucracy and the armed forces also support ideologies in the same quadrant, together with some extremist religious groups, such as the Moslem Brotherhood. Like Fascist ideologists, despite egalitarian rhetoric they are basically hierarchical.

This diagram helps us understand how a wide and continuous ideological spectrum from Left to Right can be spanned within nationalist parties such as the Indian Congress or Polish Solidarity. Moreover, 'nationalism' may be effective in ethnic groups smaller than the national state (in which case it may be inconsistent with the larger loyalty): so the Scots and Basque separatists are also an ideological coalition, as are the numerous less militant parties in all parts of the world that are basically ethnic. This helps explain why the ideologies of 'Arab Socialism' and 'African Socialism' are also vague: they have to appeal to a variety of interests.

From this point of view, it is not surprising that — to take a few topical examples — 'Leftist' sections of the British Labour Party have co-operated with Enoch Powell and other 'Right-wing' Conservatives in opposing membership of the EEC. On the other hand, the map also explains tactical alliances in the upper half of the circle, e.g. in the Republic of South Africa between what is now the Progressive Federal Party (backed by Oppenheimer mining fortunes) and Marxist groups, under the banner of multi-racialism, against both extremes of Afrikaaner and Black nationalism.

Not only have political movements become in general much less monolithic. One consequence of the emergence of the nationalist dimension is greater instability. Any party may look not only horizontally but also vertically — or even diagonally — for tactical allies, depending on what happen to be the dominant issues of the day.[2] There is now much more scope for individual leadership than in the days when a politician could only co-operate with the immediate ideological neighbours on either side.

Instability has increased in international relations too. Usually, some governments are, at any one time, whatever their overt ideology, moving, perhaps with the stimulus of financial or military aid, towards the camp dominated by the United States (e.g. tendencies in the foreign policy of China) or the Soviet Union (e.g. Iran).

Because of cultural lags, the archaic Left-Right dichotomy will still be widely used when people discuss parties or governments; they will continue to categorize these as just Left or Right, progressive or reactionary. Strong vested interests (not only material) have accumulated in these perceptions, which few will abandon readily. They are also highly comforting — even grown-ups need fairy tales in which they can identify with good characters and hate the bad.

It would have been surprising if the ideological justification for nationalist ambitions had appeared in the developed countries. (List developed mercantilist arguments but this was before the First World War, and designed to create the conditions for rapid industrialization.) Nor did it emerge readily in the 'under-developed' world. As I mentioned in Chapter 1, the Harrod-Domar model, the dynamic version of Keynesian economics, provided a convenient framework for the 1950s and 1960s. This enabled the need for savings to be estimated, and thus for aid and foreign investment, which would bring with them the latest technologies: indeed, much work at that time consisted of building growth models which justified policies of donor agencies.

Harrod-Domar could also be used as a basis for planning of a sort (see Chapter 6), thus making a bow to national aspirations. But there was another, more conventional, influence at work, that of the Chicago, or purest neo-classical, school. Simon Rottenberg, as just one example, taught this doctrine in the late 1950s in Santiago, soon to be followed by Arnold Harberger, laying the intellectual foundation for the Pinochet programme; and Peter Bauer, at work in West Africa, argued for opening the doors to foreign trade and investment and avoiding planning and controls.[3] IMF economists, from the same stable, saw inflation and payments problems, already widespread, as due simply to lack of monetary discipline and wrong exchange rates. If these were put right, the basis would be established for a fast growth of output (which they have consistently confused with 'development').

Such economists — there were also Marxist examples, such as Charles Bettelheim in Cuba — helped to shape the minds of the new generation of 'Third World' economists and political leaders, especially in Latin America. These have anyway mostly been students in one of the developed countries (or in universities at home which had copied their syllabuses). In a sense, their theoretical equipment is twice removed from reality — it was developed for *other* countries, in *earlier* circumstances.

Many of the new nations, especially in tropical Africa, have for other reasons little basis for an articulate nationalist response. They are artificial creations, with boundaries set by colonial powers ruling on maps lines that cut across tribal units: these often left part of a tribe under British rule, part under French, yet, at the same time, threw traditional enemies together — for example the Kikuyu and Luo in Kenya. In some colonies, moreover, foreign groups were introduced as slaves, indentured labourers, traders, or settlers (e.g. Africans in the Caribbean; Chinese and Indians in Malaysia; Indians in Fiji and Sri Lanka; Europeans in Zimbabwe). Countries where such foreign elements are large and unassimilated easily fall under the influence of one of the superpowers. Some leaders of these hybrid countries oscillate in their allegiance, in fact. Milton Obote, for example, took a rather Marxist position in the 1960s: when I spoke to him in 1981, he told me that one of the guides he relied on was the Berg Report on Africa, sponsored by the World Bank.

The faltering of the international system is, however, stimulating the revival of traditional nationalism in North Africa and in the Middle East, or (to use a less Eurocentric term) West Asia. Transnational influences, both Western and Marxist, conflict with Moslem traditions that obviously continue to have a widespread appeal (indeed a growing one) as far east as Indonesia.

But it is in Latin America that the opposition has been most obvious. Here the superimposed culture, the Iberian branch of the European, overcame Amerindian resistance, and then in turn was weakened by the influence of another dominant power, the United States. However, the cultural assimilation to the US has never been complete. For one thing, in some countries at least, Catholicism had taken a deep hold. The linguistic barrier has also helped; so has a fairly long experience of political independence. Perhaps the very degree of US cultural penetration, unaccompanied by acceptable economic progress for the mass of the people, created the conditions for resistance.

This started to become articulate in the 1930s. The depression hit parts of Latin America very hard and the improvized measures of protection were rationalized subsequently. Towards the end of this decade, Prebisch, an Argentinian, whose works are still largely unknown to economists in industrial countries (and who once told me he had been influenced by List), developed a thesis with nationalist implications, based on an alleged chronic tendency for the terms of trade of primary producers to deteriorate.[4] The world consisted of a 'core' of industrial countries and a weak 'periphery' of exporters of primary products: the 'gap' between their average incomes would tend to grow. This justified an emphasis on industrialization and tariff protection, so Prebisch has always – and understandably – been treated as a dangerous man by officialdom in Britain and the United States. (When I was involved in setting up the Institute of Development Studies, an Under-Secretary of Trade came to my office specifically to warn me against giving the 'wrong impression' by inviting Prebisch to join the Institute's Governing Body: the reason he put forward, Prebisch's radicalism – convinced me that his presence was essential.) Subsequent research has shown that whether there has been a deterioration in relative price depends very much on what commodities and what period one is talking about, and that anyway it has not been great.[5] Actually a stronger case for import substitution lay in the lower income-elasticities of demand for most primary products, and other factors which I shall discuss later. The significance of Prebisch was, however, that he opened the door for criticism of neoclassical theory, even if his original reasons were not well founded.

The Prebisch doctrine, though far from revolutionary, in any sense, or even egalitarian in its original form, had important repercussions. There was widespread acceptance in Latin America of the over-riding need for protected industrialization to ease the balance of payments constraint on growth.[6] Moreover, some structural strains were by implication inevitable, and thus so was a degree of inflation: this was a necessary price to pay for development.

Experience in Latin America with this programme has not been encouraging. Imports of many products were, indeed, rapidly reduced, mostly consumer goods, especially in the bigger economies such as Argentina and Brazil. But dependence on imports of energy, intermediate goods, sophisticated equipment and technology, indeed usually food, increased — sometimes in absolute terms, always in the organic sense that the industrial output and employment came to depend increasingly on foreign exchange supplies and would be paralysed without them (whereas in a less industrialized country, imports, consisting mainly of finished consumer goods, can be reduced, at least temporarily, without great damage). Moreover the programme required capital on a scale that could only be provided (if sacrifices on the part of the local upper classes were ruled out) by the TNCs, which could also supply the technology.

What is more, the protective barriers, set up around markets which were not big by modern standards, created monopolistic conditions, discouraging innovation, making possible large profit margins, and weakening the resistance to increases in costs, especially wages. These consequences were most serious in smaller economies where in the period up to 1973 governments followed the same route — such as Chile — especially since financial policy was given very little attention, as will be explained in Chapter 8.

By the 1970s the 'structuralist' school which Prebisch had founded was paying much more attention to the flaws in this policy, especially two of them: its effects on income distribution and on external dependence. The 'dependency' school was an offshoot, including economists like Pinto[7] and Sunkel,[8] who had been among the original structuralists, but drawing also on Marxism (in varying degrees, according to the author concerned)[9] and Latin American sociology (such as the work of Cardoso).

The programme that this implied was more radical than that of Prebisch (at least the Prebisch of the 1950s). It included control, if not nationalization, of foreign companies that operated at strategic points in the economy, such as mining. Where implemented — to some degree in Argentina, Brazil, and Uruguay, but especially in Chile — it provoked strong United States intervention. This was able to capitalize on the financial chaos that invariably accompanied the programme, in alliance with the local military (most of whose senior officers had been US trained), a large part of the middle classes, and the privileged portion of even the working class, which had come to feel impoverished and insecure.

The result in each case was a military coup, and it raises a crucial question: how far can a nationalist, and egalitarian policy be carried without a political catastrophe? This is the issue I shall address in the chapters that follow.

THE CONSTRAINTS ON NATIONALISM

Synopsis

SECTION A argued that in the present world crisis one of the failings of neo-classical economists of various kinds is that they ignore the strength of nationalism and overstress the merits of the (US or Soviet dominated) international system. But it does not follow that any government can simply decide to opt out.

A central concept in my analysis is what I call the 'room to manoeuvre' of a government. This is the area within which policy can be varied without the government incurring costs that are excessive in relation to the potential benefits. It can be visualized as an area in the second map in the previous chapter.

To get hold of the concept, let us carry out an imaginary experiment: assume that a government in the US sphere of influence wants to change radically and quickly the development strategy, involving some 'delinking' of the country from the world economy — by expropriating foreign capital and/or controlling its entry, with associated internal redistributive measures. In other words, suppose it wants to move further leftwards and southwards in the map, into, or further into, the EN quadrant.

The determinants of the room to manoeuvre will be revealed if we ask ourselves: what retaliation would it fear and under what circumstances? How far could it safely go before the costs became excessive?

Some may think these questions trivial. But they are not at

all irrelevant to the fate of nationalist leaders. As we know from recent experience, many who embark on an autonomous strategy with naïve optimism not merely lose power in a military coup and see their policies reversed, but also forfeit their liberties (including the freedom to live in their own country), some even their lives. And the mere *possibility* of military interventions and coups (with some external inspiration and support) shapes the policies, even if only subconsciously, of governments considering much less drastic strategies. Many policies are 'unthinkable', or at least 'impractical'.

Yet such limitations are almost totally ignored in public debate. Indeed, manifestos issued by parties contesting an election (where this still occurs), typically suggest that, if they succeeded, they would be able to do pretty much what they liked, from introducing socialism to removing all controls – they would then eliminate unemployment, poverty, inflation, etc., etc.

The failure to recognize the inevitable constraints may, indeed, lead them when they have taken power to adopt policies which are unworkable; on the other hand, the constraints may suddenly loom so large that they fail to see what *can* be achieved and do little or nothing.

Even those of us not in politics are rarely explicit on what room to manoeuvre we assume. Yet different people may well be making different assumptions about what options are open in any situation: bureaucrats, for example, tend to exclude all possible policies outside a narrow range, whereas many academics assume policy to be largely or totally unconstrained. Differences over what governments *should* do are often really about what they *can* do. It is not surprising that discussion of policy options is so often sterile.

A full treatment of this issue would take a good deal of deep theorizing about economic and political structures at both international and national levels, and the interactions between them, and the dynamics of those interactions. It would mean discussing the importance of political commitment and of the administrative efficiency and integrity required by nationalist policies.

In the three chapters that follow, I shall only deal with some of the determinants of the room to manoeuvre – starting with a few, such as the origin of capital, that are obvious, but nevertheless largely neglected in the work of neo-classical economists of any kind. The latter have done very little work on external constraints on government economic policy, apart from those that are part and parcel of the working of commodity and capital markets: as the constraints are political, they will argue that this is not economics(!) This is not surprising: they disapprove of such nationalist concerns.

A good deal can be inferred from the work of dependency theorists mentioned in the previous chapter. But there is not much explicit treatment even there of the consequences of certain constraints, especially military and geographic, which do not fit too easily into their models. For example, to increase the room to manoeuvre may involve raising military expenditure. (Radicals often want *both* a more independent policy and low military spending: in many countries these aims may well be mutually exclusive.)

In the longer run military vulnerability can be reduced by raising the birth rate, which would also increase the proportion of teenagers in the population and thus make the labour force more flexible. There are of course well-known costs of a fast-growing population, but these need to be weighed against the benefits in any particular country, rather than relying uncritically on the anti-natalist advice of many international agencies, or on the views of the Reverend Malthus (another classical economist). It is undoubtedly convenient for great powers that this advice should be widely disseminated, but I am concerned with its local relevance, which is a matter of analysis, not doctrine.

Another topic widely ignored, indeed suppressed, by all conventional schools is the ethnic diversity of many nations; yet this raises very basic problems for development strategy, especially in the non-nations (mentioned in Chapter 2) which were created by the colonial powers (probably the greatest crime of colonialism, because the effects will last longest).

Dependency economists also tend to deal rather superficially with natural resources: yet it has become increasingly clear in recent years, as the relative price of oil has risen, that the degree of self-sufficiency in energy, in particular, profoundly affects a government's room to manoeuvre — the same applies to cereals. Dependence or independence in these dimensions — and also in technology — largely determines a country's place in the international hierarchy, and I shall propose a different classification from the old 'Three Worlds'.

All this implies that the possibility of autonomous policies depends very much on the particular circumstances of each country. (In fact, for some small countries with few resources, and split into quite separate ethnic groups, autonomous development is hardly possible.)

The only way to understand the determinants of the room to manoeuvre is to look at some recent examples, and I shall draw on my own experience in countries where governments were trying to pursue independent paths, with various degrees of success.

CHAPTER 3

Economic and political realities

IN order to discuss the feasibility of alternative approaches to those in the neo-classical tradition, I shall start by examining the limits, apart from those set by the quantity of available capital, to a particular country's development, and develop the argument with brief case studies.

One major influence may be the source of capital. Neo-classical economists (of at least the Chicago and Keynesian branches, and even orthodox Marxists) are strictly indifferent to where capital comes from. When evaluating projects they concentrate simply on the rate of return. In macro-economic analysis, e.g. for development plans, they use aggregate investment — which adds together indifferently the capital from foreign and domestic, public and private sources — and work out the total saving required, as if the undistributed profits of firms, even foreign firms, were available for any type of investment. (This indeed is precisely what nearly all official statistics do, following the practice recommended in the UN System of National Accounts — see Chapter 9). An economist of this type would probably, if pressed, even show some preference for foreign capital, because of the technology, management skills, etc. it brings with it.

Most dependency theorists would hardly deny that there could ever be a need for foreign capital, but they would adopt a very different approach. The school emphasizes the importance of the economic, political, and in some cases cultural links that come with certain types of capital, especially what arrives via the TNCs. I shall not review here the whole range of the effects of foreign direct investment on the balance of payments, employment, income distribution, etc.[1] I will merely glance at the likely retaliation of the TNCs when a 'host government' drastically raises taxes, or adopts pro-labour legislation, or threatens expropriation — or even indulges in rhetoric they find alarming.

They can be expected to reduce output, employment, and perhaps exports; technological imports will almost certainly cease; and the inflow of capital be replaced by an outflow. Some such reaction would be just the natural response of a risk-avoiding profit maximizer. It may, however, also be deliberately aimed at inducing policy changes — if necessary through bringing down the government.

Foreign corporations may well get support in this aim from local groups which depend on them economically, e.g. the trade unions to which their employees belong and manufacturers or farmers supplying production inputs. (In identifying such allies the work of the dependency school is useful.) They will also expect help from 'their own' government, which can use additional instruments of retaliation, from a cut-off of aid to a trade embargo or even war. Thus purely commercial conflicts rapidly become highly political: the very existence of TNCs raises the costs of some policies (one of the usually ignored disadvantages of inviting them in), and the bigger their presence, the higher these costs become.

More serious, usually, are the consequences of thousands of individual decisions that lead to receipts of foreign exchange being held up and payments expedited. The balance of payments and economic activity are thus especially sensitive to fluctuations in 'confidence', i.e. the extent to which foreign bankers, investors, and traders approve of the policies of the governments concerned, which in turn both reflects and influences the way the media report these policies. All this may come on top of the foreign exchange effects of an unbalanced budget, as the government tries to satisfy the social demands of its supporters.

A radical government cannot safely let consumption fall much, either as a whole or of certain key goods and services. As has been pointed out above, some of the working class in a dependent country are relatively privileged and, in fact, assimilated to the 'modern' sector, with its imported standards and values. Trade unions will no doubt support the delinking strategy, but still insist, very possibly with the deliberate encouragement of foreign governments (or regional or international trade union federations in which these have influence), on what they consider a minimum tolerable income. This will cover many items that are scarcely *basic* needs in physiological terms, but are still claimed to be absolutely essential.

Nor can any government permit much of a decline in the

levels of living of the professional and managerial classes, even in those items that reflect the cultural dependence described earlier. The co-operation of some will be needed, at the least their willingness to stay in the country.

In fact the expectations of various classes constitute one of the most important constraints on the room to manoeuvre.

For various reasons, therefore, exchange reserves may fall, leading to devaluation of the currency and import restrictions, which aggravate price rises, shortages, and unemployment, and justify and reinforce the deterioration in 'confidence'. Imports can usually be reduced, but the reduction is limited by resource needs which will be discussed in Chapter 5. So the government probably turns to the IMF, which will require deflationary policies as a condition of financial rescue. To reject these may strike a heavy blow to confidence; yet if it accepts them, this probably means the abandonment of radical policies.

The necessity for foreign exchange naturally also poses issues about servicing debts to foreign governments, banks, or international agencies, and permitting profit outflows. Yet the danger of retaliation may make it impractical for a government to default on such obligations, however strong the moral case for doing so may appear (especially if the obligations had been incurred by a completely different, oppressive, government, as part of a political deal that kept it in power). We do not need to speculate about the ultimate outcome. Chile (1970–3) provides the *casus classicus*,[2] not because it is unique, but because, thanks to the openness of the United States political system, especially during the national self-examination as the Watergate scandal unwound, it is so well known.

To criticize the Allende government seems to exonerate the military officers who betrayed their oaths of loyalty and the US policy-makers who supported – perhaps prompted – them, but analysing its mistakes may help others to avoid its fate. The retaliatory measures were so effective because of the economic chaos, which was (to be frank) partly due to the government itself. It undertook very ambitious social and economic development programmes without having a majority in the Chilean Congress, and thus the ability to raise taxes. It also made serious mistakes in administration, especially financial, to which I shall return in Chapter 8.

The electoral programme of the *Unidad Popular* had been drastic. It promised big wage increases without an 'imperialist' devaluation, and threatened expropriation, virtually without compensation, of US businesses, especially the subsidiaries of mining corporations. Indeed, ITT dreamt up a plot to stop President-elect Allende even taking office. This was never hatched, but when it became clear that the new government was in earnest, the US Secretary of State, Kissinger, adopted a deliberate policy of 'destabilization'. Attempts were made to block exports of copper and hold up supplies of essential imports. Banks (including the World Bank) were induced not to lend to Chile. Strikes were supported, especially of copper miners and lorry drivers. When the stage was set for a military coup, the generals also knew they could count on the help of the United States government after taking office.

There are many lessons about the determinants of room to manoeuvre that can be learned from the experience of the Allende government, which evidently strayed beyond its bounds. Thus one might have expected United States attempts to block copper exports to be crucial: actually they turned out to have little effect. Copper is a homogeneous product and thus its origin is unrecognizable; it does not deteriorate; and it is traded in a well-organized market centred in London. But in these respects it is rather unusual: embargoes on exports of some other commodities could clearly be much more successful. (The origin of bananas, as an extreme example, could hardly be concealed; also they do not keep long and have to be carried in specially refrigerated ships; they can only be sold in bulk through distribution systems controlled by a few TNCs.)

In fact Chilean copper exports did decline, but for different reasons, that are also ignored in neo-classical texts. Foreign staff left, but also shortages developed of highly specific spare parts for copper-mining machinery: to depend on a single country (more so, a single company) for technology and associated inputs creates the conditions for successful retaliation. The decline in copper production was caused in part as well by strikes, to which I have already referred.

The experience of Chile also illustrated the danger of military subversion. There is always some risk of military coups. There were 76 of these in the Third World in 1960–80 (Sivard,

1981) — and this number does not include those (e.g. in Nigeria and Peru) where there had been coups but power had later been yielded to a civilian government.

As in Chile, generals may have personal reasons for wanting to seize office, especially because of the possibilities of enrichment. They often come from a family of property-owners whose interests have been threatened by the programmes of radical governments (or even by just the threat of efficient tax collection!). They can easily persuade themselves that they are 'saving the nation' from something (or be so persuaded by colleagues).

Moreover, they are bound to be in touch with counterparts in the armed services of foreign powers, who can promise them anything from a neutral stance to direct military assistance in a coup and support after it has been successfully carried through. There is nearly always a military attaché in the embassy of the dominant country (and also in the dependent country's own embassy in Washington, Moscow, London, Paris, etc.). In the case of Latin America, friendships have often been established at joint training courses (e.g. in the US-sponsored officers' school in Panama) or in combined manoeuvres.

So one has to add to the list of constraints: 'What would the armed forces tolerate?', which requires a knowledge of their internal politics. (The problem of how to incorporate military policy in total development strategy I shall turn to in Chapter 7.)

In some circumstances, this question may not arise. For example, in Cuba, the traditional armed forces had been defeated by the revolutionaries, and when the United States government decided to attempt a military coup, it had to organize this itself — the 'Bay of Pigs' invasion. (This was carried out half-heartedly, and its repulsion greatly strengthened Castro.)

But the Cuban government faced considerable economic difficulties due to the difficulty of obtaining spare parts, transport equipment of various kinds (especially lorries and buses), industrial materials, fertilizers, and pesticides, etc. Big Soviet loans were obtained and in due course much of the capital equipment was replaced by Soviet models. But, partly because these were unfamiliar, output declined.

Even simple linguistic mistakes had consequences. Castro himself once said, in a meeting I attended, that the reason for a sharp rise in the birth rate soon after the revolution was that a big order for 'Dutch caps' had been read as an order for automotive gaskets. When I look out on a street in Havana today, I cannot help wondering how many of the young people I see would not be there but for a translator's error!

Economic conditions were hard in the late 1960s, with long queues, even for rationed products (and consequently absenteeism from work, which aggravated supply difficulties still further).[3] It is not possible to go here into the reasons for the regime's survival, but the headings would include the wavering and ineffectual policy of the US; the interest of the Soviet government in establishing a beachhead in the Caribbean; the evident integrity of the Cuban leaders, especially Castro; and above all his eventual willingness to change course (though not so much in external policy as by reintroducing tight budgetary control — see Chapter 8).

Thus the very different experiences in Chile and Cuba added much material to substantiate the concept of dependency, and drew attention to significant factors omitted in the works of mainstream economics from the discussion of policy.

A good illustration of the automatic reaction, to which I referred above, is Portugal. The revolution of 1974 was bloodless, and did not directly threaten foreign business. But there were sweeping measures of nationalization and much heady rhetoric eagerly quoted in the US and West European press. Tourist arrivals dropped sharply; the hundreds of thousands of Portuguese workers in France and elsewhere abroad held back their normal remittances; foreign banks insisted on prompt payment of obligations; and the inflow of private capital dropped, while capital outflows rose, partly in response to the nationalization of the banks. On the other hand, imports climbed as government spending increased, and importers built up inventories in anticipation of restrictions. Taken together with the effects of the loss of Portuguese colonies in Africa, and of the concurrent world economic crisis, a sizeable foreign exchange deficit was inevitable.

In this case there were big foreign exchange and gold reserves and they covered the gap for more than two years. But in due course the government, which lacked any coherent economic strategy, had to turn to the IMF. They added its weight to that of the political groups insisting on a less radical policy. At the same time, foreign agencies — official, quasi-official, and private — were pushing in the same direction. (The Frederich-Eburt-Stiftung, for example, a West German Socialist foundation, was busy helping the socialists and encouraging them to drop extremist policies and to support affiliation to the EEC.) The political pendulum gradually swung back until a centre-right coalition was in power, five years after the coup, and little remained of the 'revolution'.

This example illustrates another factor normally left out of dependency analysis, location, which affects profoundly the possibility of self-reliance. The closer a country is to those more developed, the lower the costs of transportation, especially if there are overland freight routes. This makes it easier for its exports to compete in neighbouring markets. But it also encourages dependence on imports. Industries to make intermediate products, capital goods, and arms are not easy to establish anyway, especially in a small country, and the difficulty is all the greater where distance does not provide a natural protection.

The cheapness of travelling a few hundred miles today has both advantages and disadvantages. Though for many of the individuals concerned, the migration is temporary, it can become a longer-term source of foreign exchange and employment for their country. Emigrants not only regularly remit a fraction of their wages homewards, and spend some when on visits; they bring capital back with them when they give up their work overseas. Thus migration both relieves social pressures and provides valuable foreign exchange. (Turkey is a leading example[4] — and so, of course, is Mexico.)

The foreign payments structure becomes, however, in time vulnerable to the labour and immigration policies of the government of the recipient country. Migration is also debilitating: it deprives the country from which it comes of skills and initiative, especially since a substantial fraction of migrants settle overseas. The growth of the productive sectors is inhibited by the scarcity of manpower, especially professional workers of types in demand abroad. One possible consequence is that salaries tend to rise (or remain high) relative to wages of the unskilled, which would be inconsistent with an egalitarian strategy. Another is that the economy becomes dependent on imports, even of food. And, while the expertise and capital of the returning migrant may help local industrialization, his capital may be invested in shops or real estate rather than production.

So a government of a country that has become heavily dependent on migration can hardly expect to have much room for manoeuvre, even though it did nothing itself to encourage this dependence.

Nor can one that relies on tourism; the cheapness of passenger transport makes employment and foreign exchange receipts dependent on policies in other countries. Again, though mass tourism brings foreign exchange and creates employment, it, too, has serious side effects. Work in hotels may cause labour shortages in other sectors, especially agriculture, thus affecting their production. The policies of the tourist sector, including employment practices, are — like its organization and architecture — in a degree based on foreign models, since many of its establishments, especially the bigger hotels, are usually foreign-controlled. The source, level, and type of tourism are therefore determined largely outside the country. Policy in many spheres, particularly if it involves drastic changes, may be affected by the fear of alarming or offending tourists. (Tourism also has a cultural impact which will be discussed in the following chapter.)

CHAPTER 4

Demographic and social realities

A country's room to manoeuvre is in part a function of its size. This can, of course be defined in various ways. A country with a small *area* is unlikely to have a very diversified resource base, in contrast to Canada, say, or Australia, or Brazil. Nowadays, area has to be defined to include territorial waters in view of the fishing and sub-sea mineral potential in a country's 'economic zone'. (I come back to the significance of resources in Chapter 5.) But land area is also still important. The historic experience of Russia brought out, on at least two well-known occasions, the military importance of space: a country small in this sense will have little opportunity to absorb an invading army, and thus not even much time to take diplomatic counter-measures.[1]

More important is the size of a country's *population*. Some dependency theorists, especially in the Caribbean (e.g. Lloyd Best) have gone out of their way to argue that this is irrelevant, and tacitly assume all countries to be sufficiently large for autonomous policies to be pursued. Is the explanation that they would — especially those influenced to some degree by Marxism — find it inconvenient to admit that in many countries a revolution would not be a sufficient condition for social change?

After all, population *is* an important determinant of the room to manoeuvre. It is the reservoir from which the armed forces are drawn. There are many examples of governments of countries with large populations invading those with smaller ones to ensure that 'acceptable' policies were followed. (The United States would hardly have been able to invade the Dominican Republic on several occasions, or the Soviet Union Afghanistan, if their populations had been reversed.)

It also sets, at a given level of income, the size of the *market*, which is in turn closely related to the structure of production, especially the degree of self-sufficiency possible in manufacturing vehicles and heavy equipment. If the national market is smaller than some US $10 billion, it will hardly support industries producing intermediate products such as steel, aluminium, heavy chemicals, etc. — especially if incomes are low and largely absorbed by food and other necessities. Apart from the costs of sub-optimal levels of production, many of the necessary inputs would have to be imported, and thus paid for in foreign exchange. Industrialization in such a country inevitably means, in the end, relying on specialist export-oriented industries. The TNCs will also probably become firmly entrenched: they supply the capital and technology and often provide access to the necessary markets abroad. Then many key decisions are taken overseas, and tax administration is hampered by transfer pricing (setting prices of traded goods at levels so that profits accrue in whichever country the TNC wishes — usually to minimize total tax liability, sometimes to evade exchange control).

In a country with a very small population, like Belize, even Jamaica, there are not many development options for *any* government. It is bound to be heavily dependent on foreign trade: industrialization is restricted and its armed forces tiny. So to follow a highly independent development strategy of the type indicated above might well be catastrophic.

Apart from the size of population, its *structure* also affects the room to manoeuvre. A high ratio of new entrants to the labour force, ready to learn new skills and more mobile geographically, imparts flexibility to the economy. A 'young' population in this sense may also be more ready for political innovation. Conversely, in a country such as Britain with a static population, economic and political change is more difficult: pensioners are relatively numerous, and this is a heavy burden, political as well as economic. A high birth rate (especially if it had been low half a century previously) produces a 'young' population. So Malthusian arguments, eagerly espoused by European liberals, do not necessarily apply in all national circumstances. On the other hand, from another point of view, rapid population increase raises the pressure on resources, especially land, and increases the task of labour absorption.

Stimulating demographic growth has been almost an unmentionable subject, at least in 'progressive' circles. Policies to raise the birth rate (discussed in Chapter 6) are, no doubt, against the interests of mankind in some wider sense, but there is, after all, no international institution capable of protecting such interests, and governments, especially of countries with severe social problems, are under no obligation to behave in the same way as if such an authority did, in fact, exist – or the great powers behaved responsibly (e.g. in the share they took of world resources).

Another important influence on the room to manoeuvre is the strength of traditional *culture*. This too is difficult for most on the Left to acknowledge, especially many dependency theorists: it would seem to open the door to the despised 'modernization' theories in which traditions are treated as the major obstacles to development. But culture need not be viewed in this way. The deeper the cultural roots, the longer and stronger will be the resistance to foreign styles of consumption and the accompanying dependence on imports of consumer goods, e.g. wheat flour to satisfy a mass taste for bread in a country where growing wheat is climatically impossible. The slower, too, will be the emergence of widespread demand for automobiles in countries which lack not merely the engineering capacity to manufacture them (often because of their population size), but also the oil to keep them running. Traditional values can thus preserve the room to manoeuvre by rigidifying both the level and the structure of consumer aspirations.

In all fields, imported tastes, techniques, and theories can do profound damage, if they are allowed to. Buildings may be constructed in ways that not merely require imported materials but are quite unsuitable for the climate (e.g. glass buildings in the tropics, such as Africa Hall in Addis Ababa, the headquarters of the UN Economic Commission for Africa). To offset such errors of design, air-conditioning equipment can be introduced, but again at a heavy and chronic foreign exchange cost, taking account of power and spare parts.

Such damage not only occurs in the tropics. There are now many ways in which countries are bombarded with foreign, especially US, cultural influences. This even applies to Western Europe. Films, whether shown in cinemas or on TV or video sets, are potent conveyors of tastes. So are TV programmes, especially series such as 'Dallas'. These take up a big share of station time almost everywhere, because national TV authorities cannot fill the day with acceptable programmes locally produced. To these must be added books and magazines (e.g. TIME).[2]

Still more important is international travel. Its cultural influence is not symmetrical. Business executives from developed countries, diplomats, etc., spread foreign theories, techniques, and attitudes. So do technical assistance personnel. Foreign tourists require special facilities (shops, restaurants, nightclubs, personal services) which some native citizens will also inevitably use.[3] More important, mass tourism easily destroys local culture (dress, cooking), even languages. Personal relations become commercialized (people expect tips for friendly acts, even for having their photograph taken). Dancing and singing become distorted into the sort of 'folklore' that attracts the tourists.

The effects are not at all symmetrical. The national of the developing country who goes abroad, whether as a visitor or migrant worker, is likely to acquire, not mould, foreign tastes. The values and perceptions of officials who see themselves as loyal patriots may have been to some extent shaped by foreign contacts. A course of education in another country, for example at Harvard or Moscow (or Oxford or Prague), may not merely shape the student's consumption tastes, professional habits, and ideology, but lead him or her to believe in identities of interest which do not, in fact, exist.

The corollary of this is that scholarships for foreign students are likely to prove very worthwhile to the host in relation to their cost — provided its culture is strong enough to assimilate them. An example of the return on these scholarships is the 'Berkeley mafia' in Indonesia, which, like the 'Chicago boys' in Chile, already mentioned, were all trained in economics in the same US university. Many of the Indonesian group, too, have been in key positions as Ministers, etc.

Even if he or she studies at home, a student's values and perceptions affecting development strategy will inevitably be influenced, to some extent, by ideologies originating abroad. This applies especially to students of the social sciences. Not only are foreign texts widely used: foreign theories, such as the Chicago, Keynesian, and Marxist models discussed in the previous section, are often taught — and lazily taught, in the sense that there is little discussion of their assumptions and thus their appropriateness for various local contexts.[4] Such intellectual subservience is reinforced by aspirations to publish in foreign professional journals, and by the wish to leave open the possibility, at least, of a job abroad (for example, in the World Bank or the IMF) or a directorship of a TNC subsidiary.

But the government may need to keep educated people of some professions in the country, and may consequently have to offer salaries well out of line with local levels, and these may have to be paid in due course also to those who are less mobile (e.g. administrators).[5]

It is not surprising to see the élite in most countries, especially in the tropics, totally committed to copying foreign lifestyles. Those that do not send their children to schools overseas insist on foreign syllabuses and textbooks for the national educational systems. Even history may be depicted through foreign eyes. A younger generation educated in this way is likely to be quite alienated and even to lose the possibility of communication with their compatriots, especially in rural areas. Patriotism, on which a government's room to manoeuvre really depends in the last resort, is difficult to sustain if such foreign influences run at all deep, especially if they are associated with great economic inequality, as is often the case.

There is now a transnational culture (mainly US in origin), a common 'climate of opinion' in the dominant, transnational élite,[5] including much of the professional and bureaucratic classes. This helps explain the severe cultural dualism that reduces a government's room to manoeuvre and often makes true national development difficult, if not impossible, and why the cultural currents favouring the growth-oriented, open-door strategy of 'modernization' are now very strong.

Cultural dependence not merely determines in large part the patterns of consumption and the choice of technique in every field, and stimulates the 'brain drain': it also shapes, in some degree, development strategy, and thus the whole economic structure — a point that would be unacceptable to the more doctrinaire Marxists who assert (or rather assume) that such cultural phenomena are part of the 'superstructure'. (The Marxist position was less implausible when it originated in the nineteenth century, before the transnational culture spread over the world: in any case it is still somewhat plausible in Europe, where many of these transnational currents originate).

Cultural dependence is, indeed, more fundamental than economic as a determinant of the room to manoeuvre, just as mental illness is of more basic importance, though not necessarily more serious, than a physical disease. A patient with a sick mind may be incapable of recognizing his symptoms, of willing himself to recover, or of monitoring his own progress. Analogously, an élite whose minds are stuffed with foreign values and theories may be unable to understand even the need for national development, let alone frame a development strategy in the national interest, however defined — though when a policy of interdependence leads to a crisis (which can take a long time), their nationalism may be reawakened.

Japan is, of course, the supreme example of a country where foreign influences have been admitted selectively and at a pace slow enough to be absorbed, deliberately set by an élite that has remained firmly Japanese. The country had the advantage of a highly developed national culture with deep historical roots to its patriotism: its customs and language are particularly difficult for foreigners to learn. It was spared colonization (just), and developed in time the capacity to resist foreign domination, even to survive a period of US military occupation, and virtually to exclude foreign investment and immigrants (apart from some Koreans).

Thus the roots of an independent strategy may lie not so much in the country's particular productive structure or military capability, important though these are, as in a culture strong and homogeneous enough to avoid alienation — especially dependence on an imported way of perceiving the nation's own needs.

It is difficult to achieve this in a country with great ethnic diversity (see Chapter 2). There are many such now, because of strong migration currents both during the colonial period and subsequently. In some of the 'capital surplus' countries in the Middle East (e.g. Kuwait and Saudi Arabia), more than half the labour force consists of immigrants. Most of these are on labour contracts at relatively low wages. The position of these migrants can be illustrated by a personal experience. After I had enjoyed the hospitality of a Kuwaiti Cabinet

Minister one evening, he kindly sent me back to my hotel in his Mercedes. I noticed that a small car was following us whichever way we turned, and I drew the chauffeur's attention to it. 'Don't worry', he said, 'that is *my* chauffeur: when I've parked this car in the Ministry's car park, he will run me home.' The driver of the Minister's car was of course a Kuwaiti, for security reasons (apart from patronage): he would be able to afford a Palestinian or Jordanian to drive for him.

The loyalty of these migrants to their hosts must be doubtful (they may come from a different Moslem sect, e.g. Shiites). They cannot safely be recruited into the armed forces. They may well prove a source of political unrest, rather than support, in certain types of international crises (though policies of diversifying sources of immigration have reduced this risk).

It is of course true that, if one goes back far enough, all countries are ethnic and cultural mixtures. European and (especially) US history suggests that these differences can be overcome, provided one tribe is dominant, e.g. the Anglo-Saxons in Britain, and indeed minorities have been sources of enrichment, but the process has taken centuries. (In Belgium, especially, it is still far from complete.)

In an artificial nation, as pointed out in Chapter 2, foreign cultural influences easily take hold, formerly Christianity and Mohammedanism, now imported political religions (monetarism or Marxism). This is especially so if the economic dualism corresponds to the ethnic, and one racial group (e.g. neo-European) is more closely integrated into the transnational culture. Politicians in such countries can more easily be corrupted financially too: they are less likely to have the self-respect that is engendered in a country with deep historic roots to its nationalism.

Divisions of this kind are often further aggravated by differences in *language*, themselves anyway a serious source of weakness.

For countries divided in such ways, national development in a true sense is very difficult, as it is for small ones (see above), even if economic growth is fast. The line of development may lie in regional integration (discussed in Chapter 12), since this will increase the market, and a group of neighbours that are each internally diverse may have a clearer collective identity *vis-à-vis* the outside world.

A majority has no inherent right to impose national unity on the minority (or minorities), that wants to cut itself off from a culture it feels alien, especially if it is also exploited economically. This is in fact neither a moral question nor one of law: Northern Ireland illustrates the point. There is no correct 'solution' such as social scientists search for. There are, however, possible compromises, e.g. a degree of regional autonomy, separate electoral rolls (where elections take place), 'power-sharing', confederation, etc.

The minority may do better to settle for less than full independence: it may be too small (see above) or too short of resources (see Chapter 5) to be able to enjoy true or even secure national development on its own anyway. For the majority too, a compromise may be best, especially since there may be possibilities of gradually unifying the country, by shaping policy in education and other fields in ways to be discussed in Chapter 6.

But in some circumstances allowing secession may be preferable. An unappeased minority disrupts national unity; to suppress it is expensive; and it provides a base for intervention, even military, by neighbours (especially of the same race or racial group as the minority), or by the great powers. Norway and Sweden live amicably after their separation, and Ireland could hardly have been accommodated for long within Britain, especially since we were losing the room to make big concessions, as the colonial system disintegrated.

The strength of national culture in former colonies depends on the length and nature of colonial rule. A long occupation, especially if it involved 'direct rule', not merely virtually removed the opportunity of learning from political experience, it deeply penetrated the colony with the customs and attitudes of the dominant power and was, in many cases, devastating to the national culture, especially if settlers, slaves, or indentured labour were introduced in large numbers (see Chapter 2). Nationalists who have been influenced by Marxism or other European theories often emphasize the economic exploitation of their country, neglecting the greater wrongs.

Cultural autonomy, like economic and military autonomy, also depends on a country's *location*. Dominant neighbours can exert cultural pressures, purveying products, brands, techniques, attitudes, and values to weaker neighbours. If adjacent countries do not actually share the same language, at least they probably belong to the same linguistic groups (e.g. Latin-based). Face-to-face contacts and intermarriage may be customary near a common frontier, especially if this cuts across an ethnic or linguistic minority in each country (like the Basques in France and Spain). In various professions, including politics, meetings and conferences between people from nearby countries are commonplace. Telephone conversations between neighbours are now inexpensive. Newspapers are cheap and up-to-date, if bought close to the printing works.

A domestic radio receiver can pick up transmissions from foreign stations (FM or medium-wave) within a few hundred kilometres. (It is true that broadcasts can be 'jammed', but if this is on an effective scale it is costly and difficult to conceal.) Although the range is less for television transmitters, especially if the terrain is broken, there are often links between TV systems of neighbouring countries.

Finally, where neighbours share the same language, the larger will be able to sell the other films, video tapes, books, magazines, etc., increasing cultural dependence. Often those can be priced more cheaply, since the overheads can be charged to the bigger home market. Examples are the prevalence of German cultural products in Austria, Argentinian in Uruguay, etc.

Lesotho, a country technologically weak and very small, completely surrounded by South Africa, illustrates all these points. It is not only heavily dependent on the Republic for employment (which separates family members), it is wide open to trade and vulnerable to the possible cutting of power supplies, indeed of virtually all imports.

On top of this, it is culturally penetrated — far more than, say, an island, similar in other respects, in the Indian Ocean. Streams of tourists motor across the border with the Republic (to enjoy gambling and miscegenation forbidden under the puritanical laws and customs at home). The government could not keep out South African television programmes (including news), any more than they could exclude members of South African security services. The position of Puerto Rico is similar in these respects *vis-à-vis* the United States.

There are thus reasons beyond the economic and military

why the government of a small country is very limited in its capacity to follow a strategy that would inconvenience and antagonize the government of a bigger one, especially a neighbour.

CHAPTER 5

Resources and technology

THE inherent conflicts of interest in the world were aggravated when the 'oil shocks' of 1973-4 and 1979-80 revealed the resource constraint on world economic output. World consumption of oil could not continue to double every decade as in the 1950s and 1960s. Nor could food consumption per capita continue to rise significantly, granted the slow global rate of increase in agricultural production — shortages of cereals brought about a sharp rise in food prices in 1973, in fact, before the upsurge in oil prices.

Crucial in determining any government's room to manoeuvre is whether the country is a substantial net importer or exporter of each of these key inputs, and such issues seem likely to become still more important in the future.

Oil has been especially significant in the past decade. The long-term income elasticity of demand for it is clearly still not far short of unity, despite attempts which have been made to economize on its use (smaller cars, restrictions on central heating, etc.). To increase a nation's oil output significantly in the short period is very difficult unless some wells are about to come on stream. The time lag between exploration and commercial production is several years, especially for offshore output. There are, of course, alternative sources of energy, such as natural gas, coal, hydro-electricity, solar power, etc. (Indeed, coal can be converted into oil, and this is done — at a cost — by, for example, SASOL of South Africa, in order to reduce the country's economic dependence.) But these also require much time and capital. The security problems of nuclear power have yet to be solved. Moreover, oil is far the most flexible energy source: there is still no satisfactory substitute for oil products in vehicles, nor in the chemical industry or many other sectors where they are feedstocks. It is even the origin of some of the main fertilizers needed for cereal production.

Moreover, the oil market is not at all competitive: to rely

on imports of oil probably means being dependent on one or more of the 'seven sisters'. How much it is worth paying to avoid this depends on the total development strategy, especially the weight given to self-sufficiency.

In assessing the full costs of reliance on imported oil, it should be borne in mind that foreign exchange difficulties cannot be considered transient for most economies. While no doubt the real price of oil will decline from time to time, the outlook is for underlying strength, despite the further possibilities of fuel-saving and the output potential of some fields — notably in the Gulf of Mexico. Depletion policies in OPEC members have become more restrictive, and yet their own consumption of oil is rising rapidly. The political situation in the Middle East is chronically unstable.

Food is, of course, even more of a necessity. I shall concentrate on cereals, the most basic need. It is true that virtually every country produces some cereals, and it would not be very difficult for many of them to raise output quite quickly in an emergency, at least to some extent (as Britain did during the War). However, in contrast to oil, cereal output depends heavily in the short run on the weather, and many countries, including the Soviet Union, are self-sufficient only in good years: a bad harvest may force them to seek cereals from the few large exporters (the United States, Canada, Argentina, and Australia).

Moreover, the need can be for specific cereals. Some countries that do not have a suitable climate for producing wheat have become addicted to wheat bread, and would not be satisfied by increased supplies of maize or rice! Many have become chronically dependent on food aid from the United States (under Public Law 480) to buy their wheat.

The neo-classical economist will not be greatly concerned if imports of basic foods are considerable. On his doctrine of 'comparative advantage' a country which could produce, say, tea relatively cheaply would have a higher average income (and world income would also be higher) if it sold this and imported all its cereals.

But what if the price of its leading export declines sharply? There will be a fall in real income and employment, especially if import and exchange controls are abjured, whether the mechanism is via declining money incomes (if the exchange rate is fixed) or rising prices (if it is not). The extent of the fall in economic activity will depend mainly on the price and income elasticities of demand for cereals, and on the possibility of moving resources into cereal production, especially out of tea. The fall could indeed be large (tea-pickers are not easily converted into cereal farmers!). The pressure to seek aid or commercial loans so as to mitigate it will be considerable.

The point is that the economic, and thus social and political, price of relying on imports of a necessity (the same argument would apply to oil) can be so high that governments may quite rationally try to avoid such dependency by turning a blind eye to the doctrine of comparative advantage and subsidizing cereal production at the cost of a lower average income — as governments of industrial countries indeed do.

The global food constraint may well grow more severe. The weakness of the market in the early 1980s is misleading. Supplies are already inadequate for millions of people who lack the money to buy enough to eat. In the near future, however, not enough may be available in relation even to 'effective' (monetary) demand. The first signs of basic food market imbalance appeared during the early 1970s, with sharp price rises. It is true that they moderated after 1973 when the world recession started, but in effect what has happened is that the oil constraint, and the associated monetarist policies in the leading economies, have obscured the food constraint on world economic activity.

An authoritative recent study[1] projects world food output to continue growing at about 2.2 per cent a year, very slightly faster than the growth of population, but whereas in the past an expansion of food output has been made possible partly by bringing land under cultivation, there is now little scope for this and output per acre will have to rise much more rapidly than in the past. That will, however, be difficult without increased application of fertilizers, pesticides, and other oil-based products, and higher direct consumption of energy in mechanization, water pumping, and transportation, which conjure up again the oil constraint. So food prices are likely to rise relative to those of other commodities (at a rate of over 2 per cent a year).

The same study also points out that even if food supplies continue to keep pace with demand, taking the world as a whole, shortages are likely to become more serious in many parts of the world — most of Asia and (especially) tropical Africa. To continue meeting these by imports will become more difficult in view of the prospective foreign exchange imbalances of these areas.

Although I treat oil and food as separate constraints, they are in fact gradually becoming unified because of linkages mentioned above and also the possibility of converting cassava (or manioc) into methanol, which can be used as a substitute for gasoline. There is, indeed, a big national programme in Brazil to do just this, and it is being attempted experimentally elsewhere. Its cost depends on the relative prices at any time and place of cassava and crude oil, and on whether there is spare land: otherwise cassava displaces other crops. So far, it has generally been expensive. However, this possibility puts a long-term ceiling on the oil price (like the link between the prices of natural and artificial rubber), and the ceiling will doubtless be lowered by technical progress. In the 1990s, we may be able to talk of a single solar constraint. (Ultimately the root is the same: methanol is a form of the energy transmitted to plants by the sun; oil, like coal, is a later form of the same solar energy, obtained when the plants have decayed. Of course, the energy in plants is renewable.)

There are many other key resources, notably mineral ores such as copper, iron, and bauxite, which can be bargaining assets in international power struggles (though they may also be liabilities because the great powers are often themselves dependent on these and very reluctant to lose access to them). None of them are, however, of comparable importance, and anyway much of what I say about dependence on oil and food applies also to dependence on other primary products.

There are other physical limits on the room to manoeuvre. A country with plenty of subsoil petroleum and arable land in relation to its own needs, can hardly be considered truly self-sufficient if to exploit these resources it has to rely on foreign *technology*. This includes what is embodied in exploration and mining equipment, tractors and harvesters, etc.: even the extent of mineral reserves or the acreage of cultivable land depends very much on the technology available. Moreover, technological capacity of another sort is needed to plan the optimal development of oilfields and of the agricultural sector (including decisions on what are the best sources of equipment and expertise). Also, of course, and most obviously, industrial development relies, in ways already described, on foreign technology.

Technological dependence is very closely related to other forms. The channels are mostly the cultural ones outlined in the previous chapter (overseas education, publications, etc.). Technology usually moves with the equipment and capital provided by TNCs. Governments of the countries where these companies have their head offices will try to protect them by diplomatic intervention, backed by aid to the 'host' government, in extreme cases by military means (see the discussion of Chile, above).

Dependence on foreign investment and technology are among the main constraints on a government's room to manoeuvre. This need not be very damaging if they are carefully screened as part of a strategy of industrialization that reflects national interests and if the most appropriate technologies are drawn from the most appropriate sources. (The point is essentially the same as the one made in the previous chapter about screening cultural imports.) Indeed, the initiative in technology transfer should lie with the host government. They should know what they want and where to get it — as Japanese officials did in the early stages of their highly professional industrial strategy: foreign businessmen with the presumption to take the initiative in Tokyo have faced the prospect of being delicately but forcefully snubbed. Yet, typically, ministries of agriculture, mining, and industry in other countries are purely reactive — saying 'yes' or 'no' (almost always 'yes') to whatever corporation in whatever industry based in whatever country happens to propose an investment.

They may even subsidize it, without any proper analysis. It is true that most industrial development corporations responsible for administering incentives request information about a company's plans for employment, production, exports, etc., before deciding whether or not to use their delegated power to grant tax 'holidays', cheap credit from local sources, free use of land or even buildings. But they may well not have surveyed the range of what foreign investment is possible (the government of a small country would lack the means to do so), or even analysed in any detail the economic and social effects of proposed investments. Subsequently, there is rarely much effort to see whether the promises have, in fact, been fulfilled, let alone any discussion of withdrawing privileges, even if the prospectus has been demonstrably dishonest. (Government officials may well have been subverted.[2]) The result has typically been a ragbag of industries, without any pattern and showing virtually zero integration with the rest of the economy. Yet a large role for foreign capital tends to limit drastically the flexibility of trade, as explained above, since TNCs have their own separate interests. Less formal links with them via licensing arrangements may have similar, if weaker, effects. Indeed, governments of countries where there is already a big presence of TNCs may well have lost the option of adopting the 'Japanese model' — which in any case requires a dedicated and sophisticated nationalism hardly found elsewhere (except, to some extent, in South Korea).

National technological capacity is also essential to genuine military independence. A government lacking such capacity and relying on foreign arms firms for spare parts and personnel, both operational and maintenance, even for small arms, cannot sustain for long a war which is not at least condoned by its military suppliers. (Still less can it fight a war of any length against *them*.) It also has constantly to refresh its political alliances to keep militarily up-to-date *vis-à-vis* potential enemies. Israel and Saudi Arabia are cases in point.

Perhaps, therefore, technological dependence is the most basic form after cultural dependence, to which it is linked. Indeed, we can use technological dependence as a sort of proxy for cultural dependence (which is much more difficult to measure) as well. It is, however, in contrast to natural resources and some of the other factors mentioned above (even culture), changeable to a significant degree within a generation. Moreover, it is heterogeneous: many countries (India, for example, or the Soviet Union, or for that matter Britain) are substantial exporters of some types of technology, substantial importers of others. So 'dependence on technology' is not a simple concept.

The considerations outlined above raise questions about the widely used classification of countries into three 'worlds' (developed, centrally planned, and developing). As explained in the introduction, these categories are becoming obsolete.

It may be more useful to classify countries according to whether they are chronic exporters or importers of these three key inputs — oil, cereals, and technology (see the diagram).

DIAGRAM

Illustrative Profiles of Dependence on Key Inputs (c. 1980) (I = significant chronic imports; E = significant chronic exports; O = very roughly self-sufficient)

	Oil	Cereals	Technology[a]
Least Dependent *(one I, two Es)*			
USA	I	E	E
Soviet Union	E	I	E
Moderately Dependent *(one I, one E)*			
East Germany	I	O	E
West Germany	I	O	E
Britain	O	I	E
Argentina	O	E	I
Heavily Dependent *(two Is)*			
Japan	I	I	E
Kuwait	E	I	I
Nigeria	E	I	I
Thailand	I	E	I
China	O[b]	I	I
Most Dependent *(three Is)*			
Brazil	I	I	I
Cuba	I	I	I
Poland	I	I	I
Portugal	I	I	I

Notes:

a. Dependence on technology is sometimes measured by purchases of patents. However, a country with a high indigenous technological capacity (notably Japan) can, for that very reason, be a heavy purchaser of patents without losing its economic independence: technological capacity includes the ability to select whatever foreign inventions or innovations appear useful and to decide whether to buy their patents. Here technological dependence is measured by net trade in machinery, transport equipment, and arms.

b. Potentially a significant exporter.

Sources: FAO Trade Yearbook, 1981
        UN Yearbook of International Trade Statistics, 1981

We should remember, however, that the *extent* and *nature* of dependence on each of these items are also important. The paragraphs that follow contain some brief notes on the implications of this classification.

Certain features stand out. In the first place, only the United States and the Soviet Union are net importers of just one key input, and exporters of the other two.

The US has, in fact, significant resources of energy (especially heavy crudes, and natural gas), but to develop these sufficiently to eliminate oil imports would involve enormous capital and environmental costs. (And self-sufficiency could hardly last long.) Besides, abundant oil and natural gas are available in a near neighbour, Mexico — and Trinidad and Venezuela are other exporters in the Western hemisphere. The lifestyles which have become customary in the States have also induced heavy net imports of iron ore, copper, bauxite, and many other industrially important metals, although it is in a position to secure supplies through its corporations overseas (increasingly through joint ventures).[3]

To round out the picture, we also need to look briefly at the non-economic assets of the United States. It is not only a large country with a big population: its ethnic diversity has been partially overcome by a determined policy of assimilation. However, this is no longer so successful: one of the potential vulnerabilities of the United States is its growing *chicano* population, especially in Texas (precisely its main domestic source of oil), with evidently some degree of allegiance to Mexico — due in part to exploitation by US farmers and other employers. But its responses to problems are flexible, in part because there are still relatively few constraints on the expression of dissent.

It is a moot point whether the Soviet Union is a super-power in the same class. Cereals (mainly animal feed) form its Achilles' heel and have required big import contracts, precisely with the US, in several recent years. Once it was more or less self-sufficient taking one year with another; now it is only free from imports when it has exceptionally good harvests. To eliminate imports permanently is not physically as gigantic a task as faces the United States over energy (for the reasons given above), but it requires, apparently, a big increase in agricultural investment, which has, indeed, been taking place (reversing to some extent the industrial priority inherent in Marxism). And it also needs a far-reaching reorganization of decision-making, that would be politically traumatic.

The Soviet Union is, moreover, much less independent in technology than the United States. (It is, in fact, a net importer of civilian equipment, but this is outweighed by exports of armaments.) And, though formerly a major oil exporter, it is no longer able to meet in full the oil needs of Eastern Europe and Cuba. It has big reserves (of natural gas as well as oil), but to deliver these to the markets in Europe involves dependence on West European companies to construct the pipelines (and thus on the governments there) — and, in due course to purchase the gas. However, when the pipelines come on stream, the customers will become partly dependent on the Soviet Union (as the US government has pointed out) — though this will be matched by lower dependence on other suppliers.

The reduction in Soviet economic independence in food and oil is one of the reasons why it shows less capacity to intervene in the Third World, a major development of the past ten years, to which I will return.

So even these two governments can hardly afford autarchic or isolationist policies. Moreover, although they are both militarily very powerful (because of their large populations, advanced military technology, and heavy arms spending), their security requires neighbours which are at least neutral. The United States has the advantage that it has only two neighbours with common frontiers: these both have much smaller populations and are dependent technologically and culturally on the United States (though see the point about *chicanos* above). The Soviet Union's neighbours in Europe are allies (or neutral in the case of Austria and Finland), but not those in Asia: its main military weakness is the long common frontier with China, especially in view of its minority races in Soviet Asia, about whose loyalty we know very little: the Soviet government would be gravely threatened by a really close alliance between China and the USA, as well as by further political deterioration in Eastern Europe. Apparently military insecurity was the main reason for its invasion of Afghanistan and its insistence on a military regime in Poland.

So no country is truly independent. West Germany is mostly self-sufficient in cereals, and, although it buys arms and equipment from TNCs based in the United States (as well as other European countries), it sells more equipment to the rest of the world via its own TNCs. But it is dependent on imported oil, and while NATO forces on its soil give it some protection against a Soviet invasion, they make avoiding involvement in a Soviet–US struggle almost impossible, and as long as US forces remain they rule out a dramatic change of strategy.

The physical dependence pattern of East Germany is strikingly similar, though we would have to allow here for its military weakness *vis-à-vis* West German and other NATO forces on its frontier, and (a corollary of this) heavy political dependence on the Soviet government, which could easily intervene to ensure loyalty (as it has done elsewhere in Eastern Europe).

The West German pattern could also be taken as broadly representative of a number of West European countries. Britain, however, is rather different. It is another net exporter of technology, but imports cereals (and many minerals and other industrial materials), though not oil.

Japan is often counted as a 'superpower', and certainly its per capita income (even its national income) is higher than that of the Soviet Union.[4] It has other important assets, which do not appear in the diagram: a population which is large and highly homogeneous, ethnically and linguistically. Although there is a high degree of concentration in economic power (and in access to social services), a common culture is deeply rooted in Japanese history: its people would doubtless show, as in the past, considerable cohesion during a politico-economic crisis, even one involving major sacrifices in the level of living. It is also a net exporter of capital equipment and many attractive advanced consumer goods — though (contrary to the other cases) not of many cultural products as well. Moreover, because of restrictions imposed after the war of 1941–5, it is not a manufacturer of major military equipment. Yet its population needs imported oil to keep warm, to maintain communications, to move from one place to another, as well as to produce and distribute their necessities. It is heavily dependent on cereal imports and on imports of iron ore and bauxite, mostly (in contrast to the US) by long-term contracts.[5] It faces bigger environmental constraints and costs than other countries in expanding heavy industries, the products of which may therefore increasingly need to be imported.[6] It is also militarily weak. So its government has significantly less room to manoeuvre than that of, say, France; in particular, it is more dependent on developing export markets.

Another class of country is also heavily dependent, but in a very different sense: the petroleum exporters. It is true that the members of OPEC are very diverse in several important respects, notably in the extent of their agricultural hinterland and their population base. But they also have much in common. They depend in part on migrant labour. They buy technology, arms, equipment, and the manufactures and foodstuffs needed to meet very high consumer expectations of their native populations — and the modest ones of the immigrants. Their governments are (with the exception of Libya) heavily dependent on one or more of the capitalist powers for technical (and in the last resort military) aid.

Although there is no such thing as a 'typical' oil exporter, Kuwait illustrates one type. It is a town in the desert and produces practically no food except a few vegetables. The country's production of manufactures totally fails to match its consumption. It also has to import technology for all sectors, even in order to extract its main economic asset, oil; its government has nationalized the physical assets of the petroleum companies but cannot nationalize their 'downstream' technology, or their access to world markets. It still relies on expatriate expertise, much of which is resident, and the Kuwaiti executives in each field may be too few to have the professional capacity between them even to judge the best sources of this. It is also a country with much too small a population to defend itself in such a politically unstable area as the Gulf, especially since about half consists of foreign migrants. The level of living of the Kuwaiti public (both native and migrant) has, in fact, become wholly dependent on foreign corporations and governments — though these in turn cannot exercise their power without impunity, because of the importance to them of an uninterrupted flow of oil. Moreover, Kuwait is a considerable creditor, and debts to it could not be revoked without serious damage to the whole financial system (especially since it would reawaken the fears aroused when the US government froze Iranian assets).

For the bigger countries in this group, especially Nigeria, the export surplus of oil is limited by the rapid rise of internal consumption. Their exchange rates have a chronic tendency to be overvalued and they have become heavily dependent on imports of both food and manufacturers, despite the capital available to invest in the production of these.

China has become a small-scale exporter of oil, with plans to develop its sales considerably. It tends to import more cereals than it exports, especially when the crop is low, though the average balance is small in relation to its consumption. It is heavily dependent on foreign technology, although, because of linguistic isolation and strong political organization, the public's aspirations for sophisticated consumer goods can be restrained, as was done in Japan during its critical early stages of development.

A case can also be made for considering as a separate group countries, like Argentina or Thailand, which have export surpluses of cereals (usually wheat or rice) to trade for oil and equipment, technology, etc. But since cereals are, for the reasons given above, a good deal less useful bargaining counters than oil or technology, and they usually form a small proportion of total exports, these countries can hardly be treated on a par with exporters of oil or technology (though Argentina has the advantage of being self-sufficient in oil too).

On the other hand, cereal exporters are in a distinctly different position from countries which import not only oil and technology, but also basic foodstuffs, as would be revealed in any serious crisis. Though only a few examples are shown in the diagram, the majority of countries in Africa, Asia and Latin America are dependent in all three dimensions (and culturally dependent as well). To buy these very necessary imports and to pay the interest and profits on foreign capital, they offer less essential commodities such as coffee, tea, bananas, cocoa, sugar, cotton, metal ores, and/or tourist facilities and migrant labour. They can therefore truly be termed 'dependent' countries. Portugal, like other countries in Southern Europe that are cereal importers, has basically more in common with this group than with the developed economies, where it is placed in the conventional UN classification. I have put Poland and Cuba here too: they need to import supplies of oil (which cannot be fully satisfied any more by the Soviet Union) as well as food and equipment. Cuba is heavily dependent on its sales of sugar, largely to the same countries that provide it with markets and aid.[7]

This bottom group is thus also a very mixed bag. Some large countries with a varied resource base and indigenous technological research capacity, such as Brazil, have very much greater possibilities for autonomous action than, say, Portugal, let alone Burundi or Bangladesh. The conventional category, 'developing countries', has, however, even less in common.

These physical realities count. To take a very far-fetched case, if the United States were to undergo a socialist revolution, it would still need oil as well as iron ore and various other metals from the rest of the world. The highly hypothetical post-revolutionary government in Washington would still have to finance these essential imports and could hardly afford to stop exporting technology and arms, or receiving payments of debt service and profit remittances; nor could it abandon its military and diplomatic leverage. The Soviet Union could not give it much help — and might, indeed, be more likely to come into conflict with it.

Like any government, it would be primarily concerned with its own survival, and to use the bargaining power based on its resources to protect as best it can the consumption standards of its own population, especially of the classes that form the base of its power — even if this meant perpetuating 'unequal exchange' in the world. Indeed, continued exploitation (in this sense) of overseas countries would be *especially* necessary for a US government after a social upheaval, because, while social expectations would have been aroused, these standards would be threatened by the disruption of economic activity: as the example of Cuba shows — and the same could be said of the early Soviet government, among others — a new revolutionary government inevitably faces opposition from the former ruling class and the potential emigration of technical and administrative personnel, as well as possible trade embargoes, not to speak of financial crises and military intervention (see Chapter 3).

Enough has been said, perhaps, to indicate that country classifications based on resource dependence may in general be useful, certainly for social scientists, but perhaps increasingly

for government officials and political leaders too. Such classifications provide starting points for studying what determines
a nation's room to manoeuvre, how this differs in the short
and long term, and thus what policies are feasible or might
become so and — as we shall see — what techniques of planning
would be helpful.

The emphasis suggested by this approach would be to aim
at greater national self-sufficiency, by policies directed at
consumption as well as production, rather than maximizing
economic growth, but above all to plan the strengthening of
technological and negotiating capacity. Development in the
true sense of the word may require the creation of 'uneco-
nomic' sources of energy and food and 'wasteful duplication'
of research facilities to reduce the danger of debilitating
foreign exchange crises and increase bargaining strength. Such
policies may well turn out to be justified economically as
well, if supplies of a key commodity become tight.

There is, of course, a limit to how much income is worth
trading for autonomy and security; the position of this limit
will vary according to local circumstances, especially the
accessibility of hydrocarbons and other materials, and the
fertility·of the soil, and the degree of political support internally for nationalist policies. But, as the world political and
economic situation deteriorates, this limit shifts; to aim at
greater self-sufficiency becomes increasingly worthwhile.

NATIONALIST DEVELOPMENT STRATEGIES

Synopsis

IT might be concluded from Section B that virtually no room to manoeuvre at all was left for a government with many of the following liabilities: a small population, serious ethnic divisions, location close to a super-power, few natural resources, a culturally subverted bureaucracy, high consumer expectations, and a narrow technological base. If there were any option for the government of such a country, it would not be *whether* to be dependent, but *which* external power to depend on — just as squires in the Middle Ages could sometimes only choose which baron they would serve. Even that choice would very rarely exist, because of military or economic bonds already in place.

Policy appears in fact overdetermined, increasingly so as the networks of transnational capital proliferate. Incremental change seems doomed: all one can do is wait for some ill-defined revolution, brought about by unspecified processes. There is a tendency in what one might call the 'vulgar' exponents of dependency, though not in its main theorists (Cardoso and Faletto, 1976; Sunkel, 1974), to fall into precisely this trap and blame *all* the problems of a country, even a big one, on an immutable 'international division of labour' imposed by hegemonic forces. This is not only quite enervating; it is misleading.

It overlooks the role of political leadership. Admittedly, economic, cultural, demographic, and geographic data set the stage for the political play in a dependent country, whoever

writes the script. No amount of leadership is going to transform, say, Lesotho or Jamaica or Kampuchea into a dominant
country within a few decades, or even one where a government could enjoy much independence of action — and leaders
anyway have finite lives (and usually very much shorter periods
in power).

But no government is completely without policy options,
either, especially now that the ideological map has become
more complex and new alliances, internal and external, have
become possible (see Chapter 2).

There are many examples of dependent governments in the
US sphere of influence developing trade with the Soviet Union
— Argentina for one. Conversely, a socialist one like that of
Roumania can now join international organizations dominated
by capitalist governments, such as the IMF. Advantage can be
taken of the difficulties faced by the dominant power and its
internal divisions.

What bargaining counters a government does have can be
exploited. That of a small country in a strategically important
position, like Iceland, can exact a price (not only financial)
for use of harbours, airfields, and other facilities. Another example is overflying rights. Liabilities can be converted into
assets: a government heavily in debt may be able to take
advantage of the fact that the creditor could not stand a
formal default. Even where such possibilities are few, a
government still has some scope (for example, in population
or education policy — see below) for establishing conditions
in which a *future* administration will have more room to
manoeuvre, and this is not a negligible service to the nation.

The willpower and intelligence of actual or potential political leaders evidently differ significantly.[1] The importance of
these personal characteristics follows from the very multi-
plicity of constraints and resources which have been described.
What reduces the role of the social scientist increases that of
the politician. The really able politician sees possibilities to
which academics are blind. Who would have thought in the
1950s that Castro would be able to carry out what seemed
such provocative programmes and survive?

While some national leaders clumsily arouse alarm among
the dominant powers, and provoke retaliation, often not so
much by real threat as by rhetoric, others are capable of

ignoring their advisers, daring the 'impossible' and succeeding. It requires rare skills not merely to frame an optimal set of policies, but to mobilize an adequate coalition of diverse political forces in support; to present it persuasively to the world outside; to convince the domestic public that this is all that can be achieved; and, of course, to implement it.

Dom Mintoff, for example, brilliantly exploited the military advantages of Valetta harbour, and his political base of the dockyard workers as well as the sympathies of Britons such as Lord Mountbatten, to extract payment not only from Britain and NATO in support of the public finances of Malta, a small country singularly lacking in cultivable land and other natural resources, as in technological capacity, but also (for a time) from Libya. He was noticeably more successful than his predecessor, Borg Olivier, who, facing a basically similar set of circumstances, relied mainly on emigration (to Australia) as a solution for the country's economic problems. (Mintoff once told me that the government of a small country had to decide what trump cards it held and then play them for all they are worth.) Some clearly possess these skills, which indeed they will have cultivated in the rise to a position of power. Conventional historians may not have been so wrong in focusing attention on the talents of monarchs and prime ministers![2]

It is particularly important for the leadership to be able to sense changes in constraints which open up new possibilities. Any government needing loans a quarter of a century ago had little option but to turn to the government of the United States, or the agencies it dominated. Now the governments of Japan and several West European countries can also provide finance. Since oil prices started to rise in 1973, OPEC members have been additional possible sources of support, though their governments have not in practice made a large portion of their capital available to fellow members of 'the South' (and of course they cannot meet the need for technology — or TV programmes). Moreover, loans from commercial banks have become more readily available — to 'sound' governments — as the result of the need to find destinations for 'recycled' oil supplies. Following disasters (or, from another viewpoint, victories) associated with the names Suez and Vietnam, the likelihood of military intervention (especially successful intervention) has declined.

Nor is the international system fixed for all time. Although the procedures of the IMF still reflect in some degree the politico-economic situation when this organization was established at Bretton Woods nearly four decades ago, any perceptive politician who deals with it knows that the priority attached to particular policies (e.g. a 'realistic' exchange rate) varies both from one year to the next and as between different senior members of its staff. One of the functions of political leadership is indeed to help identify feasible changes in international institutions and promote those which are constructive from their viewpoint.

Even some seemingly permanent geographical constraints can change. The volume of mineral reserves that matters is the amount that could be exploited, and this depends not only on the amount actually in the ground but also on price and technological progress — in exploration and extraction techniques, ore treatment, etc.

Evidently a condition of political success in such a complex world, full of shifting constraints, is to be pragmatic rather than dogmatic. This may not, however, be easily compatible with the dedication needed. (Pragmatism can easily be a code-word for laziness, not to speak of corruption.) The key to the reconciliation of these requirements for successful leadership is patriotism — in addition to intelligence and political skills.

Moreover, unless patriotism is deep and widespread, a government will hardly be able to get the various social classes and racial groups to co-operate in coping with constraints, especially to tolerate the hardships of any change in course that provokes retaliation. In fact, another requirement of leadership is to develop patriotism and yet not let it get out of hand and become another major constraint on policy.

Assuming (for the sake of argument) that a political leader is dedicated to his country's development and has sufficient political judgement to handle the constraints, what backing would he need from his officials?

In the 1960s, the answer would have been obvious: a good development plan. Today, 'planning' calls up memories of teams of economics graduates, who would doubtless otherwise have been unemployed, frenetically drawing up five-year plans, largely quantitative and wholly economic, to be published with a good deal of fanfare. This is often good public relations, but whether it has much impact on actual policy decisions — or should do so — is quite a different matter.

Rarely does such a team have any real authority. I remember visiting Chile as part of a European team during the Christian Democratic administration of the 1960s (a relatively enlightened and rational government). We were briefed at ODE-PLAN and one of the points made was that the plan provided for self-sufficiency in wheat by 1970. When we came to visit the Ministry of Agriculture, we asked them about this: no, they said, there was no hope of producing enough wheat by 1970, and they were in fact planning to build extra storage capacity for wheat imports. On being told of the treatment in the national plan, they replied with some asperity: we are responsible for agriculture, they should stick to planning. (Later the Ministry of Public Works told us there was no provision for building grain silos: construction was *their* responsibility, not that of the Ministry of Agriculture!)

Typically, after a year or two, a plan is a dead letter: by then, the set of assumptions (e.g. the exchange rate) and the projections (e.g. of export prices) on which it was based are clearly out of date, and the planning office is happily buckling down to prepare the next one.

The section that follows discusses the reasons for this dreary sequence, and, drawing on my work in a dozen or so planning offices in different parts of the world, suggests that it is time to move to quite a different type of planning — longer-term, less economistic, not entirely quantitative. And the object would not be necessarily — certainly not mainly — publication. Indeed the very fact that a plan is published raises doubts as to whether it deals with issues important to the government!

This change would require a different type of planning organization, more like a military staff, with ready access to the political leadership. Its responsibilities would be to advise not on ways of accelerating economic growth but on comprehensive development strategies, including areas such as the syllabuses used at various stages of education. It would also take account of the military policies devised by the defence staff, and policies for population growth (which might include its acceleration) — issues, as I have pointed out, previously almost taboo.

Any development strategy would have to respect not only

the geographical and external constraints discussed in Section B, but also financial limits to the range of policy options. The need for cautious fiscal policy is not just old-fashioned conservatism. An indifference to finance is understandable where there are acute social problems and heavy political pressures to solve them. But political leaders who ignore financial constraints pay a high price, sometimes their very lives. Moreover, social problems are usually in the end aggravated. The requirement of financial stability is one aspect of the need to cope with the internal and external pressures; this is, indeed, more imperative for a government bent on increasing its independence than for any other.

Since greater independence and far-reaching changes are on the agenda in every country now, the strategic options facing a government can hardly be illustrated by following the UN statistical manuals and producing projections of conventional national income tables, showing aggregates such as 'investment' and 'consumption'. I have already (in the Annexe to the Introduction) discussed the limited meaning and accuracy of these concepts; shortly I shall review briefly their history — this shows, *inter alia*, their origins in the Keynesian branch of neo-classicism, which I have argued earlier is becoming outmoded.

Deliberate statistical innovation is needed if the material given to decision-makers (and the public) is to throw light on the external links and policy targets that would correspond to nationalist strategies. The sort of questions now to be answered are very specific: In what sectors and areas are foreign corporations investing? Who are the illiterate and under-nourished?

The reader may well by now be aware of an apparent inconsistency in my argument. If cultural dependence is so strong, if as I said in the Introduction political leaders are no longer to be considered autonomous agents — because their minds are moulded by foreign perceptions of the country's problems that reach them through so many channels, from textbooks to television programmes, or (in the case of industrial countries) by out-of-date models of society — how can we expect them ever to see the need for a strategy of national development? Why should we bother to consider the planning machinery, financial policy, and statistical models that such a strategy would need?

One answer is, as I pointed out in the Introduction, that people are complicated, more so than one might gather from reading the works of some dependency theorists. Whatever the foreign elements in a leader's education and career, and whatever lip-service is paid to economic liberalism, or Marxism, he may actually have some perception of, even a degree of dedication to, his country's needs.

In any case, the growing crises in the world economy that I outlined in the Introduction can be expected to force governments of dependent countries to relax outward-looking policies. (Here again the 1930s provide a parallel.) The complexity of politicians that I have just mentioned will permit their latent nationalist tendencies to grow. No doubt many leaders will prove incapable of adjustment: they could well be removed by coups (or democratic processes, where these are still possible).

However, even if there is no change in official policy, some directors of planning (and statistics) may well come to see that their responsibilities include such basic work on their country's developmental requirements. After all, any military staff worth its salt has secret contingency plans for the breakdown of an alliance, unthinkable though this may be to the politicians of the moment. I would consider the British general staff guilty of grave dereliction of duty if they had not quietly prepared plans for the possibility, however remote that may seem at the moment, of war with the United States — I would also be very surprised.[3] Similarly, the blueprint for a more independent policy can be prepared by officials (just as Saburo Okita, early in 1945, secretly constructed, so he told me, with a small group of fellow Japanese economists, a plan for the reconstruction of a defeated Japan, when the idea of defeat was totally unmentionable).

CHAPTER 6

From development 'planning' to development strategy

MANY of the early post-war 'plans', outside the Soviet bloc, were, oddly enough, prepared in the colonies. The colonial powers felt little need for planning their own future, but became increasingly concerned about the economic plight of their territories, especially as nationalist criticism mounted. These colonial 'development plans' were, however, little more than lists of public infrastructure programmes, for roads, ports, schools, etc.

As the colonies became independent, the coverage of 'development plans' became broader and attention was concentrated on economic growth (still not on development in any real sense), because this suited the political forces outlined above. Typically, projections have been made for the following four or five years for selected expenditure variables covering the economy as a whole, consumption, investment, etc., and sector totals, usually accompanied by particulars of some leading projects, and references to social goals such as reducing unemployment and poverty (not quantitatively linked to the main economic analysis). The underlying model is crude, often a simplistic version of Keynesianism, with no place for the major strategic issues, especially greater self-reliance.

The 'Alliance for Progress' of the early 1960s greatly stimulated the production of 'development plans' in Latin America by making large quantities of US aid conditional on their preparation — which naturally ensured that the work of planning offices would have little real root in national reality. By the end of that decade, it was clear that the record of such plans was far from satisfactory. The growth of per capita income often diverged a long way from target (so far as one could tell from very inaccurate national income estimates of ambiguous definition — see the Annexe to the Introduction). And even where it really was fast, there was little progress towards the social objectives such as reducing unemployment.

Many plans ceased to have any administrative or even public relations significance soon after publication, and sank out of sight long before the period they presumed to cover had expired.

There are several reasons for these débâcles. The technical quality of most plans has been poor. There has been, in the first place, little rationale for the period of a plan. In the early 1960s, I was in a meeting with Kwame N'Krumah, who had just returned from the Soviet Union. He said that Khrushchev had told him that they had changed to seven-year plans. 'I said that this was a good idea and we would do the same.' (This in spite of the fact that the phases of the gigantic Volta River Project defined quite different periods for the national economy.)

Nor has there been much attempt to distinguish between factors that are beyond the government's control, targets, and the residuals obtained from a national accounting framework. Indeed, nearly all plans implicitly convey the impression that the economy is much more under government control than it really is.

Moreover, single values have usually been assumed for exogenous variables, such as export prices in the end-year of the plan period, whereas serious decision-makers would need to know the nature and extent of uncertainty, and the implications of possible extremes so as to judge how much their policies are contingent, especially on external events. In fact, some unexpected fluctuation (e.g. in export markets) is what most often makes such plans quickly obsolete.

This was true of the very short-lived 'national plan' published in Britain in 1965 by the Labour government, which totally ignored the lessons of planning elsewhere. And although the governments of most 'developed' countries do not feel the need for 'plans' of this type, many model-builders produce 'projections' which are widely used in policy debates. Their highly aggregative nature makes them almost as irrelevant to national needs.

There is little attempt in any country anywhere in the world (with the conspicuous exception of Malaysia) to concentrate on issues of distribution — between social classes or ethnic groups. Yet these issues are crucial to development. So are, in all but the smallest countries, the balances between urban and rural areas, coastal regions and the interior, etc. Macroplanning, however, and 'physical' planning (urban and regional planning) not merely typically take place in different organizations: they are usually carried out quite separately, with no regular contact — sometimes even without either department knowing what the other is doing! Nothing could reveal more clearly the fantasy in much of what has gone on under the name of 'planning'.

In the last quarter century, plans have mostly been derived from the Harrod-Domar model (see Chapter 1), which treats investment as the determinant of economic growth. Estimates of investment needs have relied heavily on incremental capital-output ratios (ICORS): as explained already, these show great variation, especially over periods as short as five years. In fact, they can have little meaning if they cover groups of industries with very different technologies, less still if they refer to the whole economy. Output is anyway also affected by many factors besides capital — e.g., apart from education, improvements in the health of the workforce. In a poor country, food production, like primary health care, is an input rather than a final product. Moreover, the ICORs in plans are typically copied from past experience — whereas development implies choosing technologies which may well be very different from those used previously.

There is usually little attempt to specify (in plans or elsewhere) policies towards foreign capital investment or the criteria for its entry, compatible with the plan objectives, even in countries where 'self-reliance' is put forward as a major development objective (see Chapter 5).

A common bias underlying all these errors is that there is little attention to the qualitative influences mentioned earlier, especially to the benefit of a greater degree of control of one's own economy; while largely unquantifiable, the value put on these may justify any consequent loss of income. In brief, the plans have not been about *development*, which surely implies social and political progress as well as economic (Seers, 1977).

The economic dimension has tended in fact, to be greatly exaggerated. Certainly, it is difficult to solve social problems without increases in certain important types of production, as pointed out in the Annexe to the Introduction, but these may carry low price-weights in the national income, which anyway also contains output of little relevance for national development. It is the *pattern* of growth that is the economic factor most significant for development.

The short-term horizon of plans has also been a source of weakness. One major reason for the uncritical welcome of foreign capital, discussed in Chapter 5, has been the customary commitment to increase the national income by some guessed percentage within the period of a presidency. Since agricultural output inevitably grows rather slowly, and the expansion of services depends largely on the productive sectors, the only way of achieving a fast rate of growth is to aim at high growth rates in manufacturing, and this can hardly be done without foreign capital (see Chapter 2).

Real development problems can hardly be confronted in less than a decade. Development of a predominantly rural African country, even in the limited sense of achieving the income levels and democratic institutions of Western Europe, must take many generations. (It did in Japan, which started with many geographical and cultural advantages and moved very rapidly.)

Decisions on crucial elements, such as the educational system, or even major capital works such as irrigation schemes, are indeed not likely to start showing much economic effect, e.g. reduced dependence on food imports, in less than two or three decades. Even to restructure Britain adequately will take us well into the next century — and then further big changes will be necessary!

This leads us to consider how to remove obstacles to the room to manoeuvre, which were discussed in Section B. *Military strength* has been largely ignored by economists, especially those working in planning offices. They tend to look on arms spending simply as something laid down by the leadership — thus opting out of a crucial area of development policy.

This is in fact an area rarely mentioned, even by dependency theorists. The reason, perhaps, is that writers in this school are very conscious of the danger that military capacity will, as so often in Latin America (or Southern or Eastern Europe), be deployed against local citizens instead of invaders, reinforcing rather than reducing political dependence. Moreover, it is difficult to arm without increasing the debt to foreign governments or banks and becoming technologically dependent on foreign arms suppliers and military training schemes, especially if these have been financed by one foreign source. To keep sophisticated aircraft and missiles in a state of alert usually requires a steady flow of spare parts from abroad, if not also foreign personnel.

But none the less it would be naïve to ignore the importance of defence capabilities. Ultimately the possibility of an autonomous economic policy depends on military strength, i.e. the size, skill, and loyalty of the armed forces and the state of their equipment. Retaliation by a major power against policies it considers hostile, such as expropriation, can take the form of direct military intervention, from bombardment to blockade or invasion, or military threats which 'destabilize' the government and compel resources to be diverted from productive ends. Governments can be unseated by such acts, or at least forced to change their policies. The impact depends in part on location, whether neighbouring governments are hostile.[1]

The possibility of military intervention and the political difficulty of replacing officers of doubtful loyalty suggest the need for policies to win over the armed forces and integrate them more closely in the state machine (even at a price). There is a dilemma here, however. One of the main demands of the military is usually new equipment — toys like Harrier vertical take-off fighters. By acceding to these demands, the government increases the army's power, including the power to overthrow itself! It is probably safer (though not without danger from another direction — alienating government supporters) to pay higher salaries to the armed forces. Anyway, it may well be advisable to diversify sources of training and of military equipment as of other kinds of equipment.

However, in certain situations (e.g. in Spain today), the danger of a coup can hardly be entirely removed without modifications of policy that would be unacceptable to members of the government itself. So long as the central thrust is evidently nationalistic, some officers may hesitate to interfere, but in many countries where more independent policies are being attempted, this will be the crucial test of political leadership.

Policy in the military sphere needs integration with those in other areas of development. The context of a development scenario, especially the degree of 'openness' to foreign capital and the related foreign policy alignments, should be consistent with military realities. (The staffwork to prepare such scenarios will be discussed in the next chapter.)

Distributional issues have also been neglected. The patriotism needed to face and survive economic or military crises can hardly be expected today of those completely excluded from such material benefits as are available in the nation concerned. The poorer a country, the more important this is, because the technology appropriate for such a country in the military sector, as in others, would necessarily be highly labour-intensive. Its government would not be able to afford much sophisticated equipment: this would cost not merely foreign exchange but dependence on a great power, and technical manpower. Consequently, it cannot plan – as the governments of the great powers certainly do – in terms of a small élite hidden in deep bunkers, dispatching nuclear missiles by pushing buttons. Its contingency plans are bound to include mass mobilization of guerrillas, armed mainly with rifles and courage (as in Vietnam or Afghanistan) to withstand the horrors of modern technology.

There are other reasons why distribution is always central to development. It is widely argued that monetary incentives, especially the fear of poverty, are necessary to induce people to study, work, and save. But the inequalities that exist at present in most countries are not merely far greater than could conceivably be required for these purposes: many of them are of types that discourage development. A highly concentrated distribution of consumer income stimulates the propensity to import, especially oil. In addition, the output of the hundreds of millions of peasants is limited by the size of their holdings, whatever effort and skill they apply: land reform is still often a necessity for raising output as well as for national unity in many countries.

Yet this does not imply that income distribution should always be made more equal, still less that trade union demands for higher wages should necessarily be conceded. Many organized workers are often well in the top half of the distribution; moreover, labour costs may be an important consideration if exports of manufactures have to be promoted, especially in industrial countries. Whether to encourage equality depends on the country concerned.

Anyway, it is not only or even principally the distribution of income that matters: the distribution of wealth, property, and political power determine access to education and various types of employment, which in turn shape future distributions in income and other dimensions. What incentive is there for a young black in the Republic of South Africa to study hard at secondary school (assuming, that is, he or she is one of the few to get into one), if there is little prospect of entering a profession? Racial inequalities are by no means unique to the Republic; even where discrimination is very much less, as in Brazil say, what possibility does a son of a plantation worker in the North-East (also probably black) see, if he looks at what has happened to the previous generation of his family and their neighbours, of ever dining at the Copacabana Palace, or even having meat regularly at home?

Two areas have not been totally neglected but have failed to receive due attention. One is *health*. The human cost of ill-health is immense, especially of malaria, enteritis, and the other mass tropical diseases. But people enfeebled by such diseases are also a strategic liability. Their output is affected in all sectors, especially where physical effort is involved, as in farming and military service. (Talk about financial incentives really seems somewhat odd when a main cause of low productivity stares us in the face!) Almost any scenario requires a health policy that concentrates on plentiful and pure water and on information to peasants about hygiene. It also reveals the need for widespread *local* health care, rather than a handful of the massive teaching hospitals beloved by most of the medical profession and administrators (not to speak of aid donors), but requiring expensive- imported equipment and specialist personnel.

The other is *education*. In the United States, which can still afford such luxuries, this can be treated as a consumer service. Customers can obtain whatever they like, provided they meet formal qualifications (often very low), at little or no financial cost to themselves. In most other countries, however, education has to be thought of as largely vocational — the preparation of people for economic roles, which would be linked to the national strategy. For example, self-reliance in food requires skills and attitudes unlikely to be created unless school curricula are designed accordingly. This does not

mean, however, just specialized technical training: but also
the acquisition of the specialist tools, such as mathematics
and clear communication of ideas orally or in writing, that
are needed in any occupation, and basic sciences over a wide
range, depending on the country concerned.

For a self-reliant strategy another consideration becomes of
major importance: education as a chief source of patriotism.
Thus the 'arts' subjects do not have as small a role as in the
economistic approach to development. On the contrary, the
centrepiece of education is history, the history of the nation
in relation to its continent and the world, ranging right up to
the present. For the typical ex-colonial country, this means
studying the pre-colonial period, the colonial regime, the
origins of immigrants, liberation, and after independence its
position *vis-à-vis* not only neighbours but also the great
powers. In the case of Britain, the scope would basically be
the same, but with special emphasis on the problems of all
social classes in adjusting to the loss of the benefits of the
colonial system and to the strains in its successor, the neo-
colonial one (see Chapter 10).

Another educational priority for development in a fundamental sense is making people familiar with their nation's
cultural heritage — myths, fables, songs, dances, carvings and
sculpture, buildings, etc. — which expresses national experience and can help inhibit the growth of cultural dependence.
In a country that still suffers from serious ethnic divisions, it
may also be important to teach understanding and respect for
the cultures of minorities. Policy on cultural education is all
the more important now that radio and television — usually
carrying foreign cultural values (even in Britain) — are eliminating the cultural life of the village community.

Since history is embodied in monuments, places of worship,
battlefields, palaces, fortresses, etc., it is important both to
maintain these properly and encourage access to them, especially by schoolchildren — as part of their curriculum. (A
notable feature of Japan is the groups of children visiting
shrines in Kyoto, Nara, etc.) Books and films by local authors
and directors should be encouraged, attractive enough to offset the appeal of imports. (The size of the market is important
again here and subsidies may well be needed.) Maintaining
national dress may be at least symbolically important, and

dietary customs that fit the culture (not to speak of the climate and agricultural system). One of the chief functions of universities is to undertake research on the national culture (and sub-cultures), teach about it, and encourage its survival and evolution.

Religion can be another safeguard of national culture, since the main influences flowing from culturally dominant nations are secular. Christianity can play this defensive role, not merely in Europe but also in some countries outside Europe, provided it has taken root. The Moslem tradition can, however, evidently be a more powerful source of cultural autonomy. Religious instruction can in any case be an educational priority.

This raises the question of *linguistic* policy which is a central issue of development planning for those countries where there are large linguistic minorities. Its significance arises not just because of the need for a means of communication, but also because language is closely associated with ethnic, religious, and geographical divisions. Linguistic policy is part of total policy on the national culture, and I shall not go into its ramifications, which depend on the local context. The possibilities include using the language of the majority as a national one, as in Malaysia; using a foreign language such as English, at least temporarily, for many official purposes, as in India; using two official languages as in Canada; three as in Switzerland, etc.

Another item on the agenda is *population*. One reason for the neglect of this, apart from the propaganda from the major industrial countries, is the customary lack of integration between military and development planning. Military arguments probably favour a larger population. So may economic arguments, since countries with small populations, and thus small markets, as was brought out in Chapter 4, are especially constrained in their development options.

In the short run it is the pace at which the population is growing that matters, not its size: the rate of expansion of the teenage population is an especially important factor in economic and political flexibility. A policy for stimulating population growth could, in principle, take various forms apart from raising the birth rate: viz. reducing mortality, or encouraging immigration (or discouraging emigration). The

death rate tends to decline gradually anyway with the improvement of food and water supplies, and better medical facilities
and hygienic practices; and presumably, if it can be reduced
further, the motive will be humanitarian not developmental.
(Indeed, a fall in the death rate, unless it is concentrated
among children, tends to produce an ageing population of
little help for military or economic purposes.)

By far the fastest way to increase the population of young
adults is by immigration. Even if it is temporary, as mostly in
the Middle East, the host country acquires cheaply much of
the economic benefit of education and upbringing, at the
cost of the labour suppliers. That, however, raises dangers of
ethnic disunity and thus cultural dependence, discussed in
Chapter 4 and above. Selective permanent immigration, such
as Australia, Canada, and the United States have practised, is
more effective for development and military purposes but
also much more expensive (the Australian government used
to subsidize fares heavily), and slower.

A nation's development strategy may alternatively imply
reducing the rate of population growth. There may be dangers
of food dependency because of shortage of land, which can
also (together with shortage of capital) threaten employment.

Long-term emigration is a policy adopted by some governments, e.g. Malta. Very few governments, even in the Middle
East, will, however, accept large numbers of migrants any
more, except those with certain professional qualifications,
and so emigration is rarely any longer a practical policy for
avoiding population pressure. But it may also be the result of
personal choice. Either way, it means a loss of human capital.
If young professionally-educated people migrate, especially
important types such as engineers, agronomists, etc., this is
serious for countries with a limited number (such as Sri
Lanka). Of course there are ways to check this outflow by
withholding passports, etc., but those held against their will
are political liabilities. The real safeguards against the 'brain
drain' are the strength of cultural attachment (especially if
the national language is a rare one), and, more generally,
patriotism. But when that is weak, a government may have
to adopt an incomes policy less egalitarian than it would
otherwise. (Seers, 1970.)

The other main alternative way of slowing population

growth, of course, is to encourage birth control. Many now subsidize the supply of contraceptives through a network of family planning clinics and have legalized abortion, though these measures may also be adopted for welfare reasons, or in response to feminist pressures. Some governments (the Jamaican for example) have conducted extensive propaganda campaigns in favour of small families, and a few have penalized those with more than a certain number of children (Singapore and China). The government of India, for a time, not merely subsidized vasectomy but virtually compelled it. The effects of such measures can never be known precisely since fertility is a complex function of income and education as well. (Indeed, one way of reducing fertility is to increase female education.)

The real point is that population policy needs conscious choice in the light of national circumstances, and these alone, not, as pointed out above, a spurious internationalism. The various dimensions of each strategic option should be mutually consistent. Thus demographic policies have implications for housing, education, the armed forces, etc., which can be worked out. The framework for doing so is discussed in the next chapter.

The pressure on governments for a thorough reconsideration of their 'development planning', involving a broadening of its aims and considerations of extra means, has been increased by what happened in the 1970s. The adjustment and collapse of the Bretton Woods system of fixed exchange rates (1971-3), soaring food prices in 1973, the 'oil shocks' of 1973-4 and 1979–80, and related increases in the prices of manufactures, together with the deterioration in markets for other commodities greatly increased the difficulty of maintaining existing policies. For many governments, already heavily in debt, it became difficult to get more credit. Indeed, for several, especially in Africa, fast growth no longer seems even a possible option, at least until the international economy recovers (and that may well raise prices of food and oil imports).

But the case for framing proper long-term development strategies has actually been strengthened, rather than weakened. I am not only referring to oil-importing economies. In countries that export oil, a conscious and coherent strategy is also more necessary than ever. The upsurge in oil prices re-inforced euphoric delusions there, and led to inevitable political pressures to spend money quickly. The results have been enormous expenditures on armed forces; capital invest-ment projects more notable for glamour than for increasing the economy's productive capacity; and previously unimagined levels of corruption. Indeed, many of these governments (Nigeria, Indonesia, Venezuela, especially Mexico) ran up high external debts precisely during the oil boom.

Experience suggests that it is almost impossible for the government of a petroleum exporter to use an upsurge in oil revenues in a way that will build up other sectors sufficiently to support their consumption levels when the volume of oil exports starts to decline, which will inevitably happen one day – in the larger ones, notably Nigeria, a day brought closer by soaring internal sales of oil, due in part to subsidiz-ation of internal sales (in relation to world prices). The exchange rate becomes over-valued in relation to wages (which tend to leap upwards), when viewed against long-term needs for self-sufficiency in agriculture and manufacturing, which needs are not reflected in market prices and not allowed for in conventional theory. Nigeria, for example, has seen the destruction of virtually all its other exports such as groundnuts, palm oil, etc. Indeed, even Venezuela, probably the best managed of the large oil exporters, is more dependent now on oil exports than it was half a century ago, despite the fact that all governments there since then have been dedicated, on paper, to *sembrar el petroleo* – literally, 'sow the oil'. (Even what appears as its main non-oil export, coffee, largely consists of beans smuggled across from Colombia.) The sagging oil market after 1981 brutally revealed the plight of this country and other large oil producers.

The case for strategic thinking is different in oil importers, but it is just as urgent. Until recently, most of them, developed or developing, could apparently drift along on the ocean currents of the world economy without catastrophe. Govern-ments of various political ideologies in the past quarter-century treated industrialization as virtually synonymous with develop-ment, and fell into the convenient practice of relying primarily on imported technologies. These are mostly energy-intensive as well as capital-intensive, and many sectors come to depend on oil-based chemicals as well (especially textiles and agriculture). Their élites also copied US and European lifestyles which have heavy requirements of oil, e.g. for motoring and air-conditioning (see above).

When the price of oil rose to over $30 a barrel, it was somewhat absurd for governments of oil-importing countries (only slightly less so for oil exporters) to continue permitting advertisements for energy-intensive forms of consumption, such as motoring, especially where cars are also imported.

This type of economic growth has always raised serious questions because of its effects on employment and income distribution. Moreover, its industrial bias (in investment, education, and price policy) has usually led to a chronic dependence on food imports. The issue now, in most oil importers, is no longer whether this pattern is desirable, since it cannot be afforded, but what should replace it.

On almost any strategy, in fact, people will probably have to do without some imported goods to which they have become accustomed — indeed, in many countries, especially in Africa, they are already foregoing these, simply for lack of adequate foreign exchange. They may have to put up with food rationing and other inconveniences so that resources can be released for other purposes. How such sacrifices are to be imposed merits very careful consideration. However, the responses so far to difficulties such as foreign exchange problems have mostly been by-products of numerous *ad hoc* emergency decisions of various departments, often taken on very short-term criteria, rather than parts of a considered development strategy.

The prospects, especially for oil and cereals, discussed in Chapter 5, reinforce the need for a thorough re-examination of not merely the content but the organization of planning, to which I now turn.

CHAPTER 7

Development staff work

IN order to meet the need for development strategies, not merely are new policies necessary, as indicated in Chapter 6, but new machinery for framing and implementing them.

The function of a planning office has thus been widely misconceived. Its main responsibility has apparently been demonstrating, by the publication of plans, to the public (sometimes more to aid agencies) a degree of government commitment to development — which may in fact hardly exist, in any true sense.

Publishing plans is actually, on the contrary, an indication that these do not deal with really important issues. The more serious the work of a planning office (as of a high command), the less likely that it will be published. For example, it might not be appropriate to reveal that certain strategies with far-reaching foreign policy implications are even under consideration — or to discuss in public the demographic or military dimensions (on which more below).

If planning offices had been treating the real issues of development (see Chapter 6), they would have principally taken the form, not of publishing 'plans', but of direct continuing advice to decision-makers, estimating how the various departmental policies under consideration might affect the country's development.

The lack of integration of planning offices into government is, in fact, striking. Most I have visited have worked in a sort of administrative vacuum, neither being consulted by the political leadership at all frequently nor enjoying ready access to it. Their unimportance is revealed by lax security at the entrance: careful scrutiny of visitors is confined to departments which matter! Some have done little more than add a pseudo-professional patina to government policies which are decided elsewhere. (They do have one other function for those in power, however: they occupy the energies of precisely the sort of young intellectual who might otherwise be a political menace.)

Political leaders, in developed and developing countries alike, typically take decisions on wages, exchange rates, monetary policy, etc., *ad hoc*, without concern for their wider effects on the pattern of development — effects which may well be considerable — indeed very often without consulting the director of planning. (One such told me that he never knew that vital economic decisions were even under consideration, such as general wage increases, until he read about them in the press!) Yet those deciding on, say, wage increases in the public sector ought to have received a brief that pointed out the wider implications, according to the country concerned — what would happen to, for example, the demand for cars, and thus the needs for investment in roads, etc., not to speak of port congestion. (This might, for example, have saved Chief Udoji in Nigeria making, in 1975, the simple — and highly popular — recommendation that wages in the public sector should be doubled.)

It is superficially surprising that there has been little coherence between different aspects of policy. The prime purpose of planning is, if we read the textbooks, to make government policies in different sectors more consistent with each other and with the main policy goals.

But whether this happens in practice depends on the machinery of government. The principal instrument for inducing coherence across the whole range of government policies, and thus providing planning with some justification, is — according to the literature on such matters — supposed to be the regular inter-departmental meeting at ministerial and 'lower' levels, in which those who take part accept its discipline, not least the obligation to reach agreements on policy and to implement them.

Anyone familiar with the way governments actually work knows that the reality is usually quite different. Ministers typically treat whatever is their policy area as their own private domain, especially those with a personal political base that is indispensable to the government. Consequently, most planning offices lack the authority to obtain the co-operation of other ministries.

I remember visiting Chile as part of an OECD team (led by Robert Buron) during the Christian Democratic administration of the 1960s — a relatively enlightened and rational government.

We were briefed at ODEPLAN and one of the points they made was that the plan provided for self-sufficiency in wheat by 1970. When we came to visit the Ministry of Agriculture, we asked them about this: no, they said, there was no hope of producing enough wheat by 1970, and they in fact expected it would be necessary to build extra storage capacity for wheat imports. On being told of the treatment in the national plan, they replied with some asperity: *we* are responsible for agriculture, *they* should stick to planning. (Later the Ministry of Public Works told us there was no provision for building grain silos: construction was *their* responsibility, not that of the Minsitry of Agriculture!)

Ministers typically are enjoying patronage which is the reward for years of political support (and/or contributions to party funds). They are not going to yield their power lightly to a group of young economics graduates. In particular, unless it has strong political support, it will be unable to match the institutional strength of the Treasury, which tends to concentrate on short-term needs.

Usually the only real instrument for achieving a degree of coherence is not the plan but the budget; yet since departmental estimates are in the first place agreed bilaterally between the Treasury and other departments, they reflect the Finance Minister's perceptions of the balance of political power — though they can also be influenced by the personal effectiveness of ministers and officials. Anyway, the budgetary process covers only one year — or at the most two or three later ones.

These administrative weaknesses (like the habit of publishing detailed 'development' plans) reflect a lack of commitment to development in any real sense. Let us leave aside the more conspicuous cases where the political leader plunders the country for the sake of himself and a few relatives and associates (e.g. Idi Amin, Bokassa) or is in the pocket of one or more TNCs (Tubman). These cases are, in fact, rare; but many other governments have not given much greater priority to national needs. Rhetorical references have often been made to increasing equality and eliminating poverty, especially by governments calling themselves 'revolutionary' or 'socialist'. But policies actually adopted have generally permitted or even encouraged the concentration of the benefits of growth in those sectors, areas, or social classes (or ethnic groups) which are already affluent, including the higher bureaucracy and the political leaders themselves. They may well use the imported ideologies mentioned in Chapter 1 to justify this: 'We must grow first; then we can redistribute later' (as if the pattern of growth were not self-reinforcing).

To talk of deliberate development strategies is rather fanciful unless there is continuous contact between political leaders and development planners, on almost a day-to-day basis. It is true that such a working relationship will still not be initiated by many political leaders, and they may even resist it. But it will be made increasingly necessary by the world crisis, and it will become feasible if ministries of planning give up the hectic task of preparing a periodic 'development plan', that is soon out-dated, and concentrate on real strategic issues.

Political leaders, especially those committed – if only by force of circumstances – to greater self-sufficiency, will increasingly be needing studies of the longer-term aspects of various policies, especially those that cut across departmental boundaries. Their intuitive judgements can be helped by estimates of the full consequences of policy options.

If the planning office is incurably addicted to arranging quantitative economic aggregates in medium-term plans, and is unable to incorporate military and other non-economic factors in a comprehensive, consistent development strategy,[1] then a separate secretariat could be created, presumably in the office of the president or prime minister, whichever is the real political leader. This would make use of the work of the planning office, but take account of additional considerations, and interpret the combined implications. In a large administration, it could include a demographer, a serving officer, an education expert, etc., as well as an economist.

Whatever its place in the administration, let me call it a 'development staff', to distinguish it from the rather discredited 'planning office' of today. It would perform functions like those of a military general staff. The latter normally prepare contingency plans to cover sudden emergencies ('war games'), but also long-term military plans in the light of expected advances in military technology, and in international relations. The staff frames medium-term programmes of organization, re-equipment, and training to implement them

— or should do so. Since these all presuppose what government policies are with respect to neighbours and great powers, they require regular discussion with the political leadership. The staff are *not* by any means required to publish their plans, though the release of summaries or extracts helps make outside technical opinion more knowledgeable, thus enabling it to be consulted, and focuses public opinion on crucial issues (e.g. the relative importance of navies).

Naturally no political leader will automatically accept the advice of the development staff (or even ought to) any more than that of the military staff. He (or she) will always take into account other considerations, according to his own judgement, for example on the sort of political support that could be mustered for a particular scenario.[2] He does need, however, whether or not he realizes it, advice on the measurable costs and benefits of any major policy option, in the light of long-term development needs. Political judgement should be what could be called 'informed intuition'.

The feasibility of a more purposive (but less quantitative) approach to development strategy depends, of course, on the perceptions and political skills of the leadership. For example, one consideration in selecting a long-term strategy may be how to handle foreign influence over the industrial sector. This may well mean analysing the costs and benefits of any proposed investments by foreign firms, and requiring the participation in ownership and/or management of local citizens. (These would be more sensitive to national needs than foreign staff, who have to conform to worldwide corporate policies — though they would need to be placed in positions of real authority, not just given posts like 'public relations' or 'labour management'.)

Weaving the various policies into a consistent whole, compatible with constraints (internal and external) and with exogenous variables, is especially important in small countries, where the penalty for strategic mistakes can be high. Yet precisely in a small country the government will lack a wide range of expertise to formulate and implement policy, especially *vis-à-vis* foreign firms. Moreover to prepare an elaborate system of detailed alternative strategies would hardly be feasible.

On the other hand, in a small country the need for

sophistication may also be less because fewer options can realistically be considered (see above). If its area is also small, it has less need for detailed regional planning.

In an administration of limited size, the development staff is anyway less likely to remain in political limbo. Face-to-face contact between the political leaders and the people is also much more feasible, which can provide the political solidarity required for a development strategy, especially if it demands sacrifice.

Let me say something more about the scenarios that can be used to illustrate long-term strategic possibilities for various types of country (of course, I do not exclude 'industrial' countries[3]). These would incorporate some of the elements of conventional plans. I would not deny that certain issues can be illustrated by quantitative projections, and some of these could be put before the public: the preparation and publication of medium-term projections provide one possible way of doing this. Input-output matrices can be useful (where they can be realistically prepared, in adequate detail). They can show what sort of economic change might be achieved in their time span, for quantifiable variables, and indicate the foreign exchange implications of individual policies or a complete scenario.[4]

But to insist on fully quantitative planning is to restrict its scope unduly. As pointed out above, significant progress towards development objectives will take far longer than the few years covered by even medium-term plans. A more appropriate horizon for policy-makers might be about the end of the century. Reaching a significantly higher level of development — for example food self-sufficiency — may well take a much longer time, but to extend projections beyond the year 2000 would involve too big a range of projections of 'exogenous' variables (after fifteen years, for example, the size of the population of working age begins to be affected by births that have not yet taken place and thus by current policy).[5]

Scenarios with this time span could show very roughly the levels of output and employment in various sectors; the pattern of imports and exports by commodity; total capital needs and sources for meeting these. But these need complementing by factors which are not quantifiable, either because of lack of data or because they are qualitative.

One example of the non-quantifiable elements that a fully worked-out development strategy would include is increasing the popular understanding of a country's political history mentioned in Chapter 6. It would also cover, for example, the extent of public ownership of the means of production; within the private sector, the division between national and foreign control; and the distribution of arable land between landowners, peasants, and co-operatives of one type or another. Such issues, which can be partially quantified, have normally been excluded from 'development plans'. Technically it was not indefensible to take the current institutional matrix as given for the few years they covered. But since the world situation has now brought onto the agenda in many countries more fundamental and longer-term issues of development, it also forces consideration of the corresponding institutional changes.

The level of detail needed depends on the country concerned. Some in the Middle East or North Africa would need projections of the supply and usage of water; in the Andean countries there might be special emphasis on transportation; in Britain on industrial restructuring. Some special areas are indicated by the previous discussions as necessitating detailed attention almost anywhere, particularly where the more political assumptions of the scenario are nationalistic.

First, how much energy could be developed from known reserves of coal, natural gas, hydropower, fuelwood, etc.? What alternatives, such as nuclear, solar, etc., might be developed within the time horizon? What consumption of fuel would be indicated by the scenario as a whole, allowing for conservation policy? What residual would need to be filled by imports (or be available, in some cases, for export)? What would be the value of this on low and high price assumptions based on a world economic analysis (drawing, if need be, on outside sources such as the World Bank's annual *World Development Report*)?

In addition, research of this type can support policies of minimizing the immediate effect of sharp rises in oil prices. It would assist, for example, decisions on whether petrol should be rationed, whether kerosene should continue to be subsidized (as it often is because of its importance for rural households).

In the case of food, attention needs to be paid to crop patterns, level of mechanization, etc., consistent with the general economic strategy, especially nutritional needs, the materials required for manufacturing, and also the availability of labour in rural areas (which may imply slowing down urbanization).

All these issues raise, of course, other questions according to local circumstances. For example, could the administration cope with petrol rationing, in view of the opportunities for corruption? What would be the opportunity costs in terms of food foregone if crops are grown for fuel? Answering these questions throws light on the government's room to manoeuvre.

The need to simulate the effects of different assumptions about oil prices is now inescapable. Whether the terms of trade become 25 per cent worse or 25 per cent better by the year 2000 will make a great deal of difference to what any government can do. Further, comprehensive contingency plans are needed for a situation in which oil suddenly became unobtainable due to a major disruption (for whatever reasons) in supplies from the Middle East.

Although there seem to be a large number of policy options and many variables, in fact the requirement of consistency rules out the vast majority of possible permutations. The range of options is, in practice, not great. If, for example, two extreme values for exogenous factors (oil prices, exports) are used, the rough outlines of 'nationalist' and 'open' strategies could be accommodated in half-a-dozen scenarios, which could be worked out in a few man-months and kept up-to-date with very little effort.

CHAPTER 8

Curbing financial irresponsibility

A prime test of a nationalist development strategy is in the financial field. It is here that expenditures and revenues have to be reconciled and the political pressures converge. Many governments attempting autonomous development paths have thrown away their room to manoeuvre by their financial policy — or the lack of one. Then internal developments can combine with external pressures to enforce a change of policy, sometimes by a military coup.

Left-wing parties typically promise sweeping social reforms before taking office, and they usually make at least some attempt to carry these out. But such programmes seem rarely to be implementable, and activists who 'raise consciousness' take on a heavy responsibility indeed, whatever the need for far-reaching social changes. If they fail to gain power, they expose workers and peasants to cruel reprisals; if they succeed, they may find themselves trapped by their own rhetoric. The greater the public desire for higher consumption and more social services, the less the government's room to manoeuvre.

A pattern is visible in the life of such governments. Getting hold of the levers of state power generates euphoria. Now at last they can subsidize food prices, launch housing schemes, increase social services, build schools and hospitals, etc. Big wage rises can be promulgated. At the same time, land can be redistributed, and foreign-owned mines and banks taken over and made to serve the national interest.

There may, of course, be very good justification for such measures. Objectively, no doubt, they are each and all highly desirable. Moreover, they are expected by the working classes, peasants, and left-wing intellegentsia that have helped the government to power. To refrain from carrying any of them out may cost vital political support, especially in the trade unions.

But a price has to be paid if several are attempted simul-taneously, especially since the civil service, inherited from the previous regime, are unlikely to be enthusiastic about the extra work or about some of the people they have to work with.

Consumer demand soars but output inevitably falls during the first phase of reorganization (e.g. in agriculture). Inflation stimulates imports and discourages exports just at a time when (see Chapter 3) the balance of payments is threatened by loss of tourist receipts and migrant remittances, etc., and capitalist organizations, especially the TNCs, carry out their own strikes: they cut investment and export capital.

Foreign exchange reserves run down and the currency is devalued — or a black market develops in foreign exchange. Import controls are tightened, causing, in due course, shortages of fuel, industrial inputs, food, etc. Living standards decline, leading eventually to political crisis and a complete reversal of policy — whether by a coup, a lost election, or simply a 'U-turn', such as is required by the IMF as the cost of a rescue operation. (I shall give examples of each.) Then the precious social gains are forfeited anyway: the position of the working classes certainly became much worse in all the cases I shall mention than before the radical government took power (though some governments that showed flexibility survived to bring about lasting social improvements later). The more faithful a left-wing government is to its supporters, the more it is likely to betray them.

As Stephany Griffith-Jones has shown,[1] it is precisely a left-wing government, not a conservative one, that most needs a deliberate and strict financial policy, especially on the budget, the rate of interest, and wages. Even apart from the importance of avoiding the economic and political consequences of inflation, monetary stability is essential if controls are to operate efficiently and the price mechanism is to work in all the sectors which cannot be controlled.

A really radical government is naturally much plotted against. There are always high-ranking officers and foreign governments only too willing to engineer its downfall, if need be by violence. They are 'to blame' for what happens, of course, but — and this is something that has to be faced — a government which loses control of the financial situation plays into their hands and sets itself up for a coup.

Those socialist governments which have survived the traumas of birth and childishness have grown up to be extremely careful about their financial health, guarding their foreign exchange reserves with scrupulous, even excessive, care and imposing balanced budgets not merely in their own accounts but throughout the range of public institutions. Indeed, from financial irresponsibility — and partly because of its effects — policy swings to a monetarist extreme, accompanied by conversion of trade unions into state agencies.

Soviet experience after the revolution of 1917 is still relevant, even for non-revolutionary governments. In the period known as 'War Communism', the inherited supply problems and price inflation were aggravated by a romantic desire to play down the importance of money or even abolish it. Only the exhaustion of the capitalist powers at the end of the First World War, plus the size and geographical remoteness of the Soviet Union, protected the revolutionary state from effective foreign intervention (such as helped topple the Bela Kun communist regime in Hungary shortly afterwards).

Yet strict financial policies had to be imposed eventually, of course. After 1922, the direction of policy was completely reversed. The New Economic Policy then adopted would in many respects have gratified even the most doctrinaire member of the IMF staff. To balance the budget, taxes were increased, part of social expenditure was made the responsibility of local authorities, and government administrative staff were reduced by more than 50 per cent. The increase in the money supply was halted — indeed, the government linked the rouble to gold; the real value of wages fell and the consequent strikes were repressed, often with violence; trade unions were brought under government control. Tax and price policies were manipulated to provide 'incentives' to peasants and traders. (These appear to have been excessively generous, reflecting a rather simplistic 'class analysis' that emphasized the need to gain the support of the peasantry and *petit bourgeoisie*.)

This bitter medicine worked. Production recovered, inflation slowed down, and foreign payments were brought back into balance. The regime survived — but, not surprisingly, the result of such a drastic version of what we would now call a 'stabilization' policy was a rapid increase in inequality and unemployment. To repress the resistance that these generated was one of the 'objective' justifications for the Stalinist terror.

In Czechoslovakia after the Second World War, a Leftist

government, at first a coalition, was set up under the wing of Soviet military power (following the Yalta conference). Yet Soviet experience of War Communism was ignored. The post-war economic shortages were confronted with a very similar *naïveté*, the Czech leaders declaring that the job of financial policy was simply to mobilize money for whatever invest-ment was physically possible. Among many gems of official wisdom, one is eminently quotable: in a planned economy, a Czech socialist proclaimed, 'there can be no inflation unless the authorities wish it'![2]

While the government did adopt some measures to reduce excess demand, credits to the public sector still grew rapidly, because of its inefficiency. Price controls were partly ineffec-tive and black markets flourished long after the war had ended. (This was in fact, used by the Communist Party as a reason for *further* nationalization.) The consequent economic problems, together with the emergence of the 'cold war' and apparently growing Soviet anxiety about the situation, led the Communists in 1948 to dispense with the coalition and rule alone. There was a shift towards financial orthodoxy which was facilitated by their control of the trade unions, but it was accompanied by (and not unrelated to) increasing political repression, which became severe in the 1950s, and has remained so (apart from a brief interlude) ever since.

In Cuba, post-revolutionary euphoria developed, reinforced, perhaps, by the Bay of Pigs victory. Thus in August 1961, at a conference on production, Regino Boti, the Minister of Economics and head of JUCEPLAN, stated that from 1962 to 1965 the total production of Cuba would grow annually by 'not less than 10 per cent and probably [!] not more than 15.5 per cent'. By 1965 per capita consumption would have risen by more than 60 per cent in comparison with 1958, and Cuba would be, in relation to its population, the most industrialized country in Latin America. He went on: 'I want to affirm that if we raise our eyes and contemplate the picture of Cuba in 10 years' time, we arrive at the conclusion that Cuba will overcome passing difficulties and within 9 or 10 years we shall achieve the highest level of living in Latin America by an ample margin, a level of living as high as almost any country in Europe'. (*Obra Revolucionaria*, No. 30, Havana, 1962, quoted in Seers *et al.*, 1964.)

A contempt developed for financial policies, in fact for money itself, more profound even than in the Soviet Union in 1918, and led to the economic difficulties outlined in Chapter 3. (In fact, per capita consumption had actually fallen by 1965, despite heavy Soviet aid.) Not merely were relatively high minimum wages set, rents abolished, and social services quickly expanded, but establishments in all sectors ceased to keep accounts. The money supply soared, and combined with falling output this led to severe shortages of consumer goods, and these in turn caused absenteeism. There was little point in a worker reporting every day at his work, or a housewife taking a job, if the family could not spend their wages anyway — moreover, they would miss many vital queues. (During this period, I went early one Sunday morning to catch a bus from Havana to Matanzas; after queuing for three hours, I realized I would never make the return journey in a day and joined a restaurant queue instead at the bus terminal, which fortunately required only two more hours of standing — for some restaurants, you had to queue all night.)

In 1970, there was apparently a good deal of social unrest in Cuba (although how much we cannot judge from outside). However, the government was helped to survive by persistent (but ineffectual) US hostility. In this case, as in the Soviet Union and Czechoslovakia, it was able to carry through an almost complete reversal of policy. In the 1970s a new insistence emerged here too on monetary incentives, balanced books, limits to the money supply, etc. — and consequently some unemployment and greater inequality — though both are still very small compared with elsewhere in the Western Hemisphere. The government's survival is thus due in no small degree to Castro's willingness (even if belated) to put his strategy into reverse — though also to the ruthless suppression of rival movements and individuals.

So experience has taught the lesson that, especially in such cases, monetary policy *does* matter, a lesson which, since it continues to be ignored, will doubtless be repeated as often as necessary. A number of populist governments which paid little attention to monetary or even financial policy (e.g. Goulart in Brazil, the first phase of the Peronist return to Argentina) fell into the trap outlined above, and were overthrown by military coups. In each case, their supporters expected big social advances, which indeed were objectively necessary. Huge wage increases were promised. Arguments that such policies would lead to inflation and/or foreign exchange crises were spurned: they reflected the 'monetarist' doctrines which the politicians concerned had attacked as socially irresponsible. After all, idle productive capacity, especially unemployed labour, was there to be mobilized, and exchange controls would make devaluation unnecessary.

Chile provides an object lesson. A number of simplistic errors were made by the economists of the Allende government. Since inflation was due to structural problems and there was spare capacity in both labour and capital, they argued, the structural reforms that were planned would reconcile monetary stability with rapid economic growth. Thus the government would be able to fulfil social promises without alienating the middle classes.

In practice, it proved impossible to carry out the reforms and mobilize the surplus capacity. For one thing, the bureaucracy lacked the skills — indeed in most cases even the inclination — necessary for far-reaching structural change. Moreover, none of the ministers had previous experience of government administration.

Unfortunately, neither did they draw on — or apparently, for the most part, even know of — the early experiences in the Soviet Union, Eastern Europe, or Cuba. Their attitudes had been formed, naturally enough, rather by the struggle against policies advocated by teams from the IMF. They saw the fundamental problems as 'structural': finance was of quite secondary importance. Theories of 'planning' then current in Latin America, propagated by the Economic Commission for Latin America, carried for some Chilean economists the implication that social problems could be solved by inverting input-output matrices and building 'consistent' projections for some imaginary future — see Chapter 7. This naïve version of Prebisch's doctrines (outlined in Chapter 2) was married to equally naïve applications of the Keynesian dictum that what was physically possible must also be financially possible, reinforcing the tendency to separate financial policy from policy for production and to down-play the former's importance. A particularly serious consequence was that interest rates were so heavily subsidized that they were lower than the rate of inflation, encouraging the adoption of capital-intensive technologies, and stimulating consumption and investment — and thus the demand for imports.

Inflation rapidly accelerated, which in turn encouraged the outflow of private capital and caused black markets to proliferate, especially in foreign exchange, though consumer goods also started to be unavailable at controlled prices. In 1972, when an international conference on the government's policies, jointly organized by the Chilean planning office (ODEPLAN) and IDS, was held in Santiago, participants from Communist countries could hardly conceal their shock at hearing Allende's Minister of Planning say that the exchange rate did not matter 'because the government controlled both exports and imports'.[3]

The government was actually by then almost impotent. Not merely was it unable to restrain demand or control wage increases. In its final months, industrial production declined because of dwindling supplies of raw materials and spare parts, and also big strikes, stimulated by the opposition. Price inflation was now so fast that it was difficult to measure, but the rate was probably over 10 per cent a week and rising: a state of 'hyper-inflation' (when public confidence in money collapses completely, as in Germany in the 1920s) seemed inevitable. Attempts to halt the soaring prices of foodstuffs aggravated shortages and caused queues. But the government could not introduce food rationing either, except on an informal basis, and housewives joined massive demonstrations of protest.

The stage was set in 1973 for a reversal of policy here too. In contrast to the earlier experiences in the Soviet Union, Czechoslovakia, and Cuba, the government continued to reject monetarist solutions. Yet the geographical position of Chile, far from the Red Army's range, made it highly vulnerable. The aim of the United States administration was to 'destabilize' a government that had carried out a virtual expropriation of US copper companies. The measures they took, including trade sanctions and encouragement to the military, have been discussed in Chapter 3 as illustrations of external constraints. In the end, monetarism *was* introduced — under a regime which brutally repressed opposition, assassinating Allende and killing, imprisoning, or exiling thousands of his government's supporters.

This account does not exonerate generals who seize power and institute state terrorism. It would be a great oversimplification to claim that financial imprudence in the 'Southern Cone' of Latin America (Argentina and Uruguay as well as Chile — and also, earlier, Brazil) caused the subsequent political coups — one would have to analyse the interactions between all the main forces, including property-owners, trade unions, ambitious generals, and the foreign interests conspiring to overthrow the governments concerned. There is no space to do this here. But certainly inflation undermined support for populist governments there, especially among the professions and the bureaucracy, and opened the door to the military plotters.

Several experiences in other parts of the world confirm the pattern of policy reversal, by one route or another. Let me briefly mention a few.

In Portugal, a big budgetary deficit after the fall of Caetano aggravated the foreign exchange difficulties that helped bring about a complete switch of policy (see Chapter 3), though more gradually and by several changes of government.

Michael Manley's government in Jamaica also let the financial situation get out of hand, partly because one of the two trade union organizations was controlled by the opposition. Simultaneously, pro-Cuban rhetoric and measures against the bauxite companies led to a flight of capital, and discouraged tourism. The government did, in fact, accept IMF conditions and try to control the financial chaos, but too late: the subsequent withdrawal of IMF support was hardly a surprise. (It was only delayed so long because Andrew Young, a friend of Manley's, had been influential in the Carter administration.) Increasing violence, as the economic situation deteriorated, set the stage for an election which swept the government out of office and brought about a predictable reversal of policy, in this case too by constitutional means.

Mildly socialist governments seem to show mild tendencies to financial irresponsibility with correspondingly milder consequences. Is it far-fetched to see certain parallels even in recent British history? The Labour government of 1974–9 could hardly be called 'socialist' but it came to power, as always, with grandiose schemes of social improvement. In the event, it could only try to shield the working class from the consequences of the country's post-colonial economic decline, and the world crisis of the 1970s, at the cost of budgetary discipline. In its closing years, policy was already starting to swing: the Chancellor, Dennis Healey, obtained from the IMF both financial and political support at the price of tighter financial policies, but wages policy collapsed, public support dwindled, and here too the government was replaced by one dedicated to financial respectability; the ultimate price of Labour's aspirations was rapidly rising unemployment. Any future Labour government, especially if it is more radical, will face similar problems (see Chapter 11).

The reality is that, when Leftist governments get into financial difficulties, their options close down. The Soviet government cannot come to their rescue (as Chilean experience showed). It has barely enough capacity to support its existing group of clients (Cuba, Ethiopia, Afghanistan, Angola, Mozambique, South Yemen, and Vietnam), even if it wanted to add others. There are, of course, many sources in the capitalist world — private and governmental — but few will nowadays provide much capital, especially to a left-wing government, until the IMF has put its seal of approval on the financial policy. The Fund staff only does this after agreement to policy changes formalized in 'letters of intent', which are then monitored by the application of 'performance tests' (as in Jamaica).

Because the Fund is so visible, left-wing economists criticise it for the fall of radical governments, pointing to its political bias in insisting on the dismantling of controls on imports, prices, etc. — but not those over wages. There is substance in these complaints, but they seem somewhat ingenuous. What can one expect from an institution controlled by the major capitalist governments? There is no secret about this control. A few governments (those of the United States, Britain, West Germany, France, and Japan) determine policy under its weighted voting system, apart from their influence on the other delegations. What ultimately sets the financial boundaries on the policies of a delinking government are that powerful and articulate bankers, industrial capitalists, etc., have a direct interest in any policies overseas which would affect their loans being serviced, or reduce access to markets or to raw materials.

So reforming the IMF would not in itself be a decisive step in opening up the choice of development strategies, and economists who claim the contrary help to mislead 'progressive' politicians — dangerously. As we have seen, there are many other ways in which policies can be changed by foreign governments: they can usually find allies high in the national power structure, not merely generals but also senior officials and some politicians.

More to the point, the need for a strict financial policy does not arise, fundamentally, because of the prejudices of the IMF staff (though they *are* prejudiced), nor even just because of the strength of the capitalist powers behind them. The IMF is not in fact an important constraint, in itself, on policy. The financial constraint arises out of the whole situation, especially the inconsistency between the expectations of the populist government's supporters, recklessly raised during revolutions or election campaigns, and the inevitable drop in living standards, at least in the short run, when it takes power. This is one of the typical internal contradictions in the development of a socialist state, and leads to a now familiar sequence of accelerating inflation, dwindling foreign exchange reserves, difficulties in financing essential imports, etc., etc.

Indeed, much of what the Fund imposes in 'conditionality' governments would have to carry out anyway, even if it did not exist — and even if there were no other external influences. (One of Manley's ministers admitted as much to me.) I have found that finance ministers who are at the end of their tether (e.g. Healey in Britain), and more so their officials, often secretly welcome powerful outside pressure on their cabinet colleagues to behave in ways at least more consistent with avoiding foreign exchange crises — especially since the government can then claim that it was coerced into accepting such unpalatable conditions. (The IMF is a useful whipping boy.)

How many more political disasters, one wonders, over how many decades, have to take place before the Left, whether in Europe or overseas, draws the lessons? The first is that integrity, if not mere prudence, requires that while still in opposition socialist leaders should not promise the public a great deal more than can actually be delivered, but should emphasize how intractable economic problems are and how much depends

on world oil prices and many other factors completely outside their control. The experiences discussed above show con-
clusively that it is not merely dishonest but dangerous to
promise big rises in living standards. Restraint in propaganda
might jeopardize the chance of political success, but we can
now see that the victory otherwise probably proves hollow
and short-lived, and can be painfully reversed. It may well be
worth waiting until one can win honestly.

Another lesson from the experience of Chile, Jamaica, etc.,
is that a proper set of economic policies, including not merely
a partially quantified scenario, but a rough budget, needs to
be worked out in anticipation of this period of disorganization.
In the absence of advance agreement on the main lines of
financial policy, all the finance minister can do is nag his colleagues not to spend quite so much — before going to the
other extreme, when the inevitable crisis breaks, and becoming
plus Friedmanite que Milton! Yet none of the many Left
parties in opposition, to my knowledge, even the British
Labour Party, take this obvious precaution.[4]

Discussion of financial programmes cannot, of course, go
very far here — much depends on the size of each economy;
the composition of its balance of payments; its productive
structure; the nature of its capital markets; the strength and
politics of its trade unions; the capacity of its public services
(and their own political interests); and the existing rate of
inflation. Points to cover, however, would include the principles and machinery for public finance, as well as for an
incomes policy; for the central bank; and for the accounts of
public corporations, which are especially vulnerable to pressure
from trade unions. These guidelines need not be brutal (i.e.
'monetarist'), especially in countries where only gradual social
change is being attempted and where there is little room to
manoeuvre, but some limits are needed to curb financial
excesses.[5]

CHAPTER 9

Statistical needs

WHAT appear to be boringly technical choices in producing statistics are often of profound importance. We cannot, with our own eyes and ears, perceive more than a minute sample of human affairs, even in our own country — and a very unrandom sample at that. So we rely on statistics in order to build and maintain our model of the world.

The data that are available mould our perceptions. When we try to construct our models, in research institutes or social science courses, or for the loose underpinning of our personal ideologies, their constituents and design depend very much on the series that statistical offices choose to prepare and publish. What is more to the point, these latter determine to a considerable degree what can be done by an economic staff. It would be very hard to develop the sort of scenarios indicated above on the basis of the statistics normally available.

Thus, a statistical policy (i.e. the policy of statistical offices) exerts a subtle but pervasive and lasting influence on political, social, and economic development. This is why the apparently dull and minor subject of statistical priorities is of crucial importance.

What is published reflects how reality has been perceived by official statisticians. These, however, have to develop an intuitive sense of what sort of data are acceptable to the political leadership. The latter have a distinct interest in throwing the spotlight on certain questions and keeping it off others. Most political leaders have preferred official statisticians not to provide material for opponents by focusing attention on social conditions, such as the quality of housing and nutrition — let alone deaths at the hands of the police. They also have reason to prefer national averages of income (and of other variables) that conceal their distribution between classes, races, or regions (depending on whichever is a sensitive subject in the country concerned). They may well also be apprehensive about the publication of data showing the degree of foreign penetration of their country. Conservative politicians (of whatever party) need a benign model of reality — and the statistics to illustrate it.

Since statistical offices are rarely strong enough to assert much professional independence, they have found it convenient to ignore black markets, illegal industries, and corrupt practices, although these may, in fact, have come to account for a large fraction of economic activity. Consequently, data on output and exports of farm crops rarely contain an allowance for marijuana or opium, for example, even though these are often (e.g. in Colombia) among the main crops, let alone for their marketing (or processing). Retail price indices usually refer just to controlled prices, which may be of little practical relevance.

Other big influences on statistical policy are the international agencies (and some of the bilateral ones). The weight of their demand is heavy, often for statistics which have neither any real significance locally nor any basis in actual measurement, though they are very possibly (e.g. income aggregates) welcome to politicians. International standards, not only in national accounts, usually reflect how problems are perceived in the industrial countries, where statistical systems have been most highly elaborated. This external demand cannot easily be ignored by a government statistician, who may believe that the preparation of certain data is almost a condition for aid — and may have his own reasons for maintaining professional links with colleagues in the agencies. So radical changes in statistical policy would involve not merely much work but also conflicts both with his government and with international agencies.

His views on statistical priorities may anyway reflect his own university education which, if it did not actually take place abroad, will probably have been greatly influenced by imported syllabuses, textbooks, standards, etc. This education, like that of his colleagues, and of the politicians and administrators including the U.N. staff with whom he deals will moreover have occurred at least a couple of decades earlier. It was in the 1950s that today's statistical systems largely began to take shape. The social problem was then almost universally seen as essentially an economic one: a fast rate of growth would somehow benefit the whole community.

For reasons already explained, development is now increasingly perceived as a much more complex process than merely raising per capita income: its social constituents, in terms of income equality and also of better nutrition, housing, literacy, etc., and the dispersion of bureaucratic power, would not necessarily be achieved by economic growth, and some governments have started to talk, at least, about 'poverty-oriented' planning. Increasing attention is also paid to self-reliance, especially since the oil shock of 1973.

Reality and perceptions of reality have therefore both changed profoundly in the past two decades. These changes require a different approach to official statistics. Before discussing what this might be, I shall explore the ideological roots of the types of data normally published in order to show that they were neither devised, nor are they likely to be suitable, for today's problems.

Once statisticians, as a profession, were in the vanguard, anticipating and helping to create the basic shifts in public understanding, in order to translate them into political initiatives. Charles Booth's classic survey of London in the nineteenth century, which revealed the scope of poverty and threw light on its causes, laid the basis for the great wave of social reforms carried out by the Lloyd George Government in the first decade of this century. National income estimates were to hand when politicians started to call for them in the 1930s (Clark, 1983).

At that time private statisticians could innovate by themselves. Now the task would be too great; it would have to be carried out by those in official statistical offices. But these are not merely protected by their residence and lifestyle from contact with social reality; they also enjoy tenure. The optimal statistical policy from the point of view of their careers is to maintain and develop the statistical structure they inherit, normally based on the manuals of the international agencies. These organizations could be playing a vital role in encouraging the translation of changing perceptions of national problems into new data collection. But their technical assistance experts tend to emphasize established international standards rather than emerging national priorities, and their own statistical offices press national statistical departments for information needed for their international tables, whether or not

these are useful locally. They do not provide much data themselves on international transactions important to national
governments but at present under-recorded, which they would
be in the best position to develop — migration (especially of
qualified personnel), the operations of multinational corporations, and transfer pricing, etc.

There are time lags in data production on top of those in
changing perceptions. It takes years to plan and implement
the collection of new types of data, and to prepare them for
publication. When new types of data are requested to meet
policy needs (oil rationing, or the elimination of poverty),
they cannot be produced at short notice. Unless a statistical
office is alert to changing realities, it will find itself unable to
meet the emerging needs of new development strategies of
the sort outlined above.

In the Annexe to the Introduction, I discussed some of the
conceptual and practical limitations of conventional measures
of economic growth; here I want to go into the associated
accounting system, the SNA which lies at the heart of most
national statistical structures and profoundly influences the
way in which professionals and laymen alike perceive reality.

Like the cosmology of Ptolemy, the SNA is both logically
coherent and practically useful — up to a point. It has a strong
rationale, bringing out the connections between economic
problems, providing opportunities for prolonged (even heated)
conceptual discussions, and serving as a convenient framework
for much data collection and empirical research.

We easily forget that, like a cosmological model, it is purely
an artefact. With more than two decades of formal existence
(and more than four since it began to take shape), it has already
acquired the authority of tradition, and questioning it seems
almost as big a heresy as that of Giordano Bruno. Yet it
represents simply one of many possible ways of arranging data,
the way that seemed convenient to economists embracing the
value judgements and espousing the theories current in the
middle of this century.

The SNA owes its origin to the realization in the 1930s
that the existing statistics in Britain were inadequate for
policies to solve the great unemployment problem of that
time — one that Keynes was depicting as due to inadequate
global demand. This necessitated a statistical revolution (just

as the present situation does) which started in fact not in Whitehall but Cambridge. A major purpose of Colin Clark, who was at Cambridge and in touch with Kahn and Keynes, was to break down the expenditure side of the national income so as to make possible quantitative verification of the Keynesian model of income generation. The propensities to consume and to invest could then be worked out; and the 'multipliers' (connecting income and investment) estimated.

The new tables were used by Keynes himself, in his pamphlet *How to Pay for the War* (1940),[1] to demonstrate that the British mobilization for war posed essentially a resource problem, rather than a financial one, and to measure how much of an effort was possible, if unemployed resources were mobilized and consumption kept in check. Anyway he succeeded in persuading Treasury officials to agree to the courageous step of publishing under official auspices a series of tables of *estimates*[2] — up to that time, official statistics were essentially *counts* of population, imports and exports, registered unemployment, etc. Basically, the same tables were also used in the discussion of how to avoid the recurrence of unemployment after the war — e.g. by Kaldor[3] who was working in Cambridge. Meanwhile, parallel work was going on in the United States, which, tackling similar problems, led to rather similar statistics. (In a number of other industrial countries, especially the Netherlands, similar work had been getting under way before the German occupation.)

The system developed into the SNA via a series of wartime and post-war conferences. A key step was the meeting in Princeton in 1945 of a committee on National Income Statistics (a sub-committee, anachronistically, of the 1939 Committee of Statistical Experts set up by the League of Nations) which produced a 'Recommended System of Accounts' based on a paper by Richard Stone, then Director of the Department of Applied Economics at Cambridge.[4] This drew on an integrated system by James Meade and himself.[5] Stone was in charge of the OEEC National Accounts Research Unit at Cambridge, which produced, in 1952, the first version of the SNA.

This accounting system, which shows a family resemblance to Colin Clark's work, was subsequently found useful for the growth model associated with Roy Harrod and Evsey Domar, which has exerted a powerful influence on planning — see Chapter 6.

Yet we should never forget these origins. The system evolved in the industrial countries, largely in Britain, indeed, very largely out of the work of a group of Cambridge economists, in the middle decades of this century. When it was published by the United Nations, a supplementary chapter on the 'Adaptation of the full system to the developing countries' was tacked on at the end — although these countries account for the great majority of the world's population. This special chapter, with a simplified set of accounts, was moreover added not primarily because there were felt to be fundamental differences in structures or problems between different parts of the world or in their statistical resources, but because it would 'take a number of developing countries many years to build the body of statistics required . . . for the full system'.[6]

It has been argued above that the Keynesian variety of the neo-classical model (including the Harrod-Domar dynamic version) is no longer widely applicable, even in Britain. Thus we cannot expect its associated accounting system to be either. Detailed structural problems were certainly not prominent in the mind of Keynes — still less of Harrod or Domar. The continued use of the system of accounts corresponding to Keynesian economics is not due to conscious decisions by various national statistical offices that the Keynesian system is appropriate for their needs, but to it being the only one at all fully worked out, and to its promotion by technical assistance experts thoroughly conversant with its principles — though not always fully aware of the purposes for which it was created, or the assumptions it implies, or the quality of basic data it requires.

The Keynesian system of accounts was indeed a vigorous intellectual response to the political needs of its time and place, especially the need to quantify issues of demand management, which was seen as the cure for unemployment. If we draw back from the context, and look at it with fresh eyes, it has some features that are rather, so to say, strange for the 1980s.

One point should be made at the outset. A special assumption of the SNA is that *reliable* statistics do in fact exist for a large fraction of the economic activities it does cover. This is particularly doubtful in the case of imputation of the own-account activities supposed to be covered (e.g. production of food, or the rental value of owner-occupied dwellings). In fact, for many countries, published tables of national accounts are largely guesswork (see the Annexe to the Introduction).

It is also tacitly assumed by most Keynesian analysts that the economy is so unified and *homogeneous* that an increase in effective demand would generate comparable volumes of increased output and employment, wherever it was injected. Such an assumption might have seemed at least defensible in a country where patterns of consumption do not differ much from district to district, or race to race; where the concentration of income is moderated by a tax and social security system; and where labour and capital are fairly mobile between sectors and districts. But these conditions cannot be assumed to be so perfectly fulfilled any more, even in most industrial countries.

Secondly, this system of accounts, like Keynesian economics is basically designed for a country which is economically independent, in the sense that all the main economic decisions are taken by nationals of that country. It recognizes, of course, the existence of transactions with the external world, including remittances of profits. But the accounts of the group of companies which are under foreign control are not considered significant enough to require separate tabulation. In some cases a single company (e.g. Bougainville Copper in Papua New Guinea) is responsible for a large and strategic share of national output — more generally large segments in several key sectors are in foreign hands. To lump their income and expenditure with those of other companies is an implicit political statement of some importance: it does not correspond to my approach here, and hardly seems justified for any country today, developed or developing.

In fact, the system tempts economists to use naïve models, especially in its treatment of *capital formation*. If the conventions are such that this alone, of all the influences on future production (discussed above), is by implication treated as *the* source of growth, it is not surprising that policy discussion and 'development plans' may ignore all the other requirements — except perhaps for expenditure on education,[7] and centre on the need for capital flows from abroad. Similarly, over-all growth targets may hide the implied destruction of household and village activities.

As I pointed out above, there may be more profound reasons for the almost universal acceptability of the SNA: the political power base of governments is often so unsure that the real issues of development are best swept under the carpet.

Few academic economists feel the necessity for a different framework either: the conventions of the SNA do not seem at all odd to those who were educated in the third quarter of this century. Even non-economists have absorbed unconsciously the theoretical models in vogue then in the industrial countries. It is somewhat ironic that today even the most nationalistic of political leaders overseas, who believe themselves exempt from any imperialist influences, are often the slaves of a defunct European economist – Keynes himself!

However, the severity of politico-economic problems is compelling a reconsideration of not merely economic theories and planning models, but also relevant data systems, just as happened in the 1930s. In the first place, let me repeat what I said in Chapter 6: the data need is not just, or in some countries even mainly, for better statistics – the nature of institutional factors such as the links between foreign and local firms are what really matter.

'Quantitative data may indeed be helpful, but they require a major shift of focus. If aggregative approaches are largely irrelevant to today's problems, it follows that national income accounts should cease to be central to the programme of a statistical office. Precisely which tasks would be more important would depend on the country concerned.

Some general priorities are implied, however, by the approach to development strategy outlined above. It will be easier to frame this if import data are available in a classification different from the main Standard International Trade Classification (SITC). The essential principle of the SITC is the nature of the materials (so that jute bags are in the same broad group as cotton shirts, household pharmaceuticals with industrial chemicals). For many statistical purposes, on the other hand, one needs an 'end use' classification that distinguishes in the first place between consumer goods, capital goods, and industrial inputs – a classification treated by the UN Statistical Office as merely a subsidiary possibility, and many statistical offices have not developed it. (Those that have are unusually late in publishing it.)

The need I have stressed above for special attention to energy and food development planning implies a corresponding priority for energy and food balance sheets, of a higher level of accuracy and much more detail than would be necessary for other data in an input-output table. What are needed moreover are not merely value figures but also physical data in 'tons of coal equivalent', proteins, etc.

The importance of social integration in a self-reliance strategy points to a greater need for 'social indicators' than would otherwise be the case (and has been customary). I am not talking here just about the usual figures of doctors per thousand of the population, hospital beds, school places, etc. These are useful up to a point but they can only tell one about the capacity of official delivery systems. Data on their utiliz-ation — numbers of consultations, bed occupancy, school attendance — are more useful but what one really needs are data on bodily condition. Clues on this are statistics of 'mor-bidity' (illnesses), but more direct measures are at-birth weights and the height and weight of children, which can often readily be collected by schools if this is not being done already. (I found in Malaysia these were being regularly measured of all children at the start of every school year, but not then tabulated!) Classification of such data is needed by race, social class, region, etc., according to the social problems of the country (and also because anthropometric norms vary by ethnic group).

Similarly, a government seriously concerned with social conditions would carry out continuous and graded literacy tests that would reveal not merely whether somebody could read a few words, but also write a letter, etc., and would also keep a record of school absenteeism.

One way of summarizing social conditions is to construct 'active life profiles' for different races, regions, etc., showing life expectancy broken down into expected periods in different states, such as school attendance, employment, etc.[8] This provides a system in some respects analogous to the SNA, but permitting much more emphasis on distribution.

Finally, more precise data are needed on 'unemployment' and 'under-employment' because of their importance as economic waste, causes of poverty, and the origin of personal frustration and political dissension. In-depth questionnaires could help establish e.g. how many married women would take work (of what type) should it be available. In primarily peasant economies, a useful approach (especially where there is seasonal variation in work) would be through time budgets (which can also be used to extend life profiles).

For the aim of self-reliance, even in a developed economy (especially a minor one such as Ireland or Greece), data are needed on such matters as the division of export receipts, especially in manufacturing or mining, between profits of foreign and local corporations, direct taxes, and government royalties. It may also be necessary to prepare separate accounts for particular key industries, such as mining, controlled by TNCs, or even for firms themselves, where one or two of them constitute the industry. These could show not only how their sales revenue is divided between wages, profits, taxes, local and foreign inputs, etc. but also the proportion of output exported.

While the SNA is of dubious value, it may well be helpful to policy-makers and social analysts if all the data for key sectors are pulled together into some economic accounting system which separates out the activities of the TNCs. The tables could also distinguish between the public and private sectors, within a framework that showed 'informal' and 'traditional' sectors separately. This framework would correspond not merely to fundamental differences in the structure of inputs, in the sources of income and employment, and in political interests. It would also reflect statistical reality, because it would not add together data of very different degrees and types of reliability. For the modern economy, especially its multinational sector, there are usually fairly reliable statistics at least in the hands of the firms — this is an area in which the use of statistical resources would have a high yield. Production which is not marketed and has to be valued by imputation may best be left in the physical terms which form the first step in imputation (see above) rather than being guessed and added to income. A cash aggregate would be more useful anyway for certain types of research, e.g. into import propensities, taxable capacity, etc.

It would also be helpful in many countries to distinguish

for statistical purposes urban and rural areas, or advanced and backward regions (such as São Paolo and the north-east of Brazil). Especially where there is pressure for local autonomy, e.g. in the Basque regions, separate tables would be helpful (though whether to publish them is another matter). Where it is important, the income of different races could be distinguished.

Another change corresponding to development needs would be to cease treating some expenditure separately as fixed capital formation, which can only be justified as explained above, on the assumption that it is the sole determinant of growth. This would imply relaxing the definition of 'savings'; which is neither meaningful nor easy to estimate.

It might be more useful to estimate the surplus above 'subsistence' available for various uses – luxury consumption, security, building food stocks, fixed capital formation, education, etc. This is one of the main determinants of a government's room to manoeuvre – see Section B. To measure it would, of course, be difficult, because 'subsistence' is a relative concept, but for highly significant categories even order-of-magnitude estimates are worthwhile. (They would not in fact be all that arbitrary in countries where there is an official poverty line.) This approach would yield an aggregate national income net of what should be considered the first charge on income, the cost of maintaining human (rather than physical) capital.

The crucial problem is not, however, one of devising a new and ideal system: it is to get official statisticians to think about what they are doing. They tend to be extremely conservative in their professional behaviour, even if politically they are radicals. As pointed out above, they belong to a class which the existing frameworks suit (or at least have suited until the crises of the 1980s). Moreover, while they may not realize that they are the slaves of Keynes, they do sense that it would take them a great deal of mental effort and time to construct and quantify a system *ab initio*.

Besides, many users of statistics want to make comparisons with some time in the past, even if the data are unsatisfactory, or with other countries, and would resist such changes – though these needs can largely be met by providing estimates for some categories on both the new and old bases for an overlap period.

We should not, however, assume that resistance to statistical change lasts, any more than it did in the past. Even in the leading industrial countries, structural problems now seem formidable, making Keynesian analysis obviously less applicable and global aggregates thus less useful. Moreover, substantial parts of West European economies, too, are now controlled by foreign corporations.

The responsiveness of statistical offices to new perceptions of development problems is, of course, also constrained by shortage of resources — of qualified and experienced statistical officers who can design and carry out surveys, of equipment, of finance for fieldwork. This is not quite as severe a problem as it appears. Many surveys could be carried out by unemployed secondary school or university graduates, at relatively low cost (especially in fuel or foreign exchange), indeed easing the often critical problem of youth unemployment at the same time. Although some of the work, e.g. converting accounts of foreign companies into economically analysable tables, requires special professional skills, it may be possible to provide these by transferring the officers at present trying to prepare national income data of rather little use.

A more serious difficulty may be confidentiality. Sometimes this can be handled by grouping the information about at least three companies. But no macro-economic statistics about Papua New Guinea, say, would be worth much without data on the income and expenditure of Bougainville Copper.

This is, however, a problem mainly when considering publication. The crucial responsibility of a statistical office is to act as an information gatherer for government, which may well need such data for its own use, especially in any strategy of self-reliance. However, a statistical office has, like a department of justice or of audit or planning (see the synopsis of this section), a responsibility to the public, over and above its responsibility either for publication or to the administration currently in power, and should be prepared, if need be, to compile data which are not required by, or indeed convenient to, the government of the day, even if they cannot be published.

EXTENDED NATIONALISM

Synopsis

IN the first decade after the end of the war, when the globe was divided into three 'worlds', this corresponded to reality. The centrally planned countries were ruled by Communist Parties which obediently followed the lead of their comrades in Moscow, and had characteristically different economic systems, in which each production unit was assigned an annual target.

In the rest of the world, the profit motive still reigned, but two distinct groups could be identified. One was much richer than the other; too much has been made of comparisons in per capita incomes, but there was little doubt about the contrast if one looked at dimensions such as degree of industrialization, reliance on exports of primary products, fiscal systems, and sources of technology, let alone such social indicators on literacy, mortality, etc., as were available.

Besides, many of the developed countries were still imperial powers, even if their empires were crumbling, and nearly all the other countries (then called by the unflattering term 'underdeveloped') had been colonies, the majority in fact until very recently. Rarely explicit in diplomatic fora was an underlying perception in both camps that the great majority in the developed countries were white, of European stock, whereas the great majority in the other group (with the conspicuous exception of the Southern Cone of Latin America) were not.

This frame for looking at the world has been until now curiously convenient for the governments of each type of country. Its usefulness to the élites ruling the developing countries does not need spelling out: it created the presumption that they would receive concessions in trade, etc., and in particular, large quantities of resources would be passed to them as aid. Not merely would they be able to use some of this themselves: they would be able to dispense it as patronage.

Secondly, the framework separated the Soviet government and its East European allies from the rest of Europe, and relieved them from the responsibility of making such transfers themselves — but allowed them to continue criticizing the 'imperialist powers' as exploiters.

What is superficially somewhat surprising is that there was widespread acceptance of such a perceptual frame in the developed countries too. But it suited powerful interests. Naturally it was convenient for foreign offices: it justified parliamentary appropriations that helped to save the ex-colonies from Soviet domination. The emerging TNCs not only wanted to keep open the non-socialist world economy (which can without dogma be called 'neo-colonial'), they were glad there was some other source of capital and technical assistance to create the schools, roads, power plants, etc., necessary to support their activities.

Yet this also provided a moral programme for European liberals and socialists, who were keen to purge themselves of guilt about both the colonial past and the inequalities of the present. Indeed it gave them a stage for a world role — a version, though much diminished, of the part that their fore-fathers (the 'liberal imperialists') could play in the days of empire. Many of the heads of state of former colonies, notably Nehru, later Nyerere, for example, were well known in Europe: they were seen as socialists in the West European tradition, who would respect democratic rights. Inequalities overseas were gross indeed (reflecting in part the pay structure inherited from the colonial services), but they would soon be reduced, as they had been in Europe.

This extraordinary international coalition (the political breadth of which must be historically unique) included a part of academia. Some social scientists, economists in particular, in both developed and developing countries, showed the governments of the developing countries how to 'plan' growth, along the lines criticized in the previous section.

The third quarter of this century was the hey-day of the well-intentioned intervener, abroad as well as at home: the 'scientific' approach to social problems, the roots of which were discussed in Chapter 1, was in the ascendant. Social problems only had to be properly specified and analysed for them to be solved. In particular, research into economic and social problems, based on imported analytical techniques, could help to raise the economic and social levels in developing countries to those in the developed countries, which were seen as basically satisfactory. A cosy philosophy of internationalism reinforced modernization. There were ultimately no unmanageable conflicts of interest within or between countries; in the ever-expanding world made possible by scientific discoveries, all could advance − those furthest behind, indeed, the quickest. The only obstacles were the cultural traditions that (temporarily) stood in the way of progress, especially nationalism, militarism, and philoprogenitive attitudes, as explained above.

Events have been undermining the three-world classification, the basis of this way of perceiving world problems. The categories of developed and developing countries have been becoming more heterogeneous and thus now overlap, whatever dimension one looks at. The per capita income of some developing countries, e.g. Abu Dhabi, is now higher than that of the USA, and Singapore is more urbanized than most of Western Europe. Indeed, Japan has leapt from underdeveloped to highly developed; Argentina and Brazil have become in many economic dimensions, including technological capacity, more developed than Greece or Portugal.

There has also been some convergence between the systems of the capitalist and socialist countries. The former, both developed and developing, have been showing gradual centralization of economic and political power and growing public sectors, despite temporary periods of 'denationalization' in Britain and the USA, whereas the socialist countries are becoming − in varying degrees − decentralized, as well as increasingly dependent on imported capital and technology. Hungary is a conspicuous example; China, Algeria, and Yugoslavia have been anomalies for some time, hard to fit into any of the official categories, and the same is now true of Roumania.

The second major change has been political. Whereas in the first decades after independence at least the forms of parliamentary democracy were mostly preserved — and they flourished in parts of Latin America, for example Chile — the characteristic government of developing countries is now dictatorship, sometimes civilian, but mostly military, and in any case repressive, often savagely so. As far as one can tell, inequalities have become greater: in many countries the poorest 20 per cent of the population are little better off, if indeed there has been any improvement at all (except in the reduced prevalence of a few endemic diseases), whereas the élites have been adapting their lifestyle to the rising standards of their counterparts in the industrial countries (with the additional advantage of cheap domestic services and, in many countries, cheap petrol). Corruption has become rampant (it exists in various forms in the developed countries, of course, but relatively on a much smaller scale).

A programme for reforming the neo-colonial system, such as the New International Economic Order, would help them maintain this lifestyle and their political control, but it no longer has much, if any, moral content. (It would doubtless benefit some of the poor, too, but at the cost of perpetuating their subjugation.)

So academic progressives have become disillusioned, and the old coalition has been undermined. Moreover, few in the developed countries any longer see their own societies as sufficiently successful either to act as a model or to provide great quantities of resources to help the rest of the world.

The framework is still useful to those with political and commercial motives for subsidizing the governments of developing countries. Indeed, there is now an additional justification — many private banks have lent heavily abroad and are worried about the prospects of the debts being serviced, let alone repaid. A more general argument (e.g. in the Brandt Report) is that rising incomes in the South would help reflate the economies of the North: but if the 'Northern' governments wanted a boom (some of them seem far from keen), they could manage it much more efficiently by increasing their domestic expenditures. The result of a worldwide reflation might well be to reveal the oil and food shortages that lurk near the surface, and could generate a politically embarrassing return of inflation. Moreover, if aid were massively increased, its suppliers might not all gain trade correspondingly — Britain, in particular, might lose out.

Yet large-scale aid may not be a necessary price to keep the neo-colonial system alive. The Soviet Union has evidently become less influential in the world scene: it no longer has much oil to offer, even to its Communist partners. Besides, the survival of this system seems unlikely to continue being in the interests of many in the industrial countries, who find it means heavy outflows of capital, growing volumes of imports of manufactures, and increasing competition in the world market.

I argue in Chapter 11 that the best survival policy for Western Europe, Britain in particular, lies in strengthening and further enlarging the European Community, though to make this viable will require a development strategy with many dimensions, as yet hardly touched on in Community politics, especially industrial and redistributive (to integrate the new members properly), but also in the fields of education and population — reflecting the policies discussed in the first nine chapters.

The concluding chapter suggests the possibility of a united Europe, Western and Eastern, as not only fulfilling economic logic, but also creating a better basis for peace, both for Europe and the rest of the world. Perhaps one can see a set of regional blocs starting to emerge, each largely (but not wholly) self-sufficient, a more stable system than the existing one.

CHAPTER 10

The colonial system and its successor

I have already discussed various aspects of the colonial system. I want to examine it briefly here as the forerunner and shaper of the post-war world system.

Let us remind ourselves of its essential elements. It provided in the first place trading opportunities — European manufactures (including guns) being exchanged for primary products, tea, sugar, bananas, etc., but above all gold, silver, and later copper, tin, rubber, and other industrial materials. European entrepreneurs, administrators, and people with professional skills went abroad to the plantations and mines, where they could take advantage of cheap native labour. In some areas, European farmers and traders became settlers. In language used by Prebisch (see Chapter 2), Europe was the 'core' of the system.

It was highly compartmentalized: economic opportunities in the British Colonies were very largely restricted to 'our' companies, and similarly for the French and the others, by colonial currency and trading regimes. The 'periphery' was most of the rest of the world. In its initial phase, colonial administrations had been set up in South Asia and the Americas; the Austrian Empire covered part of the Balkans; and Russian rule extended eastwards towards the Pacific. In the late eighteenth century, nationalist demands for independence had grown in the American continent from the settler populations (not the indigenous) who resented the political subordination to the metropolis, and the inhibitions on their own economic progress. The Spanish and Portuguese governments were unable to maintain control of their South American colonies, and Britain of most of its territory in North America. The losses were partly attributable to sheer distance and expense, though also to clumsiness and delays in reacting to settler demands (and in the case of Portugal and Spain, the weakening of their technological pre-eminence).

In the nineteenth century the system entered a second

phase, with the opening of another continent, Africa. British and French armies, in particular, established colonies, with scant attention to tribal boundaries, as has already been pointed out. In the South, and to some extent in the North and Kenya, Europeans settled in numbers — as they were doing in Australia and New Zealand.

The framework for financial transactions was the gold standard. Convertibility suited the main European powers, especially Britain, because of their technical leadership, and it permitted a period of price stability, from 1815 to 1914, in the sense that despite trends in some commodities and sharp movements from time to time in the general price level, the latter showed little long-term tendency.

The system was very profitable to the colonial powers. It required, of course, heavy policing: the real guardian of the colonial system was the Royal Navy (which, on occasion, fired shells to punish those, e.g. Venezuelans, whose governments defaulted on debt service). But the benefits of the original trading pattern (manufactures for primary products) became augmented by profits on the growing investments.

It is true that the ultimate root of the whole system was industrial leadership (including leadership in military technology), but the colonial system for a long time both stimulated and supplemented this. Its profits helped finance research in science and technology, and investment in new plant and machinery. They also helped pay for the armed forces to punish rebellions and ward off rival powers.

When I say that the colonial powers benefited, I refer to almost the whole population. In fact, because of the way the system functioned, wages started to diverge considerably from those in the colonies, as did social expenditures. Living standards rose for all classes and a broadening suffrage could be permitted without a violent struggle. But the technical leadership was slipping away by the opening years of this century. One reason was that the life of a gentleman, in Britain for example, drawing the dividends of the Empire (directly or indirectly), with a career in the armed forces or Oxbridge or the great bureaucracies at home or overseas, was more attractive than sweating to maintain the industrial supremacy on which colonial dominance ultimately depended. (As late as the 1960s, when I was teaching at Oxford, a student said to me that he was not going to get a good degree, so he would have to go into business!)

Europeans could enjoy the luxury of paternalism: the colonial offices proclaimed their role as bringing civilization to Africa and Asia. The peoples of the colonies would be gently, but firmly, guided up a long constitutional ladder, enjoying gradually increasing political responsibility, until they were deemed fit to govern themselves, using parliamentary institutions and bureaucratic systems based on those of their imperial masters. They would be helped along the way by colonial administrators, soldiers, officals of colonial companies, and missionaries (the last often providing health and educational services, as well as religion), and in many cases by financial aid too. During the unspecified, but certainly lengthy, time this would take — indeed, even afterwards — they would naturally remain part of the Empire concerned.

These perceptions were the basis of colonial policy in all spheres from constitutional commissions to currency boards and higher education.

A number of European rivals had, however, arrived on the scene, notably Germany, and were overtaking in technical fields Britain, France, Russia, and the Netherlands. Germany was too late to acquire colonies, except for a couple in Africa, and the German leadership felt entitled to take over from Britain and France. This now meant a bitter and costly war, in the course of which two empires, the Russian and Austrian, collapsed, although the new Bolshevik government, in the immediate post-war chaos, successfully took over almost the whole of the Tsarist one. Britain and France had been weakened, not merely by loss of assets and accumulation of debt, but by the death of millions of men, including tens of thousands who would have become the leaders of the two Empires — politically, administratively, and in the professions. Meanwhile, the United States came through virtually unscathed: it hardly needed colonies because of its own vast hinterland, but it became a formidable industrial competitor.

The post-1918 boom greatly expanded industrial capacity, but subsequently this could not be fully utilized and investment fell sharply in the industrial countries, pulling down the whole income structure and causing heavy unemployment. The depression was especially severe in Britain, where in 1925 the gold standard had been re-established with the pound at its pre-1914 parity to the US dollar ($4.80 to the £) and thus seriously overvalued. (One can rarely say with certainty that any economic policy was wrong from all points of view, but surely this is true of the decision to 'look the dollar in the face'.)

Yet the well-known events of the early 1930s showed that Britain had, in fact, lost control of the system. Exports contracted, sterling was (belatedly) devalued, and defaults by overseas debtors went unpunished. Nationalist movements were now growing in the colonial empire, especially the Congress Party in India, erupting into demonstrations and, in places, violent protests.

The system came under external pressures too. What finally overthrew it was the renewed challenge from Germany, where militarism was stimulated by the economic strains of the depression, and from another later industrializer, Japan, whose armies proceeded to occupy most of the colonies in South-East Asia, including Malaysia, Vietnam, and Indonesia.

Although the main colonial powers, Britain and France, 'won' again in the end, they did so with considerably greater difficulty than in the first round. They depended much more heavily, not only on US military and civil supplies, and later its intervention (after Pearl Harbour), but also the great Soviet resistance to the German invasion (which was an historic blunder from the German point of view, comparable to the British return to the gold standard – quite apart from its brutality).

The colonial empires had to be diminished after 1945. To nationalist pressure was added US insistence on opening up the colonial trading systems, and nearly all the colonies became independent in the next two decades, starting with India, Pakistan, Burma, Ceylon, and Indonesia, and then most of the rest of Asia and Africa in the next two decades. (Only the old Russian empire still survives.)

The lesson to which I want to draw attention – because it is very relevant today – is the cost of not letting go of empires in the 1930s – unemployment at home and external military threats. With hindsight, the colonial empires were doomed as soon as Germany reached British and French technical standards. Even though the empires survived in a formal sense for

another thirty to fifty years after 1914, they were hencefor-
ward of very doubtful net value economically. Moreover,
they focused political attention in the metropolis on military
strength, rather than the essential technical predominance.

There were spectacular defeats after 1945 for the colonial
powers when they tried to maintain particular overseas pos-
sessions – the Dutch government, with British assistance,
misguidedly tried to re-occupy Indonesia. There were several
such attempts: Algeria (France), the Suez Canal (Britain and
France), Vietnam (France and later the United States). But,
taking the world as a whole (a conspicuous exception being
Portugal), the governments of the metropolitan countries
relaxed their hold without a great struggle. The lessons of the
past seemed at last to have been learned.

The new system that was taking shape can properly be
called 'neo-colonial'. This had been foreshadowed by developments in the western hemisphere. After the imperial powers
had conceded independence in Latin America, their manufactures could still be exchanged for primary products. Investments could still be made overseas, and profits remitted
homewards. The same happened after independence in Asia
and Africa. At Bretton Woods, moreover, a modified form of
the gold standard was established, with fixed exchange rates
linking currencies which were convertible (or to become so).

The main economic difference was that the barriers around
the old empires (e.g. the 'sterling area') were coming down, and
trade patterns were becoming more diversified, so the United
States – later Germany and Japan, still later the NICs – could
take full advantage of trade with Africa and (especially) Asia.

There was also a big political change: the dominant power
in the new system was the United States, and the dollar
replaced the pound as the main international currency. Britain
was at first the junior partner, and later, as they recovered
from the war, other industrial countries collectively formed
with them a new and bigger 'core'.

Additional forms of cultural dependence emerged – a
great expansion of scholarships for study in the industrial
countries, especially the United States, widening circulation
of periodicals, mushrooming of tourism, conferences, etc.,
and more recently TV linkages.

Paternalism could still be exercised. The governments of

the industrial countries accepted special 'responsibilities' — as had the colonial powers earlier — to help the Third World develop. Since the economic sinews of the colonial system remained essentially unchanged, the set of perceptions formed to defend them in a morally acceptable way was transferred with only marginal adjustment. The newly-independent countries needed, it was believed, even more technical and financial help. There was an additional reason: the Soviet Union had ended the war as one of the military victors and might well prove capable of pulling them into its sphere of influence, depriving the developed countries of the resources and markets they needed. There was also, to be fair, a humanitarian element, as pointed out in the synopsis.

To supplement the agencies of the former colonial powers, technical assistance departments were created in the United Nations system. But capital started to flow through quite different international channels, which fitted better the international realities. Whereas in the United Nations all governments are nominally equal and have the same voting power (except for a curious anomaly under which two of the Soviet republics were made members, which has effectively given the Soviet government three votes), in the World Bank, matters are very different: those of the developed countries which provide most of the capital form a separate 'class' with much bigger votes and heavier representation among Executive Directors and in the staff itself. Moreover, none of the East European group belong (except for Roumania and Hungary, which joined only recently — and, of course, Yugoslavia). The International Monetary Fund has similar structures of voting, directors, and staff. The 'conditionality' (see Chapter 8) on its loans, to meet short-term foreign exchange needs, includes the dismantling of exchange controls and other measures to keep borrowers firmly integrated into the neo-colonial system.

The governments of the developed countries also gave OECD the function of co-ordinating donor policy towards the Third World; a special Development Assistance Committee establishes standards for the volume and terms of aid and collects and publishes aid statistics. Aid targets were set (e.g. 0.7 per cent of donor's GNP), to encourage the governments of all the industrial countries to take a share in financing the system.

In the first two decades after the war, the new system was still fairly cheap for Western Europe (very cheap for Japan). The United States government carried the main military burden, yet could afford to respect the interests of the others, and helped them overthrow a number of nationalist politicians (e.g. Lumumba, Mossedeq, Soekano) — though there was always a price for some countries in the Western alliance (e.g. yielding some of the BP oil wells in Iran to US firms). But during the 1960s, the deterioration of the competitive power of the US *vis-à-vis* Japan and West Germany, combined with the rising costs of policing the system, were undermining internal support in the US itself. The dwindling of its room to man-oeuvre had been aggravated by the economic and moral costs of choosing Vietnam as a battleground (another historic blunder).

The same administration, moreover, expanded welfare services at home (the 'Great Society'), showing that United States governments are not prepared to (indeed cannot) give the management of the international system an over-riding priority, as a super-power should, if it is to remain one. The combination of external and internal expansion led to a fall in US reserves of gold, an international realignment of ex-change rates in 1971, and finally (in 1973) the abandonment of the system of fixed rates.

But the system has become increasingly expensive to the other industrial powers, too, especially Britain. It is true that all classes in Britain have benefited from the neo-colonial system as they did from its forerunner: investments abroad, access to markets, and the supply of cheap primary products have made possible not only considerable profits but also our current wage levels and the welfare state. (If aid has been necessary to preserve the system, it has been a bargain.)

But to accommodate the sharp rise in the price of oil, heavy loans have been required, mostly from private sources, that cannot be serviced, let alone repaid (see Table 3). These loans multiplied some thirty-fold in a decade.

The system's 'rules of the game' require an open door policy on imports of manufactures as well as exports of capital. These are linked: many of the imports into Western Europe from Singapore, etc., are the products of West European firms manufacturing there, set up with capital that is needed by the European economy.

The liberal trading rules also involve a big deficit with Japan, and Western Europe's surplus in trade in manufactures (the ratio of its exports to its imports of manufactures) is being eroded (see Table 5), and one industry after another — originally textiles and TV sets, now cars — destroyed. Moreover, the high European demand for imports, especially oil, has to be depressed by deflationary policy. The rise in industrial output in OECD countries first slowed up, then virtually halted, and the social cost of the consequent unemployment has been becoming intolerable, sharply so in the recent past (see Table 1). Moreover, really high returns on overseas investments in plantations and mines have become rare, in part because of the increased sophistication of Third World negotiators and tax inspectors.

In any case, these interests overseas are no longer secure. We lack the military power to protect them; even Britain, with France the most heavily armed country in Western Europe, depended on the co-operation of the United States over the South Atlantic. It is decreasingly likely that such co-operation will be given on terms that are politically acceptable to European leaders, in view of the internal pressures on US governments.

The Brandt Report (1980), a fairly representative internationalist programme for meeting the crises, argues for helping the South on two quite separate grounds: that it is in *their* interest, and that it is in *ours*. The Report seemed, in fact, to be based on the traditional liberal tenet, which according to Sir Isaiah Berlin is the chief legacy of the Enlightenment, that the interests of all human beings are basically common. (This naïve belief has been battered in the course of this century, especially since the constraints in energy and other resources emerged.)

There is no case whatever on welfare grounds for aid to the NICs. Their income levels are quite adequate now to eliminate dire poverty: that this does certainly still exist is due to the policies followed, not lack of resources. Aiding such governments would merely allow them to continue oil-intensive and socially-divisive growth policies and maintain fascist-type systems; it would also permit them to service their colossal debts to the private banks: this would not merely be, in effect, a transfer from the publics of the North to the bankers, it

would restore the 'creditworthiness' of the debtors and remove
the main obstacle to continuing the recent pace and patterns
of growth. Finally, it would help them subsidize their onslaught
on European markets.

But the moral argument for aid has become weak in general,
anyway. The Brandt Report, like most internationalist
pamphlets, bases its case on the poverty of *countries*, but
advocates aid to *governments*. After billions of pounds of aid,
military regimes are both much more common in the Third
World than they were twenty years ago, and much more
vicious.

Ruth Sivard (1982) classified 52 countries as 'military
dominated'.[1] A large majority (49) are classed in various
degrees 'repressive', because of 'a consistent pattern of vio-
lation of their human rights' or of those 'relating to personal
safety', judging from the prevalence of arbitrary arrest and
imprisonment, denial of public trial, invasion of the home. Of
these 30 are shown as 'highly repressive' because of the use of
'torture, brutality and other forms of physical abuse'. As the
source points out, 'military power wedded to political power
turns inward to terrorize the people it is intended to protect'
(op. cit.).

But that is not all. It should be noted that the figures do
not include another 33 governments which did not meet the
criteria for being 'military dominated', but were still classed
as 'repressive' or 'highly repressive'. An obvious example is
Iran.

One may quibble about whether particular governments
are 'repressive', but the general picture is incontravertible.
There are now only a handful of countries where, say, the
result of a general election is at all unpredictable, or it is safe
to criticize publicly the political leadership, and this number
is dwindling.

Most of the military-dominated governments receive a
good deal of financial support from abroad. Some of these
governments have been borrowing heavily from private
sources, which is now reflected in high ratios of debt service
to exports of goods and services, reaching in the case of Brazil
over 30 per cent, and over 20 per cent for Bolivia, Algeria,
Chile, Burma, etc. Broadly those military governments which
were not eligible for private loans received official aid — in

some cases very substantial amounts: according to the latest DAC figures, Bangladesh, Pakistan, and Turkey — all 'highly repressive' military governments — each received more than $1 billion in 1980, and another, Indonesia, not much less. A few, e.g. Turkey and Zaire, drew substantially on private loans as well.

To continue propping up governments listed can hardly be in the interests of their subjects. This is not just a Eurocentric bias in favour of democracy: governments which do not permit criticism are unlikely to be flexible enough to face the storms that lie ahead.

The Brandt Report not only advocated increases in aid: it also commended both the UNIDO proposals, under which the South's share of industrial production would more than double before the end of the century, and those of UNCSTD, to raise the South's share in R & D six-fold. TNCs were expected to invest more overseas, to make technology available to the South, to give up market allocation, to abjure tax havens, to allow transfer pricing to be monitored, etc., etc. The governments of developed countries were to open their doors even wider to manufacturers from the NICs. Aid flows should be greatly raised, made increasingly automatic, and channelled largely through multinational institutions.

The Brandt Commission, ignoring the social problems of the North, in effect invited its governments to yield their power. Indeed, the Report proposed that borrowing countries (by which it meant their *governments*: a crucial confusion) should have a 'greater role in decision-making and management' (p. 218) of financial institutions. Curiously, from a Northern point of view, 'more equal representation' of the South in the Bank and the Fund was described as a measure that would not merely 'create consensus' but 'build confidence' in these institutions!

Further questions are raised by the claim that it is in *the North*'s interest to create purchasing power in the South, which would flow back as demand for northern goods, and halt the recession. There is certainly a good basis for this in Keynesian logic. But as the Report itself pointed out, one might well ask why, if the inflationary consequences of greater demand can be tolerated, this could not equally well be created within the North itself; then it could be concentrated on problem regions.

My misgivings are in fact more profound. No evidence whatever is put forward for the assumption that Northern governments wish to reduce unemployment, even in their own countries. The governments concerned have justified monetarist policies as being designed to 'fight inflation' and set the stage for economic growth. But this does not quite ring true. Would any sane government with that ultimate objective forego for years much investment in their industries, on which eventually growth depends, just to reduce by a few points the annual rise in the consumer price index – to rates which they may not be able to maintain anyway?

An alternative hypothesis would be that to run the neo-colonial system is very difficult now, without heavy unemployment. It would not be necessarily ignorant or short-sighted for governments in the North to calculate (though it might be unwise to state publicly) that a rise of even 5 per cent in the national products of OECD countries would make OPEC and its member governments far too powerful, and also lead to sharply higher prices for metals (as well as agricultural products). And two of the main political forces (financial capitalists and senior bureaucrats, as well as many professional people) are not discomforted by a recession: it reduces the strength of the trade unions, and the financiers welcome the strength of Northern currencies. One way of looking at the oil price rise is that it provides an excuse for shifting the burden of trying to prolong the life of the neo-colonial system onto other classes, while blaming the Arabs!

There are more profound reasons for doubting the advantages to the North of any financial plan for the world economy that – incidentally – salvages the governments and élites of the NICs. This would facilitate the growing import penetration of our markets, which has been referred to above.

Far and away the most persuasive argument for large-scale aid and trade concessions is the concealed message of the Report, the unmentionable political one; namely that these are necessary to shore up the neo-colonial system, whatever the social costs. It is not at all obvious that Western support of various kinds (including aid) can, in fact, ensure the survival of dictatorships in the South: there are many examples to the contrary, from Batista to Somoza. Anyway, it is not clear either that the system would be threatened now if aid were substantially reduced and other concessions to Southern governments withheld.

It no longer appears likely that many countries in the Third World would 'go Communist' if their economic difficulties increased. Certainly, some political leaders there were attracted in the 1950s by the socialist system that was forming in Eastern Europe. The Soviet government was able to supply not only arms and various other manufactures, but also (then) oil, while other governments in the system were starting to offer exports of various kinds on credit — manufactures from East Germany (which took on a role within the bloc analogous to West Germany within the neo-colonial system of the West), primary products from Bulgaria and Roumania.

The Soviet government appeared capable of extending the system. They had passed the US in space technology (demonstrated by the launching of Sputnik I), suggesting that they could do the same in other sectors. Considerable supplies were being poured into Cuba — food, oils, arms, and equipment for agriculture, fisheries, the nickel mines, etc. For a time, Moscow seemed poised to expand into Africa too: large-scale aid to Nasser was followed by support for the revolutionary governments in Ethiopia, Angola, and Mozambique, even for Idi Amin. An immense effort helped save the Hanoi regime.

But by the mid-1970s, the Soviet government was facing considerable economic problems at home (not to speak of Eastern Europe). It found, like its capitalist counterparts, that running its own neo-colonial system is expensive. Despite considerable quantities of Soviet financial and technical help (and a very high price for sugar), Cuba has shown little capacity for paying its creditors, Eastern or Western. In Egypt, Indonesia, Somalia, and Uganda, large quantities of Soviet aid have had to be written off, with apparently no lasting political benefits.

One early sign that the Soviet government at least had taken the point was that Allende returned virtually empty-handed from a desperate trip to Moscow. Another signal was the muted reaction to the bombing of North Vietnam (later to the South Atlantic war too).

The Soviet exportable surplus of oil has dwindled, forcing the other members to buy oil for hard currencies — and thus to find export markets — outside the Soviet zone, a road pioneered by Romania, Hungary, and Poland. But this occurred at precisely the same time as these export markets were ceasing to expand and competition in them was becoming more aggressive. The consequence for East European governments was heavy indebtedness, as among governments of the Third World. The problem of servicing these debts became acute, especially since the type of 'planning' used had become highly bureaucratic and incapable of adjusting to changing circumstances.[2] In Poland, of course, the cracks in the system have become more evident, with serious declines in living standards, which can only be imposed by martial law.

Mugabe, for one, got the message, which Algerians had registered earlier, and which was now starkly clear: there is really nowhere that a government of the Third World, however 'Marxist', can turn for the capital and technology it needs, except to the North, especially the United States.

There is only one argument in favour of aid likely to appeal to Northern interests now: it would enable rich debtors, such as the governments of Mexico, Brazil, and Argentina, to service their debts to transnational banks. Those private banks which have incautiously lent large sums abroad are pointing to the danger of a major financial crisis. Thus Willard Butcher, President and Chief Executive of Chase Manhattan, pointed out (1980) that 'both the World Bank and the IMF will need additional financing in the relatively near future on a hitherto unprecedented scale', and called for 'the partnership of the world's private banks as well as the political and financial mechanisms of the world's international institutions and the sovereign governments themselves. . . . Are we willing to wait until a specific country cannot meet its debts before we take action?' This must be a veiled reference to Mexico or Brazil: the anxiety is scarcely concealed. A study by Morgan Guaranty Trust Co. (1980), recommending less stringent conditions on IMF loans, stated that 'The industrial countries should avoid an overly restrictive approach to developing country financing that would multiply recessionary forces affecting their own economies.'

Even those not very sympathetic to banks are asking what might happen if a major debtor defaults. Would that not start a worldwide chain of bankruptcies as the collapse of the Credit

Anstalt did just over half a century ago, helping to precipitate a really serious crisis in the world economy? I doubt this. Governments nowadays do not let big banks collapse.

We, more than those in other industrial countries, are finding, in fact, that the costs of the system are becoming uncomfortably high, in part because of the weakness of our manufacturing industries. Its rules, strictly applied, would stop any major reflating of the British economy in the 1980s: if expansion were attempted, especially a unilateral expansion, unmanageable foreign exchange difficulties would soon appear (which could hardly be solved by a unilateral imposition of import and exchange controls).

We should be prepared to let go of this system in its turn, now that it has also become too expensive. The lesson of history is that it is most unwise to try to hold on to an international system when the basis for it has been eroded. I shall now turn to examine the alternatives (and come back in Chapter 12 to relations with the Third World).

CHAPTER 11

The development of Western Europe

THE neo-colonial system will not disappear rapidly or all at one time; its predecessor, the colonial system, took half a century to disintegrate, and some of its institutions (e.g. the gold standard) began to collapse decades before political independence was given to (or won by) all the colonies (and that process is still not quite complete – viz. Hong Kong, not to speak of the Russian colonies in Asia. Besides, since the neo-colonial system is less formal, its disintegration is less evident).

We can probably date the beginning of this disintegration at about 1970, when it became clear that the United States government could neither sustain its satellite administration in Saigon, nor maintain the dollar exchange system. More fundamentally, its technological leadership was no longer unchallenged. Thus the system started to leave the centre of the stage before its fore-runner had made its final bow.

The Reagan administration is attempting to reassert US authority, but the costs are high in terms of unemployment, as was the similar attempt of the British government to assert its authority in the inter-war period, during the decline of the colonial system.

The disintegration has gone far enough to leave Britain even more exposed. We have inherited an economic structure created in the colonial period, highly dependent on exports of financial services and industrial products to pay for essential imports. Perhaps even more seriously, we are still burdened with many of the grandiose attitudes of the period – including global paternalism and the delusion (on the part of the Conservatives) that if the economy were 'free' we could take on the world. The public also acquired, in that period and during its neo-colonial successor, confident expectations of high wages and comprehensive social services. Yet all this has to be carried without an adequate technological base.

We even managed to have an oil boom without solving the

foreign exchange problem, which is only in abeyance because of the low level of industrial activity. As someone often overseas, I see Britain as others do — an aged lion, padding feebly along, barely able to keep up with the pride (the industrial countries), seemingly too confused to decide what to do to survive. A number of other animals, once the lion's prey (and well mindful of this) wait hopefully for the old beast to stagger and collapse, so that they can tear him to pieces. Sometimes they miscalculate — as over the South Atlantic — but one day they could succeed.

Certainly, the *laissez-faire* strategy based on neo-classical economics, with sterling fully convertible and easy access to British markets for manufactures, has failed to produce a solution to Britain's problems: it seems to imply unemployment permanently over three million.

It is tempting to react as the Labour Party has done, drawing on the work of some Cambridge economists, by proposing reflation within a siege economy, protecting weak British industries by import controls and withdrawing from the European Community. As any reader of the earlier sections of this book will appreciate, big questions are raised about the feasibility of this programme: we cannot assume we have infinite room to manoeuvre. Imports of food and industrial materials will have to grow if unemployment is to be reduced. It is true that if we could purchase freely in world markets, unhampered by Community regulations, we could buy some foodstuffs, notably cereals, meat, and sugar, more cheaply — at least temporarily — but we already buy at world prices agricultural materials (cotton, jute, etc.), and metal ores (e.g. copper and tin), so the saving would not be great. Yet the exchange controls implicit in this policy would damage our exports of financial services, now a very big foreign exchange earner. The policy would require, in addition, substantial aid and military spending, especially an expanded Royal Navy, to safeguard supplies of essential commodities, since we would no longer be able to rely on the United States.

That this is not just speculation was revealed by the late Frank McElhone, Labour Party front-bench spokesman on overseas development, who said (answering a warning by Gunnar Myrdal and myself about the dangers of increasing aid to the Third World) that when the Labour Party was returned to office, it would double British aid and 'take on obstructive governments' (i.e. those that did not adopt policies the British government thought appropriate in the country concerned).[1]

We would have to re-establish a substantial export surplus in manufactures. We could, indeed, cut down on imports of Japanese goods (though there are other ways of doing this, as I shall explain below), and on our imported industrial products from the Continent, but we would have to expect our exports there to fall at least as much, especially since the pressure to innovate would be weakened. We would be, in fact, if not in formal terms, resigning from GATT, and could hardly expect its members to continue to give us 'most favoured nation' treatment. Governments in many other parts of the world, especially the USA, would certainly retaliate against British protectionism.

As one small example, a British quota on Indonesian textile exports led the government there to cancel orders for textile machinery and aircraft. The then Trade Minister, John Nott, stated: 'The Indonesians have no right . . . to retaliate in this way, but they did . . . and it hurts.' (He raised the quota by 181 per cent.)[2]

Finally, the need to open up new markets for manufactures would require monetary control, including a ceiling on public expenditure. Labour governments have not shown themselves capable of imposing this for long. Nor does there appear much recognition of the need for this in the Party's debates.

There would also have to be tight restraint on wages. Yet in the colonial and neo-colonial periods, the trade unions became accustomed to high and rising wages as a matter of right. Since the trade unions are its political base, another Labour government could hardly be expected to impose the necessary discipline. They would be in a particularly weak position to do so if industry becomes heavily protected, which would reduce its exposure to competition in home markets.

It is also obvious from my earlier analysis that great risks indeed would be involved in an expansionist programme which would imply major organizational difficulties (e.g. because of the re-orientation of exports, as a result of leaving the Community, let alone further measures of nationalization), as well as external hostility. Why would such a programme be any more successful than that of Chile or Portugal or Poland – or

its own forerunner headed by Callaghan? The ultimate outcome, by one route or another, has generally been *lower* real
wages, *fewer* social services — and usually authoritarian
regimes to impose them.

What we need to do is to identify the tide running in the
outside world and turn so that we can run with it. The South
Atlantic crisis demonstrated once again the familiar lesson of
this century, the strength of nationalist feeling, and its capacity
to cover deep class and ideological chasms. Moreover, this
emotion was not confined to Argentina and Britain: Latin
American governments backed Argentina, European ones
Britain — even if with considerable reservations in some cases.
Loyalty can emerge between peoples of different nations and
very different ideologies but similar ethnic and cultural
patterns.

I shall call this 'extended nationalism': it provides us with
a clue. A much more realistic refuge is staring us in the face,
reflation within a largely self-sufficient economy, indeed, but
on a *continental*, not a *national*, scale.

In the Community, technology and capital could more
easily be mobilized, especially for the development of oil and
other minerals. Behind the continental ramparts there would
be markets large enough to match the super-powers — e.g. for
planes and other sophisticated engineering products. The
Community market would provide Britain with a competitive
challenge that would be demanding, without being overwhelming. The protected development of Europe would
provide orders for the capital goods industries, such as steel,
of the industrial heartland, in particular Clydeside, the North-
East and South Wales, rather than the USA or Japan.

Economic activity could be safely expanded without devaluation: indeed, the inflationary effect might well be slight.
Such a bloc could become capable of covering its energy and
food needs at stable prices, if it used its market size and its
technology to organize long-term purchase agreements and
joint production plans with foreign governments. It could,
because of its bargaining power, limit the penetration of
European industrial sectors by Japan, the USA, and the NICs,[3]
which has helped cause the diminishing export surplus in
Community manufactures — see Table 5. The Community
could protect its domestic market without losing access to

overseas markets or sources of supply. (Note the acceptance abroad, albeit reluctant, of the Multi-Fibre Arrangement.)

Community regulation of industrial output, currently applied in steel, will surely spread to an increasing number of industries, backed by higher tariffs. Community initiatives, at present small-scale and tentative (e.g. in electronics), could be greatly increased. So could European education in technical and scientific subjects.

This would mean in effect a policy of increasing Community self-reliance, the logical counterpart of 'South-South' co-operation, or 'collective self-reliance', which is increasingly (and understandably) being promoted in the rest of the world.

But it would not mean, of course, complete economic independence. Indeed, cutting down imports of manufactures would release foreign exchange for the purchase of more primary products, which would indeed be needed to support the expansion. Many countries of the Third World would thus receive more foreign exchange, but by exports rather than loans, i.e. in ways that involve less European interference in their affairs.

I can only sketch briefly here the other measures necessary. The first point is that we must not fall into the trap of treating economic planning as solely a supply-side phenomenon. Information campaigns, fiscal policy, etc., could be used to reduce the import content of consumption and steer it towards sectors which could help provide employment.

Inflows of non-European capital could be monitored by a special department of the Brussels Secretariat, and, where they threaten strategic sectors, prevented. The frantic and expensive competition for Japanese investment can and should be ended. Detailed Community exchange controls would not be easy to administer (especially since capital movements in and out of Switzerland would be hard to monitor). But the TNCs based in Europe could be dissuaded from financing the creation of industrial plant overseas that competed with our own industries. Secondly, it should be possible to reduce the dependence of our interest rates on those of the US — a dependence which keeps activity in Europe depressed.

Yet a member government would still not be able to create demand without limit: indeed, if the European Monetary System is strengthened, expansive financial policies of the sort described in Chapter 8 could be made virtually impossible (though a more powerful EMS would have a damaging effect on some peripheral economies of Europe unless Community financial institutions are adapted in ways I shall describe shortly).

In a more homogeneous Europe, pursuing compatible financial policies, not merely much trade, but also most transactions for services would be internal. Then the European Currency Unit (ECU) could be used as a currency of both account and settlement, greatly reducing the need for US dollars: it could in fact develop sufficient strength to be largely unaffected by fluctuations in the dollar. Then the EMS could eventually acquire some of the functions of a European Central Bank with its own reserves, capable of reinforcing Community economic policies.

It is particularly important that a big fraction of future increases in output — whether due to increased integration or not — goes into investments and technical education to fortify the West European economy and increase employment, rather than raising living standards of those already in jobs a further notch, especially in its richer areas: that would reduce still further the room to manoeuvre.

Jean Monnet and other progenitors of the Community might well even approve of a more protected Community as the way to achieve in the 1980s their ultimate aim — European peace, prosperity, and independence. Such a Community would be, of course, less 'liberal' than they envisaged, but one must allow for the likely effects on their thinking, too, of the events and trends of the past decade, especially the greatly increased strength of OPEC, the continued export thrust by Japan and the NICs, and the foreign policy trends in the Soviet Union and the United States. (The last quarter of this century is making mercantilists of us all — really the only question is what to protect: the nation or the continent?)

It would also, on my argument, be more egalitarian than they thought necessary. They did not foresee the need to transfer revenue-raising powers from member governments though these might well have been easier to take over in the early, dynamic years. The neo-classical proposition that the profits of growth would 'trickle down' sufficiently to mitigate inequality, a proposition discredited in other continents, has obviously proved ill founded in Western Europe too, where there are still vivid contrasts between the core (e.g. Düsseldorf) and the periphery (for example, Calabria). A shift of income towards the periphery should help produce patterns of consumption with high labour content and lower need for imports from outside Europe.

There are no effective institutions at the Community level to redistribute income.[4] The main head of Community expenditure, the CAP, has turned out on balance somewhat regressive. Although the Regional and Social Funds have redistributive aspects, their effect is negligible. Somewhat surprisingly, a large part of their outlays, too, are made in the richest countries. (From 1960 to 1976, the main beneficiary of the Social Fund was none other than West Germany which took, in fact, 44 per cent of the total grants, as well as substantial grants from the Regional Funds for allegedly impoverished German regions.[5]) Moreover, the European Monetary System could, like the gold standard, easily increase continental inequality (because it inhibits exchange controls) in the absence of policies to stop this happening.

This will become a more serious issue with the Community's further enlargement. If it is to be strong and viable, its new members need *really* integrating into it — now Greece, later Portugal and Spain. (The same applies to Ireland.)

At the time of writing, the Community's basic response to the problem imposed by the three poorer recruits seems to be: 'What must we concede to them?', not 'What do they need to become fully integrated into the Community?' This is true even of the West German establishment, who have most to gain economically from increased access to new markets.

If, however, the political will and leadership to assimilate Southern Italy have been lacking, why should we expect them to appear on the scale needed to develop most of Portugal, especially in a period when governments are dedicated to restrictive financial policies? In concrete terms, even if there are no major changes in the Community, sacrifices will be required from many in the Nine whose jobs are anyway precarious (e.g. textile workers) or who rely on subsidies from the Community budget for products that can be produced in Southern Europe (wine, for example). Some of those currently benefiting from the Regional and Social Funds (and the 'structural' part of CAP spending) will be affected because new operational criteria will have to be employed. We must expect competition for the Community's meagre financial resources between the Three and the poorer regions of the Nine.

Yet, if there were no major reforms in the Community, dualism would, after the second enlargement is complete, grow more serious; indeed, a sort of local neo-colonial system would appear. Wage levels would stay much lower than in the Nine, and the new members would continue to depend heavily, perhaps increasingly, not only on tourism but also labour migration. During the transition years, legal barriers will remain, but, ultimately, one result of a severely split Community would presumably be an uncomfortably heavy migration towards West Germany and France. Moreover, the business of the Community would become more difficult to transact than at present, further impairing its capacity to deal with external challenges: the exact constitutional arrangements for the future have yet to be defined, but the new recruits will hardly lack ways of making known their needs if these are neglected.[6] Secession might become an increasing possibility, and if it got under way it would not necessarily stop at the Pyrenees.

There is an alternative scenario for the end of the century, that of true integration. This would require a reformed fiscal system for the Community with a much larger budget. It would be particularly necessary to support the development of regions with critical economic problems, and also the reconstruction of the agricultural and industrial sectors of the new members. But these are already strongly linked to the Nine by trade. Although the economic argument of the Brandt Report — that it is in the interests of rich countries to help the development of the poorer, and that 'massive transfers' of funds would flow back to the donors in export orders stimulating *their* industries — is open to various political and economic, not to say logical, objections (set out above), these objections are less cogent when the argument is applied inside Europe: here there really are some 'mutual interests'. While the social problems of the new members are very real, they are less insoluble than those of the Third World. Their élites are much less dependent on links with the industrial powers, so to strengthen them by aid programmes need not imply supporting political repression, as would reinforcing the governments of the Third World (for reasons I explained earlier). On the contrary, in their case aid seems essential to avoid relapses into dictatorships such as all three have known (quite recently).

So it is in the European periphery that the case for aid, in technology as well as capital, is strong. But this is not just a matter of money. In any policy area, we need to avoid a grudging spirit. For example, as a strengthened industrial regime emerges (a Common Industrial Policy) it could be used to increase industrial output in Southern Europe, including locating new industries there.

The new members should not be looked on as liabilities. Chapter 6 drew attention to the importance of the demographic dimension to development strategy. The first nine members of the Community, with the exception of Ireland, have static and ageing populations, with relatively low numbers of young people entering the labour force and the electorate (or available for military service), and increasing numbers of pensioners. This can be partly changed by more generous family allowances, maternity leave, etc., but the total picture is being improved automatically and much more quickly by the entrance of new members, with a higher birth rate and younger populations, and thus greater economic and political flexibility.

Secondly, a Community of Twelve will be able to meet more of its own requirements of cotton, wool, iron ore, copper, antimony, manganese, mercury, and tungsten, as well as semi-tropical fruits and vegetables, such as citrus and tomatoes. On the other hand, certain agricultural surpluses of the Nine could more easily be absorbed — provided, of course, that the CAP is reformed so that enlargement does not lead to higher production in the Three of foodstuffs already in surplus.

The Community will remain, it is true, a big importer of many key industrial materials, although in the future self-sufficiency could increase: there are considerable possibilities of further resource development in the Three, especially of minerals.

A third advantage of shifting power towards the Community is that it could help meet the needs of its cultural minorities, making it less likely that they will remain chronically disaffected. Such minorities could be better served by a continental political system than a national one: the Basques or Northern Ireland Catholics might well be more peaceful if governed from Brussels rather than Madrid or London.

Yet there is a big question mark about the foundations of a more integrated Europe, when we consider the querulous Community debates at all levels, from meetings of the heads of states, to the European Parliament and sector committees.

To what extent do people feel themselves 'Europeans', willing to transfer patriotic loyalties to continental institutions (as most United States minorities have been prepared to accept assimilation)? This is hardly a question which can be put in quantifiable terms, but it is already a fundamental one about the Community of Ten, and will be raised more acutely as it becomes bigger. The viability of a group of countries with pretensions to integration ultimately depends in the end on the answer, and the larger and more heterogeneous the group of countries, the more important this is.

An intuitive, but hardly controversial, reaction is that the sense of being a European does not seem, anywhere in the continent, nearly strong enough to carry a big political and economic superstructure. We must not forget the linguistic frontiers, which are more durable than customs barriers, nor the traditional enmities, e.g. between the British and the French. A Briton, say, who goes 'to Europe' for his holiday, perceives contrasts not similarities, and very probably remains firmly in the group of compatriots on the package tour. Such cultural diversity reinforces economic interests behind the resistance to policies that would integrate the Community.

I can only speculate about the possibilities of this limited nationalism being overcome. A visitor from Africa or Asia is likely to be struck by the similarities of life-styles in Europe — brands of consumer goods, clothing fashions, architectural design, popular music, and (by comparison with the rest of the world) values and attitudes, including a persistent belief in the rule of law and in the possibility of peaceful settlement of disputes. The moral values of even Europeans who call themselves atheists are profoundly affected by Christian traditions.

The ideologies of communists and conservatives seem to us far apart, even within, say, France, but this contrast looks a good deal less striking when we turn to the values and attitudes of (say) Iranian mullahs or the cadres of the Khmer Rouge or Argentinian generals or many of the African dictators. This is not surprising. Not only is there a long tradition of political debate, but the main European ideologies, Marxism and economic liberalism, have, as explained in Chapter 1, a common root in nineteenth-century Europe.

Because of common legacies and experiences in Europe (covering the Three as well as the Nine), cultural differences are really quite marginal relative to those separating us from other continents. I am *not* saying that our culture is superior — it clearly contains tendencies to violence, illustrated not merely by the history of warfare but current football hooliganism and street crime. My point is that it is evidently different.

There is also now a more noticeable cultural contrast between the United States on the one hand, and the countries of Western Europe on the other, despite the invasion of cinema and TV screens by US products. One difference is that US treatment of social, especially economic, questions is more technocratic and quantitative: 'models' have to be constructed and 'rigorously' applied. Secondly (and somewhat inconsistently) there is a more moralistic approach to international relations, especially where the Communist bloc is concerned. Even a Briton notices this, and we speak the same language (though is it still the same language? — one is always unconsciously making subtle translations of what Americans say, because the divergence in culture means that words have acquired different overtones).

One important indication that greater integration is possible is that it has already gone some way. Community spokesmen put forward distinctively Community policies (e.g. on the Middle East, Central America, Southern Africa, and the South Atlantic). The factors that have increasingly produced these policies, and led the Community to act as a bargaining agent, will continue to operate in the coming decades. Soviet hostility is hardly going to disappear. The interests of the United States and Europe are unlikely to start converging: indeed, political trends in the United States seem bound to lead to growing friction. The Reagan administration's policies have compelled Community members to co-operate, e.g. on the gasline to the Soviet Union. The competition of Japan (and the NICs) will predictably affect additional European industries, until tariff barriers are raised here. The Community's need for inexpensive and secure supplies of energy is hardly likely to abate. Joint action in defence of what will be seen as *European* interests in an increasingly insecure world will almost certainly become more common.

Moreover, there may well be more regimes like those of Idi Amin and Bokassa, and incidents in the Third World that have shocked public opinion (like the assassination of Europeans in Katanga) may grow more frequent. These incidents are in fact exceptional; it is clearly unfair of the European media to play them up as they do, and ignore the positive side of the Third World, (just as internationalists ignore its darker side), but I am concerned with the effects of this treatment, not its fairness.

Struggles between Southern governments and their opponents will no doubt continue to overflow into the streets of Paris, London, etc., causing hijacking and murders.

There will be more reports of incidents in Western Europe itself like the riots of Iranian students here first against the Shah, then against the Ayatollah — and probably against the Mojahedin too, if and when they come to power.

Co-operation between EEC anti-terrorist agencies will neccessarily grow, but a more important point is that so will a realization of European identity.

I suggest, therefore, as a tentative working hypothesis, that the cultural foundations will prove adequate. We would appear likely to gain more than we could lose by making this assumption. The feeling of European identity can, moreover, be actively fostered, in ways indicated in Chapter 6 — through stressing European history in the schools; through language instruction, especially in English, French, and German, and organizing many more exchange visits between schoolchildren. Of major importance is to increase the links between national TV networks, especially the number of programmes designed for European audiences, not merely documentaries and sports events but also fictional series. Video possibilities also need exploiting.

So a European Development Strategy is required with most

of the features (economic, financial, demographic, cultural, social, statistical) mentioned in Section C, in connection with national policies. (I shall turn to military aspects in the next chapter.) Even though the political basis for it does not yet exist, alternative scenarios could be prepared in readiness, on the basis of different assumptions about political and economic trends overseas.

But for European strategies to be adopted and implemented, the level of debate in meetings of Community politicians, especially heads of state, will have to be lifted well above bargaining about how much the British budgetary contribution should be, farm prices, fish catches, and obstacles to trade in apples, wine, etc. If senior politicians behave like auditors and customs officers, then new ideas will have to be developed outside, in informal conferences and working parties, while we wait for the logic of events to produce European leaders capable of grasping and exploiting it.

Reforms of political machinery are certainly implied by closer integration, covering the status of the European Parliament and the procedures of the Council of Ministers, which I do not have the space (or, indeed, the competence) to pursue here. Also a proper Community planning staff is needed, and considerable development of Community-wide statistics — with greater harmonization of definitions.

The importance of leadership, mentioned at the beginning of Section C, applies in Europe too. Perhaps it will come from Germany, which has most to gain from an expansion of the European economy[7] — but also most to sacrifice in a redistribution of income and power.[8] This raises the historical spectre of German domination — but we should bear in mind that although it is the strongest single country, there are two others in the Community of nearly comparable magnitude (France and Britain), and another two of medium size (Italy and the Netherlands): it would be different if the population of West Germany were, say, 40 per cent of the total. In any case, the historical memories to which I referred encourage the politicians of both Germany and the rest of the Community to keep a watchful eye open for a revival of German domination.

Whatever individual leadership of Europe arises, the initiative could well come from a British government: we are the country with little real alternative (and some of us will, perhaps, see it in due course).

CHAPTER 12

Europe in a world of regional blocs

LET us take a step further. Does not the basic politico-economic rationale of the Treaty of Rome, and of the first two enlargements, also apply to a still bigger Community?

An immediate issue is posed by the pending Turkish application. The economic task of integrating Turkey into the Community would be formidable in view of the social and economic conditions in some Turkish provinces deep in Asia, compared to which even North Portugal seems highly developed. The population size, more than 40 million, and the rate of population growth (over 2 per cent a year) are by no means assets in a view of these economic and social levels. Indeed, the task of truly integrating Turkey into the Community would be so great as to weaken the resolve to tackle the much more manageable absorption of Southern Europe.

In fact, it is doubtful whether such integration is possible. Cultural traditions in Turkey are very different indeed, not only from the linguistic angle. The entrance of a Moslem country would create a cultural mixture that really would make the whole programme of European integration problematic, not to speak of its traditional enmity with Greece.

The case for a positive response to a Turkish application would have to rest almost entirely on military grounds. Certainly, there has to be a military dimension to any plausible strategy for Western Europe, but there are other ways of tackling strategic vulnerability. Alleviating poverty in Southern Europe is one.

But much more important is to overcome the fundamental East-West division in Europe. The task is still, as in the 1950s, to eliminate the danger of war. Now the war would no longer be Franco-German: the obvious danger is of a war between the Soviet Union and the United States, with Europe as the battlefield. This prospect would become considerably less threatening if a broader European economy covered the countries of Eastern Europe as well, in due course.

An economic grouping on that scale — not necessarily taking the form of a mammoth Community — would naturally be much more independent of the United States, and distinctive European interests could more easily be protected.

There would then be a market of the size beyond the plans of the founders of the EEC. It would have a combined GNP of some $4,000 billion (1980 figures), against $2,500 billion for the United States, and $1,200 billion for Japan. It would be still more self-sufficent than a Community of a dozen, especially in wool, iron ore, and copper. The additional countries are ones which never became so dependent on colonial patterns of trade. (Here again, the potential for self-sufficiency would be yet greater if we allowed for the resources that *could* be developed.)

Eastern Europe would, moreover, because of its unsuccessful farming record, provide, like Southern Europe, a natural outlet for agricultural surpluses of the western countries — as it already is on a small scale. Its pent-up demand for meat, dairy products and wine is high, whereas it could help meet Western Europe's needs for maize. The demographic consequences would also be similar to the second enlargement: Eastern Europe (except for East Germany) is, like Southern Europe, younger and more dynamic.

Closer economic integration needs complementing by non-aggression pacts which would make both NATO and the Warsaw Pact obsolete. Medium-range nuclear weapons could be eliminated. After all, neither Western nor Eastern Europe has interests identical with its patrons, nor any interest at all in being destroyed in the furtherance of the aims of the latter. A Community that was really independent and economically secure could negotiate with the Soviet and United States governments for the supervized and mutual removal of missiles from Europe (including the SS-20s on Soviet soil trained on Europe).

The costs to either the United States or the Soviet Union of trying to absorb and administer this group would be the main deterrent. However, it would need, of course, adequate conventional armed forces too, and a greater self-sufficiency in non-nuclear arms, notably military aircraft and tanks, under a joint European command. (This would not necessarily mean unified armed forces: a structure like that of NATO could take its place — without the United States, Canada, or Turkey.) A more integrated Community would also reduce the competition among its members to promote exports of arms, and it could press the governments of the USA, Canada, and the Soviet Union to co-operate in restricting such sales.

An independent group, without close affiliation to either super-power, could also attract Austria and Finland, and the governments of Sweden and Norway might, some time in the coming decades, find remaining outside a more united Europe unsafe — for basically the same reasons as a future Labour government in Britain would (see Chapter 11).

But there are obvious difficulties in the way of the formation of a greater Europe. Would the ideological differences stop it? What would be the attitude in other countries to a Germany which was reunited — *de facto* if not *de jure*? Would not the Soviet government veto such a development? Would the cultural heterogeneity not be too great?

Let us take these in turn. The economies of the EEC are being increasingly 'managed', despite the temporary dominance of *laissez-faire* in some of them. The public sector continues to spread. On the other hand, 'free' markets and decentralized decision-making are spreading in the East, again whatever the proclaimed ideology, and these ultimately imply political changes that would, in turn, reinforce this trend: they will be brought about, as a Marxist would predict, by the internal contradictions of socialism, between the emerging socio-economic system there and the old political system.[1]

Integration in the real sense is slowly happening anyway. The TNCs have been embarking on joint ventures in Eastern Europe, and West European (especially West German) brands are increasingly visible. The governments of CMEA have been borrowing heavily from the private banks of the West. Much West European currency is circulating in Eastern Europe. Tourist and student exchanges have been growing. Greater integration into Western Europe would undoubtedly have a popular appeal, especially if the Community had developed proper mechanisms for social development and used them in Southern Europe.

Certainly formal affiliation poses great difficulties. But this is not really the issue. The early relations between the Nine and each of the Three consisted of specially tailored agreements, which ran for years before the latter applied for membership; meanwhile the economic logic of integration continued to operate. That could also be the pattern for developing relationships with the governments of Eastern Europe — such an agreement already exists with Yugoslavia. Various types of association are possible, short of full membership, but involving closer economic and political links and permitting, for example, access to the European Investment Bank. Agreements could become in due course more comprehensive, until, eventually, a single East European government might apply for membership and be followed by others, one at a time. Anyway, the Community could hardly face a big further enlargement until it has digested Southern Europe, which must take a decade at least. (The second enlargement might turn out to have the additional historical justification of compelling the Community to remove institutional obstacles to its further expansion.)

Relations between the Germanies in particular are surely going to continue their gradual convergence, even if there are temporary setbacks, and despite the likelihood that reunification will not soon be on the agenda. Besides, the strong cultural (even family) ties between East and West Germany, their consumption levels and styles are less dissimilar than within either Western or Eastern Europe. There would indeed be a certain logic in a German economy as the geographical hub of an integrated Europe, with its internal trade stimulated by the new Rhine/Danube Canal.[2] This development might not appear such a political threat to neighbouring countries, provided adequate mechanisms had by then been created for spreading the profits of the core, and also truly democratic controls, especially a considerable strengthening of the European Parliament. (The status of this at present reminds one of that of the English Parliament under Charles I — until he needed his budgets approved.)

No doubt the Soviet government would view such a suggestion with considerable anxiety, but it is clearly not completely in control of its own neo-colonial system. It cannot provide the capital, the technology, or the markets these countries need to meet consumer aspirations (now, not even all the oil they require). It has become heavily dependent on importing wheat from the US.

If continental integration is gradual, the costs to the Soviet government of intervening, especially by military action, to stop any particular step, might well appear too high. (The basic arguments that must have persuaded Stalin of the dangers of trying to make these countries part of the Soviet Union, like the small Baltic States, would still seem cogent.) Besides, the Soviet government might see a neutral bloc to the South-West as a partial 'Finlandization' of the continent.

Is it, anyway, quite inconceivable that political developments within the Soviet Union, especially the growing independence of its Asian Republics, will ultimately lead to links between the Community and the European Soviet Republics, especially the Ukraine but including Russia itself? It is difficult to judge from outside, but the heavy presence of Russians in each of the Republics (who always hold key positions in the local administrative and party structures) may be both symptom and cause of separatist tendencies, which would hardly be surprising in view of the cultural differences and the Russians' hardly concealed disdain for Asians (which could be exploited by a stronger China).

Certainly, the affiliation of Northern and Eastern Europe would increase the Community's cultural diversity. But cultural patterns in the countries concerned do not show much greater heterogeneity than those in the Nine. Here, too, there would be common religious origins (whatever the official attitudes to these), not to speak of the common membership several of them once shared in the kingdoms of Central Europe, apart from the common basic ideological roots (see Chapter 1).

To sum up, an expanding Community, with growing internal homogeneity, self-sufficiency and bargaining power, provides one coherent answer to the historic challenge which the loss of empire has posed for Europeans, especially the British. In this way, welfare services and political democracy, which rested in part on the colonial, then the neo-colonial, system, could survive here.

As Western Europe develops its resource base (even just the Twelve) the customary interventions of its member governments in the political and economic affairs of overseas countries, which is certainly becoming less feasible, should be less necessary. This, together with the effects of the economic expansion of the Community, could be much more important to most of the Third World than what happened to the volume of aid and other capital flows, or to trade barriers on manufactures. Indeed, import controls on industrial products would be consistent with an expansion of imports of many types of primary product.

It could well be to the benefit of all parties if the European TNCs engaged in manufacturing and mining were induced to invest *inside* the Community, especially along its periphery, rather than in other continents. Governments elsewhere are much less capable of rejecting economically or socially undesirable projects put forward by the TNCs, or of monitoring their operations (e.g. by checking 'transfer pricing'), or of ensuring that technology of the right kind is employed.

Thus what appears to be a Eurocentric scenario could be beneficial to the Third World, at least in the longer run. It would not be hard to improve on past performance. Our contribution to overseas development may well have been on balance negative, even since decolonization. The impact varies of course, but in general high technology is injected into the 'modern sector', aggravating geographical dualism and economic inequality. The beneficial effects of aid on some parts of the recipient population have often been outweighed by the consequences of political support for governments that fit into the neo-colonial system (see Chapter 10). A good deal of European capital and covert political support has been extended to the government of South Africa, affecting the whole of the southern part of the continent.[3]

As has been indicated in Chapter 10, now that the neo-colonial system is disintegrating, the most constructive European policy in the 1980s would be to adopt less paternalistic policies towards the Third World. One of the most significant implications of the second enlargement, as explained in Chapter 11, is that it permits, and may compel, a degree of disengagement, including a running down of aid programmes in the South.

Types of aid that have primarily political or commercial justifications (constituting now a large majority of the total) could well be reduced, with advantage to both sides. This does not imply its sharp and total elimination: while that would reduce the income of many who live off corruption and high distribution margins, and reduce the patronage of military cliques, it would also hurt some of the really poor. Aid targets are really meaningless (because aid covers so many sins), but an aim of letting it decline to about 0.1 per cent of donors' GNP by the end of the century would concentrate the minds of the policy-makers and may be the sort of magnitude that would be consistent with the scenario I am outlining.

There is a growing demand for 'self-reliance' in the Third World. Our correct response is to respect this, and — so far as we can — reduce, not increase, our contacts. If we could give up the temptation to meddle in the affairs of overseas countries — a meddling that, in fact, is often counter-productive — we would certainly save on military expenditures as well as aid budgets, and need to make fewer trade concessions.

It might well be argued that some North-South contacts are beneficial to the South — even that they offset the damage done by political and cultural interventions by the great powers. Thus European (and for that matter United States) priests and nuns have done a great deal in Latin America, politically as well as socially, to offset the financial and military aid given to the dictatorships and the commercial loans. It would also be possible to argue that much technical advice offsets the damage done by European monetarists (or Marxists).

The trouble with justifications of intervention is, however, that they can be used by those who want to strengthen the neo-colonial system for their own reasons. Besides, more basically, who are we to judge what is, and what is not, a justifiable intervention? — we really lack the knowledge, no less than the right, to do this.

I make one major exception, however, in favour of human rights. There is little doubt that outside intervention, whether in the form of resolutions, deputations, or letters, has some influence in encouraging the application of proper legal process to political prisoners. If one can do anything to lessen, even marginally, the torture, inhumane imprisonment, and execution of people for political reasons (often personal vendettas) which continues on a massive scale in the Third World, then the obligation to do this seems to me to over-ride the arguments against intervention in the affairs of other countries, especially since administrations that behave in this way are often supported from Europe and cannot ignore European delegations.

The Community could also itself play a positive role in establishing a more durable world economic order, with international taxation gradually taking the place of aid, and expenditures based on criteria such as infant mortality rates (perhaps tied to loans for basic health care). Europe would certainly gain from a stable new international order, even (or especially?) if it is less colonial. Admittedly, many dictatorships would automatically benefit — but they would not receive aid *because* they adopted policies conducive to the survival of the neo-colonial system.

I will close by speculating on what sort of a world system might replace the neo-colonial one. Europe may prove to be the first of a new series of regional blocs. While the world crises encourage self-sufficiency, this can hardly be achieved on a national basis, indeed that is more implausible overseas than in Europe. Only a handful of nation-states are big enough for manufactures such as aircraft: the United States and the Soviet Union are leading examples, although India and China could well join them in the twenty-first century.

As we have seen, it is politically uncertain whether Europe (even its Western part) will develop in this way. Elsewhere it is even more problematic, and for the same basic reasons. The links within other regional groupings are so far mostly economic. They are each even more lopsided than the Community, consisting essentially of a weak ring around a highly advanced core. The core of the Latin American region is Brazil and Argentina (with Mexico a separate base to the North); of East Asia, Japan; of the South Pacific, Australia. There are colonial-type relations between each regional core and its periphery: the core sells advanced manufactures and takes in less sophisticated products, foodstuffs, and raw materials. There are also strong labour flows towards the centre to work in its factories; and tourist flows mainly in the opposite direction, just as in Europe. Indeed, the balance of payments of the regional periphery is heavily dependent on remittances from migrants working in the factories of the core and on tourist expenditures.[4]

While the big nation-states have some political machinery for integration, the regional groups, by contrast, have even fewer means than the Community of overcoming these disparities, e.g. by transferring to the periphery the profits of core manufacturing operations (and also of financial and transport institutions with headquarters in core countries). Regional banks provide some capital on concessional terms, but very little in relation to needs. The UN has Regional Commissions, but they do not fit the regional economic patterns; their powers are limited; and their coverage is too big. (Even the Latin American Commission includes the United States as well as Britain and France.) The responsibility for aid programmes to alleviate poverty in each area best lies in the governments of local rich countries — they have some long-term interest in doing so.

A region like Latin America trades more with the outside world than they would need to if their resources were properly developed, and internal trade encouraged. Much of the capital generated in some regions — again Latin America is an example — flows elsewhere (whereas many governments in the same regions have to borrow, usually expensively, from outside).

No region has developed (again with the partial exception of the two European systems) collective representation in international affairs. There are regional political organizations, such as the Organization of American States and the Organization of African Unity, but they hardly fulfil this role. (The former includes the United States.) Finally, there are no effective common defence arrangements (except for each of the two Europes, and even these each include outside powers).

Such weaknesses may well be overcome if the economic pressures continue to grow and great power policies become increasingly threatening. There are already a few indications of progress in this direction, apart from those already mentioned in connection with Europe. Aid programmes of the oil exporters of the Middle East show a concentration on neighbouring countries, and Mexico, together with Venezuela, has arranged to supply cheap oil to countries in the Caribbean. In the 1960s, intra-regional trade (for developing countries) increased markedly, and this rise accelerated in the 1970s: if we consider non-fuel products (since fuel trade has been relatively small within regions), there was a rise in intra-regional trade between 1970 and 1979 from 15 per cent to 20 per cent of the total developing country exports.[5]

As one example of institutional development, a Latin American organization for regional co-operation has emerged without US membership — SELA, based in Caracas, working on food self-sufficiency and energy development.

But regional blocs will only be viable in the long run if they show some cultural cohesion — in terms of common ethnic origins, language, customs, and historical experience — at least enough to be able to 'communicate' despite linguistic differences (so that the members understand each other's problems).

I have neither the space nor the knowledge to discuss what would be the appropriate membership for regional systems in other parts of the world, still less how they ought to be organized. Indeed, it would be an impertinence for me to do so — the usual impertinence of the citizen of a former colonial power trying to arrange the affairs of other people. Those blocs that have a realistic basis will appear and shape themselves. They may be quite different from the existing regional systems of trade.

What a European can say, however, is that it will be costly for all parties if we fail to grasp the logic of these trends, and try to preserve the neo-colonial system by political or military intervention or by aid programmes (or some combination of these, as is usually the case) — just as expensive as the slowness to recognize, earlier in the century, the breakdown of colonialism. (The temptations for such intervention may be considerable.)

A world system of large regional economies, with a minimum of 200 million people each, would be more symmetrical, even if not completely so: none would dominate, though some would be stronger than others.

Such a system should be more stable. There is no certainty about this — one could imagine (as in Orwell's 1984) war between such blocs, perhaps between alliances of them — but if such a system does emerge, I will certainly feel more confident that my grandchildren will grow up to be adults.

Notes

INTRODUCTION

1. The data in Table 1 are not quite comparable between countries because of reasons given in its notes, but changes for each country can be compared over time.

2. IBRD (1982) shows average calorie consumption in 1977 to have been 83 per cent of 'requirements' as estimated by FAO, less than for Bangladesh. In view of the uncertainty about even how many people there are in Nigeria (let alone how much food is produced — or what 'requirements' are) this can be little more than a guess, but the impression it conveys cannot be wildly incorrect.

3. Iraq shows daily calorie supply in 1977 as 90 per cent of FAO norms, Saudi Arabia 87 per cent (ibid.). In Saudi Arabia 84 per cent had access to safe water in the mid-1970s, in Iraq only 62 per cent.

4. Seers (1981a). I would not now defend the quantitative projections there in detail, but the general conclusion stands.

5. Quoted in Blades (1974: 70-1, para. 185). See also Van Arkadie (1972-3: 17).

6. But note Sir John Hicks's sharp comment: 'It is the business of the theoretical economist to be able to criticise the practice of [the income tax] authorities: he has no right to be found in their comany himself' (1946: 180, n. 1).

7. UN Statistical Office (1968: 96, paras. 6.19-6.20).

8. Blades (op. cit.) omitted consideration of barter trade on the ground that it appears relatively unimportant. But in South Asia, for example, itinerant monks who exchange religious services for rice seem numerous, even to the casual observer.

9. See Blades (op. cit.). In Malawi, for example, it has been assumed that the number of livestock home-slaughtered is twice the number of carcasses marketed, and that (analogously) total output of milk equals twice the volume sold (paras. 58, 60). In Cyprus, the estimate of the value of animals shot by hunters has been based on the total cost of that year's issue of hunting licences plus the sale of cartridges (para. 70)!

10. Even in India, despite the labours of the National Sample Survey and of district agricultural and fiscal officers, in 1974 only about half the national income was covered by primary data, according to J. N. Tewari ('Data Base for the Fifth Plan', *Economic and Political Weekly*, 26 Jan. 1974, p. 103), though the proportion must now be somewhat higher.

11. Kravis *et al.* (1982). See the exchange on problems of international real income comparison between Samuelson (1974) and Balassa (1974).

CHAPTER 1

1. Keynes (1964: 383).
2. Bill Warren's position on various issues illustrates this point. See Warren (1973, 1980).
3. I define 'development' as including social and political progress, and increased national autonomy in Seers (1977).
4. This can be true even for a decade: the aggregate ICOR, in 1960-70, ranged from 16 for Uruguay to 1.8 for Saudi Arabia (UNCTAD Secretariat 1972:29).
5. Jolly and Seers (1969).

CHAPTER 2

1. As Sir Isaiah Berlin has pointed out: 'Consciously or not, Marx all his life underestimated nationalism as an independent force — an illusion which led his followers in the twentieth century to a faulty analysis of Fascism and National Socialism' (Berlin, 1980: 'Benjamin Disraeli, Karl Marx and the Search for Identity'). This is ascribed, like Marx's well-known anti-Semitism, to the desire to bury his Jewish origins. Sir Isaiah's work is full of perceptive remarks on nationalism.
2. For this reason, the conventional dichotomy has not become completely irrelevant. Thus the attempt of the Allende government in Chile to achieve a major shift in the distribution of economic power provoked a basically Left-Right confrontation by welding together military fascists and economic liberals, exemplified by the presence of 'Chicago boys' (such as Cauas, de Castro, and Bardon) in the Pinochet cabinet. See Chapter 8.
3. I must confess, however, that in one respect at least I did (even?) more damage in West Africa than Bauer. In 1951, just after Nkrumah took office, I was sitting with him (and Dick Ross, then a colleague at Oxford), looking at a long list of very desirable investment projects. Nkrumah asked us (he was then quite a humble man) how he could possibly finance these. We replied in typical Keynesian manner, 'Why not borrow the funds the Cocoa Marketing Board has on deposit in London?' Nkrumah was astonished: 'Can I do that?' In subsequent visits to Ghana, I saw what was done with the money (Black Star Square, the convention centre, the Tema highway, the shipping line, etc.) and noted the growth of corruption. I could also see the continued poverty of the cocoa farmers in Ashanti (especially in contrast with their counterparts in the Ivory Coast). Since this method of raising money was widely copied, and usually with fairly disastrous results for the economy and thus the political system, as in Ghana itself, I must admit to having made my own small contribution to the present chaos in Africa — by naïvely applying a British economic model, without regard to local circumstances.
4. See also Singer (1950).
5. See Spraos (1980). It is true that some countries show a deterioration

(especially if the period covers the past decade), but the net effect over the decades is relatively very small. In Bosworth and Lawrence (1982) recent research is reviewed relevant to the thesis, though without mentioning Prebisch (or Singer), and the authors conclude (p. 37) that even when fuel prices are excluded, 'the relative prices of primary commodities during the 1975–9 period is almost identical to that of a century earlier.'

6. In this respect it not merely echoed the mercantilism of earlier spokesmen of 'late industrializers' such as List, but foreshadowed the arguments of the 'New Cambridge School' (Godley, Cripps, *et al.*) against the de-industrialization of Britain. This link, still not really appreciated in Cambridge, was strikingly brought out in 1981 when the Mexican Ministry of Industry hired several Cambridge economists as consultants, to apply their model and add foreign authority to the case for import controls. (Latin American economists, many of whom had advocated these for decades, would have been cheaper, but less persuasive.)

7. For a recent example of his work, see Pinto (1980).

8. Sunkel (1974).

9. Palma (1981) gives an excellent comprehensive survey, though perhaps he still exaggerates somewhat the influence of Marxism (even in this version of his paper, which down-played it somewhat in comparison with Palma, 1978).

CHAPTER 3

1. Criticisms of foreign direct investment and some counter-arguments are well summarized in Biersteker (1978), with empirical material from Nigeria.

2. See, for example, Fagan (1975).

3. These problems are sketched in Seers (1974). The supply shortages, in part due to financial mismanagement, are discussed below in Chapter 8.

4. See Paine (1974).

CHAPTER 4

1. Other geographical factors may also be important, such as the physical nature of the frontier or coastline, the cover given to guerilla forces by mountains and forests. And its economic vulnerability depends on climate (including the risk of hurricanes, droughts, earthquakes, etc.).

2. Figures for 1970 show that in West European countries, a high proportion of TV series were imported (over 90 per cent for countries with rather limited linguistic markets such as the Scandinavian countries, and the leading source was always the USA — with Britain usually second. Seers *et al.*, 1979).

3. In Cuba, special shops (and restaurants) are available only to tourists. Such shops are open to local residents too in Poland, to mop up their foreign exchange, e.g. sent by relatives abroad.

4. Seers (1962).
5. See Seers (1970).
6. Fuenzalida (1981).

CHAPTER 5

1. US Council on Environmental Quality (US Dept. of State, 1980).
2. The government of Trinidad once sent a promising young official overseas to learn about the oil industry. When he returned the oil companies noted that negotiations were no longer so one-sided. The managing director of one offered the official a post with a much bigger salary than he was receiving. Being rather nationalistic, he turned the offer down, but reluctantly and without telling his wife. A few days later, the wife was invited to tea with the wife of the oil executive, who said at one point, 'My dear, I can't help noticing that you are not very well off. I think your husband was heroic . . . ' The husband is now in the United States (though he assured me that he was not working for an oil company with concessions in Trinidad!)
3. These sources are not as secure as in the 1960s when minerals were nearly all obtained from fully-owned subsidiaries of Bethlehem, Anaconda, Reynolds, etc. See Radish (1982).
4. For industrial countries, national income data are less inaccurate — and more meaningful — than in the rest of the world.
5. See Radish (op. cit.).
6. Japanese External Trade Organization (1974).
7. Trade and aid are difficult to separate, especially in this case. Under a 1975 agreement with the Soviet Union, Cuba has guaranteed to supply part of its crop at a price that has been relatively high, indexed to Soviet export prices (including oil) — though paid partly in inconvertible roubles.

SECTION C: SYNOPSIS

1. For brevity, I write of individual political leaders: a full analysis would allow for the existence of more than one centre of power, the role of party bureaucracies, etc.
2. 'At any given moment . . . the sudden decision of his will introduced into the course of events a new, unexpected and changeable force, which may alter that course, but which cannot be measured in itself' (Sainte-Beuve, quoted in G. V. Plekhanov, *The Role of the Individual in History*, London, Camelot Press, 1940). Plekanhov, although a Marshevik, was respected by Lenin.
3. It is well known that there is a special code word in Britain for documents *not* to be shown to US officials (a fact that throws interesting light on the degree of British dependence, since by implication any other document may be so revealed, without any of the fuss over 'spying').

CHAPTER 6

1.   However, military threat can have an effect opposite from what is intended. It can help a government mobilize support and impose sacrifice, as has undoubtedly been the case in Taiwan, South Korea, and Hong Kong. Conversely, great-power support, especially military aid can be debilitating.

CHAPTER 7

1.   Sometimes the 'Director of Planning' is, in fact, a political appointment, but that raises other problems: one is that each new director would have to spend many months familiarizing himself with the work already done. The development of planning, as of military staffwork, requires a certain continuity.
2.   This underlines the need for security precautions: a political leader may well pay a political price if it is known that he has turned down professional advice (as in the area of military policy).
3.   For example, see Economic Planning Agency (Japanese Government, 1981).
4.   In countries where there are major divisions, e.g. ethnic or regional, the extended form of these tables — the 'social accounting matrix' — may be valuable. I devised an early version of this in putting together the Zambia Report (1961), and found it particularly useful because of the very different consumption levels and patterns of the European and African populations.
5.   In some cases much rougher projections for 40 or 50 years might, however, help to bring out strategic alternatives.

CHAPTER 8

1.   In the discussions that follow of Soviet, Czech and Chilean experience, I drew heavily on her book (Griffith-Jones, 1981), to which an early version of part of this chapter was a preface. Stephany was herself a bank official in the Allende regime.
2.   Ibid., p. 87.
3.   See Zammit (1973).
4.   When I was acting as adviser to the 'Keep Left' group of MPs, in the late 1940s (subsequently the 'Bevanites'), I prepared for them rough sets of projections showing what sets of policies might be compatible with a foreign exchange balance, but I would not claim that these were either technically good or effective in limiting aspirations.
5.   These guidelines are even more urgently necessary in a period such as the early 1980s: world trade has levelled off, cheap loans are hard to obtain, and the IMF has tightened its 'conditionality'.

CHAPTER 9

1.   The brilliant weaving of economic, social, and political analysis, with

apt use of statistics and evident ethical concern, together with a lucid and elegant style, make this still a model for all of us who write on economic problems — and, indeed, the policy package is not entirely irrelevant today (though such a programme of national self-sufficiency and social equality can be adopted by a conservative political leader in wartime more easily than by a socialist one in time of peace).

2. H.M. Treasury (1941). Keynes had published some of the basic analysis using a national accounting system in his 1939 *Economic Journal* article (with a note in the March 1940 issue which reconciles his estimates with Colin Clark's). Estimates had been prepared already in the Treasury for some years, but not published.

3. Kaldor (1944: Appendix C, pp. 344–401).

4. Another link was Sir Harry Campion's post-war move from the Central Statistical Office to direct the United Nations Statistical Office.

5. Meade and Stone (1941: 216–33).

6. United Nations (1968). In view of the distribution of world population, it would be more appropriate if UN manuals in this field were so constructed that they needed at the end a chapter on 'The adaptation of the system of the *developed* countries'.

7. See Jolly and Seers (1969).

8. A technique for comparing life profiles of periods spent in different stages (education, employment, etc.) between different sexes, religions, etc., is outlined in Seers (1977). An international research programme in this area is under way: see Seers (1982).

CHAPTER 10

1. 'In establishing the list of military-dominated governments . . . the following criteria were considered: existence of a state of martial law; key political leadership by military officers; regimes established by military coups; a legal system based on military courts; links between military forces and political police' (Sivard, 1982, p. 36). It is pointed out that such classification is in part a matter of subjective judgement. Some Communist governments — Albania, Afghanistan, South Yemen — are classified as 'highly repressive', the remainder 'repressive'.

2. Hungary is a partial exception here, having pursued 'decentralization' further than the others. I have, in fact, been somewhat startled to hear senior Hungarian economists talking about 'removing price distortions' (relative to world prices), just like any neo-classical economist — an easy transition for the reasons explained in Chapter 1.

CHAPTER 11

1. *The Guardian*, 7 July 1982.

2. *Far Eastern Economic Review*, 16 Jan. 1981.

3. It would, however, be dangerous to leave Japan with no export

surplus in its-trade with industrial countries to help cover its considerable need for imports of primary products. Such problems have constituted a major reason for Japanese militarism in the past, when, moreover, it was more self-sufficient.

4. Seers *et al.* (1979).
5. European Communities (1981). Its share has, however, fallen sharply since then — though not to zero, which is what it ought to be.
6. Because of this possibility, there has been some talk of a formal junior category of membership with fewer rights (which has, indeed, also been considered for Britain). But this would scarcely be compatible with potential European economic prosperity, let alone its political stability and world influence.
7. Begg *et al.* (1981).
8. A 'Marshall Plan' for the Mediterranean was adopted by the West German Social Democratic Party, though not the West German Social Democratic government.

CHAPTER 12

1. Brucan (1979).
2. The Nazis' plan for a 'New Order' was unacceptable to the people of other European countries, because it implied German political domination imposed by force; still, economically, it had a certain rationale.
3. Banks in the EEC and their subsidiaries (more than 200 altogether) lent a total of more than $10 billion to South Africa from 1972 to 1978 (Corporate Data Exchange Inc., 1979).
4. The East Asian system is largely exceptional in these respects: Japan excludes immigrants, except for a few from South Korea, and its tourists mostly go much further afield when they take holidays abroad.
5. UNCTAD (1981). The regions of developing countries are Western Hemisphere, North Africa, Other Africa, West Asia, South Asia, and East Asia.

The papers from which each chapter derives

I have drawn on various of my published papers for this book. Those on which each chapter was based are as follows:

1. 'The Cultural Lag in Economics', in J. Pajetska and C. H. Feinstein (eds.), *The Relevance of Economic Theories* (London: Macmillan, 1980), Chapter 1.

    'The Congruence of Marxism and Other Neo-Classical Doctrines' in A. Hirschman *et al.*, *Towards a New Strategy of Development* (New York: Pergamon, 1980; also as *IDS Discussion Paper* 136, Brighton, 1978).

2. Do.

3. 'Development Options: The Strengths and Weaknesses of Development Theories in Explaining a Government's Room to Manoeuvre', in D. Seers (ed.), *Dependency Theory: A Critical Reassessment* (London: Frances Pinter, 1981).[1]

4. Do.

5. 'Patterns of Dependence', in J. Villamil (ed.), *Transnational Capitalism and National Development: Studies in the Theory of Dependency* (Hassocks: Harvester Press, 1979).

6. 'The New Role of Development Planning, With Special Reference to Small Countries', in B. Jamal (ed.), *Problems and Policies in Small Economies* (London: Croom Helm, 1982).

7. Do.

8. 'The Tendency to Financial Irresponsibility of Socialist Governments and its Political Consequences', in Stephany Griffith-Jones, *The Role of Finance in the Transition to Socialism* (London: Frances Pinter, 1981, Preface; also as *IDS Discussion Paper* 161, Brighton, 1981).

9. 'The Political Economy of National Accounting', in A. Cairncross and M. Puri (eds.), *Employment, Income Distribution and Development Strategy: Problems of Developing Countries, Essays in Honour of H. W. Singer* (London: Macmillan, 1975).[2]

1. Also drawn on for the synopsis of Section C.
2. Also the main source for the Annexe to the Introduction ('A technical note on economic growth').

10. 'North-South: Muddling Morality and Mutuality' (review of the Brandt Report), *Third World Quarterly*, 2.4 (Oct. 1980).

'A Second Look at the 'Third World' in *Development Policy Review*, London, Sage for ODI, 1983).

11. 'The Second Enlargement in Historical Perspective', in *The Second Enlargement of the EEC: The Integration of Unequal Partners*, D. Seers and C. Vaitsos (eds.), (London: Macmillan, 1982; Spanish version, *La Segunda Ampliacion de la CEE: Integracion de Socios Desiguales*, Banco Exterior de Espagna, Madrid, 1981; also as *IDS Discussion Paper* 158, Brighton, 1981).

12. Do.

Many of these have been so extensively revised, cut, and supplemented for this book that they are hardly recognizable — and I would prefer to stand by the new versions. However, the reader would find in the originals not only additional material but also greater detail on sources of information.

Statistical tables
LIST OF TABLES

TABLE 1
Unemployment in Major OECD Economies, 1970 to 1981[a]

		1970	*1980*	*1981[b]*
EEC (9)	no. (m.)	2.1	6.8	9.0
	rate	2.0%	6.2%	8.1%
France	no. (m.)	0.3	1.5	1.8
	rate	1.3%	6.4%	7.8%
West Germany	no. (m.)	0.1	0.9	1.3
	rate	0.6%	3.4%	4.9%
UK[c]	no. (m.)	0.6	1.8	2.7
	rate	2.7%	7.5%	10.5%
USA	no. (m.)	4.1	7.6	8.2
	rate	4.9%	7.1%	7.6%
Japan	no. (m.)	0.6	1.1	1.3
	rate	1.1%	2.0%	2.2%

Notes:

a. Annual averages. Rates given as percentage of total labour force for Japan: otherwise of civilian labour force. Comparability between countries is limited by differences between definitions of unemployment due in part to the sources of unemployment data. (For the USA and Japan these are gathered by labour force sample surveys: for France, West Germany, the UK, and most other EEC countries, the major sources are employment office statistics.)

b. Preliminary.

c. Includes 'temporarily laid off'.

Sources: Statistical Office of the European Communities (1982). OECD Department of Economics and Statistics (1982a and 1982b).

TABLE 2

Index Numbers of Industrial Production:[a] *Major OECD Economies and World, 1960 to 1981* (1975 = 100)

	1960		1970		1975		1980	1981
USA	56	//	92		100		125	128
JAPAN	26	//	92	//	100		142	146
FRANCE	53	//	88		100		118	117
W. GERMANY	57	//	95		100	//	117	116
UK	63	//	86	//	100		108	103
OECD total	53		91		100		123	124
WORLD	42		82		100		125	126

Notes:

a. Excludes construction. Index numbers to base 1975, given here, are derived from series with a variety of base years, generally by using the ratio of index numbers in overlap years to link the respective series. See sources for details. Other breaks in series (due for instance to changes in coverage), as given in OECD sources, are indicated here by //. See notes in following sources for serious gaps in comparability.

Sources:

OECD Statistics Division, *Main Economic Indicators* (various issues, Paris).

— (1980), *Main Economic Indicators: Historical Statistics 1960–1979* (Paris). 'Coverage and weighting pattern of the index were extensively modified with effect from 1963'; in 1982, data covered 78% of total industry. Because of new methods of collection, data from 1978 not quite comparable with previous years.

World:

UN Department of Economic and Social Affairs (Statistical Office, 1975), *Statistical Yearbook 1974* (New York).

— Monthly Bulletin of Statistics (various issues, New York). Excludes Albania, China, Democratic People's Republic of Korea (1960–80), and also Mongolia and Democratic Republic of Vietnam (1960–70).

TABLE 3

THE EXTERNAL DEBT AND DEBT SERVICE[a] OF DEVELOPING
COUNTRIES, 1970 AND 1981 ($ bn.)

| | end 1970 | | end 1981 | |
	Selected NICs[b]	All developing countries[c]	Selected NICs[b]	All developing countries[c]
Outstanding debt — total	11.1	49.4	129.1	368.2
(of which, from private sources)	(6.4)	(15.8)	(102.0)	(199.6)
Debt service	2.1	5.3	(24.1)	59.2

Notes:

  a. Public and publicly-guaranteed.

  b. Argentina, Brazil, South Korea, Malaysia, Mexico, Philippines.

  c. Includes seven 'advanced Mediterranean economies': excludes Afghanistan, Iran, Iraq, Spain, and Taiwan.

Source: Material kindly provided by the World Bank.

TABLE 4

BALANCE OF TRADE IN MANUFACTURES:[a] EEC (9) AND UK
WITH REST OF WORLD, 1960 TO 1980

| Ecu. bn. | EEC (9) | | of which | UK | | |
	Imports M	Exports X	Ratio X/M	Imports M	Exports X	Ratio X/M
1960	8.4	21.5	2.6	2.8	6.9	2.5
1965	13.2	29.1	2.2	4.3	8.5	2.0
1970	26.1	47.6	1.8	7.5	11.8	1.6
1975	48.8	103.1	2.1	13.4	20.6	1.5
1980	118.7	183.0	1.5	30.4	38.7	1.3

Note:

  a. S.I.T.C. groups 5 to 8, viz. Chemicals, Manufactured Goods classified by material, Machinery and Transport Equipment, Other manufactured goods.

Source: Statistical Office of the European Communities (1981), *Monthly External Trade Bulletin*, Special Number, 1958–80 (Luxembourg).

Bibliography

Balassa, Bela (1974): 'The Rule of Four-Ninths: a Rejoinder', *Economic Journal*, 84.

Balassa, Bela (1981): *The Newly Industrializing Countries in the World Economy* (New York: Pergamon).

Baran, Paul (1957): *The Political Economy of Growth* (New York: Monthly Review Press).

Begg, Iain *et al.* (1981): 'The European Community: Problems and Prospects, *Cambridge Economic Policy Review*, Vol. 7, No. 2.

Berlin, Sir Isaiah (1980): *Against the Current* (New York, Viking Press).

Biersteker, Thomas (1978): *Distortion or Development? Contending Perspectives on the Multinational Corporation* (Cambridge, Mass.: M.I.T. Press).

Blades, Derek W. (1974): 'Non Monetary (Subsistence) Activities in the National Accounts of Developing Countries', OECD Development Centre mimeo (Paris).

Blades, Derek W., Johnston, D.D., and Marczewski, E. (1974): 'Service Activities in Developing Countries', OECD Development Centre mimeo (Paris).

Bosworth, B.P. and Lawrence, R.Z. (1982): *Commodity Prices and the New Inflation* (Washington, Brookings Institution).

Brandt Commission (1980): *North-South: a Programme for Survival: Report of the Independent Commission on International Development Issues*, chaired by W. Brandt (London: Pan).

Bressand, A. (1982): 'Rich Interests and Third World Development Finance', in R. Cassen *et al.* (eds.), *Rich Country Interests and Third World Development* (Lodon: Croom Helm).

Brown, Lester R. (1975): *The Politics and Responsibility of the North American Breadbasket*, Worldwatch Paper 2 (Washington D.C.: Worldwatch Institute).

Brucan, S. (1979): 'The Strategies of Development in Eastern Europe', *IFDA Dossier*, 13 (Nyon).

Butcher, Willard (1980): 'How OPEC Can Help in Recycling', *Euromoney* (October).

Cardoso, F.H. and Faletto, E. (1970): *Dependencia y Desarrollo en America Latina* (Mexico: Siglo XXI Editiones).

Chenery, H. *et al.* (1974): *Redistribution With Growth* (London: Oxford University Press).

Clark, Colin (1932): *The National Income 1924-31* (London: Macmillan).

Clark, Colin (1937): *National Income and Outlay* (London: Macmillan).

Clark, Colin (1983): 'Development Economics — the Early Years', in G. Meier and D. Seers (eds.), *The Pioneers of Development Economics* (Washington D.C.: IBRD).

Corporate Data Exchange Inc. (1979): *Bank Loans to South Africa 1972-78* (New York: CDE).

Economic Planning Agency (1981): (Japanese Government), *Scenarios 1990, Japan*, Report to Social Policy Bureau (Tokyo).

European Community (1981): *The Social Policy of the European Community*, 2nd. edn. (Luxembourg).

Eysenck, H.J. (1954): *The Psychology of Politics* (London: Routledge).

Fagan, Richard (1975): 'The United States and Chile: Roots and Branches', *Foreign Affairs*, 53.

Fuenzalida, Edmundo (1981): 'Incorporation into the Contemporary Stage of the Modern World System: Conditions, Processes and Mechanisms' (unpublished note).

Griffith-Jones, Stephany (1981): *The Role of Finance in the Transition to Socialism* (London: Frances Pinter).

Hicks, J.R. (1946): *Value and Capital*, 2nd. edn. (Oxford: Clarendon Press).

H. M. Treasury (1941): *An Analysis of the Sources of War Finance and an Estimate of National Income and Expenditure 1938-40* (London: H.M.S.O.).

IBRD *et al.* (1975): *A System of International Comparisons of Gross Product and Purchasing Power*, UN International Comparison Project, Phase II (Baltimore: John Hopkins U.P.).

IBRD (1982): *World Development Report 1982* (Washington D.C.: IBRD).

ILO (1970): *Towards Full Employment in Colombia* (Geneva).

ILO (1972): *Employment, Income and Equality: A Strategy for Expanding Productive Employment in Kenya* (Geneva).

ILO (1981): *First Things First: Report to the Government of Nigeria by a JASPA Basic Needs Mission* (Addis Ababa).

Japan External Trade Research Organization (1974): *Japan's Industrial Structure — A Long-Range Vision* (Tokyo).

Jaszi, G. (1958): 'The Conceptual Basis of the Accounts: A Re-Examination', in Conference on Income and Wealth, *A Critique of the United States Income and Product Accounts*, Studies in Income and Wealth, Vol. 22 (Princeton U.P.).

Jayawardena, Lal (1980): 'Institutional Mechanisms for the Utilisation of OPEC Surpluses' (unpublished note). See also Commonwealth Secretariat (1980), *The World Economic Crisis: A Commonwealth Perspective*, Report of a Group of Experts, chaired by H. W. Arndt, Chapter 3, 'The Balance of Payments Problems' (London).

Jolly, A. Richard and Seers, Dudley (1969): 'The Treatment of Education in National Accounting', *Review of Income and Wealth*, Series 12, 3.

Kaldor, N. (1944): 'The Quantitative Aspects of the Full Employment Problem in Britain', in W. H. Beveridge (ed.), *Full Employment in a Free Society* (London: Allen & Unwin).

Kaser, M. (1961): 'A Survey of the National Accounts of Eastern Europe', in International Association for Research in Income and Wealth, *Income and Wealth*, Series IX, ed. P. Deane (London: Bowes and Bowes).

Kendrick, John (1974): 'The Accounting Treatment of Human Investment and Capital', *Review of Income and Wealth*, Series 20, 4.

Keynes, J.M. (1939): 'The Income and Fiscal Potential of Great Britain', *Economic Journal*, 49.

Keynes, J.M. (1940): *How to Pay for the War: A Radical Plan for the Chancellor of the Exchequer* (London: Macmillan).

Keynes, J.M. (1964): *The General Theory of Employment, Interest and Money* (London: Macmillan).

Killick, Tony (1981): 'Eurocurrency Market Recycling of OPEC Surpluses to Developing Countries: Fact or Myth?', in C. Stevens (ed.), *The EEC and the Third World: a Survey* (London: Hodder and Stoughton).

Kravis, I.B. *et al.* (1982): *World Product and Income: International Comparisons of Real Gross Product* (Baltimore: John Hopkins U.P.).

Kuznets, Simon (1941): *National Income and Its Composition 1919–1938* (New York: National Bureau of Economic Research).

Kuznets, Simon (1945): *National Product in Wartime* (New York: National Bureau of Economic Research).

Kuznets, Simon (1951): 'Government Product and National Income', in International Association for Research in Income and Wealth, *Income and Wealth*, Series 1, ed. E. Lundberg (Cambridge: Bowes and Bowes).

Kuznets, Simon (1971): 'Problems in Comparing Recent Growth Rates for Developed and Less Developed Countries', *Economic Development and Cultural Change*, 20.

Mansour, Fawzy (1980): 'Third World Revolt and Self Reliant Auto-Centered Strategy of Development', in A. Hirschman *et al.*, *Towards a New Strategy of Development* (New York: Pergamon).

Meade, J.R. and Stone, R. (1941): 'The Construction of Tables of National Income Expenditure, Savings and Investment', *Economic Journal*, 51.

Meier, G. and Seers, D. (eds.), (1983): *The Pioneers of Development Economics* (Washington D.C.: IBRD).

Morgan Guaranty Trust Co. (1980): *World Financial Markets*, September (New York).

OECD Interfutures (1979): *Facing the Future: Mastering the Probable and Managing the Unpredictable* (Paris).

OECD Statistics Division (1980): *Main Economic Indicators: Historical Statistics 1960–1979* (Paris).

OECD Department of Economics and Statistics (1982a): *Labour Force Statistics 1969-1980* (Paris).

OECD Department of Economics and Statistics (1982b): *Labour Force Statistics*, Quarterly Supplement 1982/III (Paris).

OPEC Statistics Unit (1981): *Annual Statistical Bulletin 1980* (Vienna).

Paine, Suzanne (1974): *Exporting Workers: The Turkish Case*, University of Cambridge, Department of Applied Economics, Occasional Paper 41 (Cambridge U.P.).

Palma, Gabriel (1978): 'Dependency: a Formal Theory of Underdevelopment', *World Development*, 6. 7/8.

Palma, Gabriel (1981): 'Dependency and Development: A Critical Overview' in D. Seers (ed.), *Dependency Theory: A Critical Reassessment* (London: Frances Pinter).

Pinto, A. (1980): 'The Opening Up of Latin America to the Exterior', *CEPAL Review*, 11.

Popov, Z. (1975): 'National Accounting Systems in Eastern European Socialist Countries', IDS mimeo (Brighton).

Prebisch, Raul (forthcoming): 'Five Stages in My Thinking on Development' in G. Meier and D. Seers (eds.), *The Pioneers of Development Economics* (Washington D.C.: IBRD).

Pyatt, G., Roe, A.R., and Associates (1978): *Social Accounting for Development Planning: with Special Reference to Sri Lanka* (Cambridge U.P.).

Robbins, L. (1953): *The Economic Impact on Underdeveloped Societies* (Oxford: Blackwell).

Samuelson, Paul A. (1974): 'Analytical Notes on International Real-Incomes Measures', *Economic Journal*, 84.

Seers, Dudley (1951): *The Levelling of Incomes* (Oxford: Blackwell).

Seers, Dudley (1962): 'The Limitations of the Special Case', *Bulletin of the Oxford Institute of Economics and Statistics*; reprinted in Martin and Knapp (eds.), *The Teaching of Development Economics* (Cass, 1967), and 'Las Limitaciones del Caso Especial' in *Economia*, XXII.1 (1964).

Seers, Dudley (1964), *et al.*: *Cuba: The Economic and Social Revolution* (Chapel Hill: U. of North Carolina Press).

Seers, Dudley (1970): 'The Transmission of Inequality', in R. Gardiner *et al.* (eds.), *Africa and the World* (Oxford U.P.).; also in *EKISTICS*, 180 and 214.

Seers, Dudley (1974): 'Cuba', in Chenery, H. *et al.*, *Redistribution With Growth* (London: Oxford U.P.).

Seers, Dudley (1977): 'Life Expectancy as an Integrating Concept in Social and Demographic Analysis and Planning', *Review of Income and Wealth*, Series 23, 3.

Seers, Dudley (1977): 'The New Meaning of Development', *International Development Review*, 19. 3.; also in Lehman (ed.) *Development*

Theory: Four Critical Studies (Cass, 1979), and in *Political Perspective*, Vol. 6, no. 2.

Seers, Dudley (1980a): 'Theoretical Aspects of Unequal Development at Different Spatial Levels', in D. Seers and C. Vaitsos (eds.), *Integration and Unequal Development: The Experience of the EEC* (London: Macmillan).

Seers, Dudley (1980b): 'North-South: Muddling Morality and Mutuality', *Third World Quarterly*, 2. 4.

Seers, Dudley (1981a): 'Alternative Scenarios for Developing Countries: The Fundamental Issues, in V. Bickley and P. J. Philip (eds.), *Cultural Relations in the Global Community: Problems and Prospects* (New Delhi: Abinhav Publications).

Seers, Dudley (1981b): 'Inflation: A Sketch for the Theory of World Inflation', *IDS Discussion Paper* 169 (Brighton).

Seers, Dudley (1981c): 'The Life Cycle of a Petroleum Economy and Its Implications for Development', *Research for Development*, 1. 1 (Journal of the Nigerian Institute of Social and Economic Research).

Seers, Dudley (1982): 'Active Life Profiles for Different Social Groups: A Contribution to Demographic Accounting, a Frame for Social Indicators and a Tool of Social and Economic Analysis', *IDS Discussion Paper* 178 (Brighton).

Seers, D., Schaffer, B., and Kiljunen, M.-L. (eds.) (1979): *Underdeveloped Europe: Studies in Core-Periphery Relations* (Hassocks: Harvester).

Shourie, A. (1974): 'Sri Lanka's National Accounts', *Marga*, 2, 3 (Colombo).

Singer, H.W. (1937) (joint author): *Men Without Work: A Report to the Pilgrim Trust* (Cambridge U.P.).

Singer, H.W. (1940): *Unemployment and the Unemployed* (London: King).

Singer, H.W. (1950): 'The Distributions of Gains Between Investing and Borrowing Countries', *American Economic Review*, 40 (proceedings).

Singer, H.W. (1969): 'Keynesian Models of Economic Development and Their Limitations', UN Asian Institute for Economic Development and Planning, *Occasional Paper*, 1. 2 (Bangkok) (reprinted (1970) as *IDS Communication*, No. 54 (Brighton)).

Sivard, Ruth L. (1981): *World Military and Social Expenditures* (Leesburg, Va.: World Priorities).

Spraos, J. (1980): 'The Statistical Debate on the Net Barter Terms of Trade between Primary Commodities and Manufactures', *Economic Journal*, Vol 90, no. 357, p. 107.

Statistical Office of the European Communities (1982): *Employment and Unemployment: Statistical Bulletin*, 3/1982 (Luxembourg).

Sunkel, O. (1974): 'External Economic Relations and the Process of Development: A Latin-American View', in R. B. Williamson *et al.* (eds.), *Latin American-US Economic Interactions: Conflict, Accom-*

modation and Policies for the Future (Washington D.C.: American Enterprise Institute for Public Policy Research).

Tewari, J.N. (1974): 'Data Base for the Fifth Plan', *Economic and Political Weekly*, 26 Jan. (Bombay).

UNCTAD Secretariat (1972): *Trade Prospects and Capital Needs of Developing Countries During the Second United Nations Development Decade* (TD/118/Supp. 3/Rev. 1), (New York).

UNCTAD Secretariat (1981): *Trade and Development Report 1981* (New York).

UN Department of Economic and Social Affairs (1973): *The Inter-National Development Strategy: First Overall Review and Appraisal of Issues and Policies* (E/AC.54/L.60), (New York).

UN Department of Economic and Social Affairs (1975): *Statistical Yearbook 1974* (New York).

UN/ECA/FAO (1964): *Report of the UN/ECA/FAO Economic Survey Mission on the Economic Development of Zambia* (Dudley Seers, leader), (Lusaka: Government of the Republic of Zambia).

UN Statistical Office (1968): *A System of National Accounts* (E.69, XVII. 3), (New York).

US Council on Environmental Quality/US Department of State (1980): *The Global 2000 Report to the President*, Vol. 1 (Washington D.C.: Government Printing Office).

Van Arkadie, Brian (1972-3): 'National Accounting and Development Planning', *Development and Change*, 4. 2.

Warren, Bill (1973): 'Imperialism and Capitalist Industrialization', *New Left Review*, 81.

Warren, Bill (1980): *Imperialism: A Pioneer of Capitalism* (ed. J. Sender), (London: Verso).

Wyeth, John (1980): 'Development Strategies and Specialisation in Small Countries: A Case Study of Belize', unpublished doctoral thesis, University of Sussex.

Zammit, J. Ann (1973): (ed.), *The Chilean Road to Socialism* (Brighton: IDS).

Index

Academics: on room to manoeuvre, 56
Accumulation: *See* Investment
Administration, government: in Chile
(1970-3), 61; and failure of conventional planning, 112-13; and
national independence, 13; planning offices in, 111; weak, under
Allende (Chile), 124
Afghanistan: and Soviet military insecurity, 85
Africa: colonialism in, 149; Soviet
role in, limited, 159; North, nationalism in, 51; tropical, nationalism
weak in, 51
Agricultural policy: in continental
European bloc, 177; in enlarged
European Community, 170
Agricultural production: global, short-
fall in, 77; and health care, 104;
and land distribution, 103
Agriculture: discrimination against, 3;
export price instability in, 78-9;
in national income estimates, 22,
24
Aid: case for reducing, 181-2; in enlarged European Community, 169-
70; and growth models, 50; to
military governments, 156-7; in
neo-colonial system, 16, 146-7,
153; to newly-industrializing
countries, criticized, 155-6; to
petroleum-exporting countries, 87;
politically harmful, 181; and private
banks, 160; and regional integration, 184; and statistical policy,
131; suits TNCs' interests, 144; and
three-world classification, 144;
United States, food, 78; United
States, and conventional planning,
98
Allende, Salvador (Chile): government
of, 61-3; fall of, 124-5. *See also*
Chile
Alliance for Progress: and conventional
planning, 98

Argentina: economic performance of,
2; trades with Soviet Union, 92; as
resource exporter, 88
Armed forces: and external dependence, 63; securing allegiance of,
102. *See also* Military capacity
Art, indigenous: in nationalist development strategy, 105
Austria: and European integration, 178
Authoritarianism: *See* Political repression

Balance of payments: and migration,
65; and radical development strategy, 60; and socialist financial
policy, 120
Balogh, Thomas: influenced author, xi
Bananas, exports of: and political
embargo, 62
Banks, commercial: international
loans by, 93; lending to newly-
industrializing countries, 2
Bargaining capacity, 1, 90; and mineral
resources, 80; and strategic location, 92
Basques: and European integration,
171
Bauer, Peter: and neo-classical internationalism, 50
Bay of Pigs (Cuba): US invasion at, 63
Berg Report (World Bank): influence
of, 51
Berlin, Sir Isaiah: on nationalism, 187
n. 1 (Ch. 2)
Bettelheim, Charles: influence of, 51
Birth control: and nationalist development strategy, 107-8. *See also*
population policy
Black markets: official statistics ignore,
131
Booth, Charles: statistical work of, and
social reform, 132
'Brain drain': *See* Emigration
Brandt Report: arguments of, dis-
puted, 146, 155-8; and neo-colonial

Brandt Report (*cont.*):
system, 158; in European context, 169
Brandt, Willi: internationalism of, criticised, 16
Brazil: economic performance of, 2
Bretton Woods system: and neo-colonial system, 152; and post-war liberalism, 32
Bribes: *See* Corruption
Britain: benefits from neo-colonial system, 14–15, 154; decolonization by, 15; dependent on United States, 155, 189 n. 3 (Section C); and European development strategy, 165, 174–5; and gold standard, 15; in liberal world economy; 15; limited room to manoeuvre of, 86; monetarism in, 15; nationalist strategy for, criticized, 163–5; 'national plan' in, 99; neo-classical ideology in, 33; neo-colonial system penalises, 161; and possible war with United States, 97; post-colonial decline of, 162–3; System of National Accounts emerges in, 135; technological weakness of, 14, 15; view of Prebisch in, 52
Broadcasting: and cultural dependence, 105, 188 n. 2 (Ch. 4); cultural penetration by, 75; in European development strategy, 173
Bureaucracy: as class, in socialist countries, 34; underestimates room to manoeuvre, 56

Cambridge School, economics of: in Latin America, 188 n. 6 (Ch. 2); in Britain, 163
Capital: and determination of output, 100; international, private, and national financial policy, 127; in national accounting, 136; neo-classical doctrines overemphasize, 44; source of, 59
Capitalist countries: appeal of Marxism in, 35; benefit from colonialism, 149; control IMF, 127; converge with socialist countries, 145; retreat from neo-colonial system, 147; and three-world classification, 143, 144. *See also* Developed countries
Cassava: as energy source, 80

Cereals, exports of: and room to manoeuvre, 88
Cereals, imports of: dependence on, 57, 78–9; Soviet, 8, 84, 179
Chicago school, economics of: as neo-classical doctrine, 33–45; inimical to nationalism, 50–1
Chicanos (United States): as potential constraint, 84
Chile: Chicago school economists in, 50, 187 n. 2 (Ch. 2); and financial indiscipline, 14, 124–5; planning ineffectual in, 95, 112–13; protectionism in, 53; and room to manoeuvre (1970–3), 61–3; and Soviet Union, 159; US destabilization in, 62
China: room to manoeuvre of, limited, 88; national incentives in, 49; and Soviet security, 85
Clark, Colin: as scientist, 43; and System of National Accounts, 134
Club of Rome: on limits to growth, 8
Colonial system: 148–52; British retreat from, 15; and conventional planning, 98; as core–periphery relationship, 148; cost of, to colonialist powers, 151–2, 185; cultural impact of, 74; creates hybrid states, 57; independent European development supersedes, 180; and national identity, 51; and three-world classification, 143
Comparative advantage: doctrine of, inadequate, 78–9
Consumption pattern: and cultural identity, 69; and European development strategy, 166, 168; and import dependence, 3, 110
Convertibility: and colonial system, 149; and neo-colonial system, 152
Copper, exports of: and Allende government (Chile), 62
Corruption: ethnic divisions encourage, 73; increases in Third World countries, 4; official statistics ignore, 130; in petroleum-exporting countries, 5; private-sector, 5; in socialist countries, 7; and technological dependence, 82, 189 n. 2 (Ch. 5); and three-world classification, 146
Countries, classification of: by input

dependence, 83–90; 'three-world', 82

Coups, military: in Third World, 62–3. *See also* Military intervention

Crisis, international economic: and colonial system (1930s), 150, 151; and conventional planning, 108; and developing-country debt, 160; and ideological change, 47; and nationalist development strategy, 97

Cuba: financial policy in, 122–3; national incentives in, 49; room to manoeuvre for, 12, 63–4, 88–9; Soviet aid to, 159; sugar exports from, 189 n. 7 (Ch. 5)

Cultural dependence, 4, 69–72; in artificial nations, 73; and colonial rule, 74; and ethnic differentiation, 72–3; and geographical location, 74–5; and immigration, 107; and Keynes' influence, 137; and language, 75; in neo-colonial system, 152; and professional salaries, 71; and statistical policy, 131; and technological dependence, 81, 82

Cultural identity: and continental European integration, 171–2, 173, 180; and independent development, 72–6; and Japanese development, 86; in Latin America, 52; and nationalist development strategy, 105–6; and professsional emigration, 107; and regional integration, 17, 165, 185; in Third World élites, 11; versus internationalism, 145

Cultural lags: in neo-classical economics, 31–2, 45

Culture: and educational system, 105–6; European distinctive, 172; neo-classical doctrines ignore, 44; and country's room to manoeuvre, 69, 71

Czechoslovakia: socialist financial policy in, 122

Debt, external: and aid, 146; as bargaining counter, 92; of military governments, 156; of newly-industrializing countries 2; of petroleum-exporting countries, 3, 109; default on, 61; of socialist countries, 8, 160;

undermines neo-colonial system, 154. *See also* Finance external

Dependence: armed forces' role in, 63; structure of external exchange defines, 88; for socialist governments, 127; and System of National Accounts, 136. *See also* Room to manoeuvre

Dependency school: belittles cultural factors, 69; criticised, 57, 91; and Cuban, Chilean experience, 64; on foreign capital, 59; ignores population size, 67; influenced author, xi; sources of, 53

Deprivation, social: and internationalism, 10–11

Destabilization: by US in Chile, 62

Developed countries: development path of, unique, 4; and neo-colonial system, 14; planning attempts in, 99; support TNCs, 60, 81; Third World students in, 70

Developing countries: and System of National Accounts, 135

Development: time-scale of, 101; meaning of, 90, 100, 132, 187 n. 3 (Ch. 1)

Development policy: neo-classical economism in, 40

Development staff: for integrated European bloc, 174; place of, in government, 114–16; role in strategic planning, 111–18

Development strategy, 3; and changing international prices, 108–10; compared with military planning, 114–15; constraints on, 56–8, 117–18; and country size, 68, 115–16; and cultural dependence, 71–2; and ethnic differentiation, 57; for European Community, 17, 147, 165–71, 173–4; financial programme in, 129; and foreign 'confidence', 60; institutional issues in, 117; and military intervention, 54, 56; and patriotism, 94; and political leadership, 114–15; quantitative analysis in, 116; requires confidentiality, 111, 141, 190 n. 2 (Ch. 7); and statistical policy, 137–40. *See also* Independent development

Development strategy: nationalist, 95–

Development strategy (*cont.*):
7, 101–10; financial policy in, 119–
29; and international economic
crisis, 97; linguistic policy in, 106;
and military planning, 102–3; population policy in, 106–8; and religion,
106; time horizon for, 101
Dictatorships: *See* Political repression
Diem, President (Vietnam): costs of
repression under, 7
Disarmament, nuclear: and continental
European integration, 18, 177
Dissidents: appeal of neo-classical
models to, 35
Distribution: conventional planning
ignores, 99–100; and life expectancy
measures, 138; and nationalist
development strategy, 103–4; official statistics conceal, 130. *See also*
Income distribution
Dynamics: in Marxist analysis, 45

Ecology: *See* Environmentalism
Economic growth: concept and
measurement of, criticized, 4, 18–
27; and concepts of development,
131–2; in conventional planning,
98; global, limits on, 2; IMF view
of, 51; its relationship with development, 21, 40–1; and social inequality, 4; models of, and aid, 50;
in neo-classical doctrine, 37, 43;
and oil, food imports, 109–10;
pattern of, versus aggregate value,
100–1; rapid, inimical to development, 21. *See also* National income estimates
Economics, conventional capitalist:
affinity with Marxism, 9; broad
appeal of, 34–6; factors ignored by,
3–4; hostile to nationalism, 30;
origins of, 9; supposed rigour in,
32; and technological dominance, 9
Economics, teaching of: national income concepts in, 26
Economism: in conventional planning,
94, 100–1; and neo-classical doctrine, 39–40, 44
Education: in European development
strategy, 166, 167, 173; and fertility, 108; in nationalist development strategy, 104–5; and statistical
policy, 138; and foreign cultural

influences, 70–1; in national accounting, 43–4
Egalitarianism: in taxonomy of ideologies, 45–50
Empiricism: vs neo-classical position-
ism, 43
Energy: constrains development strategy, 117; as global constraint, 8;
imports of, by independent
European bloc, 165; and room to
manoeuvre, 57, 77; statistical treatment of, 138; substitutable sources
of, 80
Environmental constraints: in Japan,
86–7
Environmentalism, 8; East, West leaderships reject, 37
Equilibrium: concept of, in Chicago-
school economics, 45
Ethnic differentiation: and cultural
dependence, 72–3; education helps
allay, 105; and European Community integration, 171; and neo-
classical doctrine, 57; and Soviet
military security, 85; statistical
treatment of, 140; in United States,
84
Ethnic separatism: and independent
development, 74; neo-classical disdain for, 10
Europe, continent of: Nazi 'New Order'
for, 192, n. 2 (Ch. 12); as regional
bloc, 176–80
Europe, Eastern: appeal of neo-classical
economics in, 35; ideological change
in, 178; possible integration with
European Community, 176–80; and
Western financial links, 178. *See
also* Socialist countries
Europe, Western: Marxism in, 35, 48;
cultural dependence in, 69; independent development of, 162–
75; need for integration of, 16–17;
neo-classical doctrine formed in,
38; and neo-colonial system, 154,
155; and United States, 172
European Community: economic inter-
ventionism in, 178; expansion of
benefits Third World, 180–1; and
extended nationalism, 17, 18;
extension of, to Eastern Europe,
178–9, 180; independent development strategy for, 165–71, 173–4;

and international peace, 18; and
new world economic order, 183; at
odds with United States, 172;
regional policy ineffectual in, 168;
and retreat from neo-colonial system, 147; and Turkey, 176; unified
external policies of, 172-3. *See also*
Europe, continent of

European Community, enlargement of,
169-74; and disengagement from
Third World, 181; industrial policy
for, 170; requirements for, 168-71,
172

European Currency Unit: in independent European bloc, 167

European Monetary System: and
regional inequality, 168; strengthened, in European development
strategy, 166-7

European Parliament: and continental
European integration, 179

Exchange controls: and Bretton Woods
system, 32; removed in Britain, 15

Exchange rates: and neo-colonial system, 154; of petroleum-exporting
countries, 88

Fascism: in taxonomy of ideologies, 49

Feminism: and neo-classical ideology,
37

Finance, external: in European development strategy, 166-7; for
military governments, 156-7; new
sources of, 93. *See also* Debt,
external

Financial policy: in Chile, 124-5; in
Cuba, 64, 122-3; in Czechoslovakia,
post-1945, 122; discipline needed
in, 119-29, 190 n. 5 (Ch. 8); displaces planning, 113; in IMF analysis, 51; for independent European
bloc, 166-7; in Jamaica, 126; in
nationalist development strategy,
14, 96, 129; in Portugal, 126; in
socialist states, 14, 121-3, 128;
weak, in Latin America, 54

Finland: and European integration,
178

Food: consumption of, constrained,
77; in development strategy, 118;
global supply of, constrained, 79; as
input to production, 100; in
national income estimates, 21;
and oil constraint, 80; output of,
and development, 21; regional
shortages of, 79-80; statistical
treatment of, 21-2, 138; supply of,
and room to manoeuvre, 78-80;
83-90

Food, imports of: by independent
European bloc, 165; neo-classical
view of, 78; by petroleum-exporting
countries, 3; and room to manoeuvre, 88-9; Third World, 3

Foreign capital: alternative views of,
59; and Harrod-Domar model, 50;
and IMF approval, 127; in Latin
American development, 53

Foreign exchange: and British economy, 161; constrains socialist
development, 60-1, 120; and
development strategy, 110; and
European regional integration,
166-7; and populist financial
policies, 124; and Portuguese revolution (1974), 64-5; and oil imports,
78

Foreign investment: constrains trade
flows, 82; in conventional planning,
100; and development strategy,
115; in independent European bloc,
166; as political expedient, 101;
statistical treatment of, 27, 139;
System of National Accounts ignores, 136. *See also* TNCs

Freidrich-Ebert-Stiftung (West Germany): role in Portugal, 65

Futurology: and neo-classical doctrine,
42

Gandhi, Mahatma: and British retreat
from Empire, 15

General Agreement on Tariffs and
Trade (GATT): and post-war economic liberalism, 32

Geography: neo-classical doctrines ignore, 44; and room to manoeuvre,
67, 188 n. 1 (Ch. 4)

Germany: challenges old colonial system, 150, 151; and East-West
European integration, 179

Germany, East: constraints on, 86

Germany, West: constraints on, 85-6;
and European regional policy, 168;
influences Portugal, 65; and strategy
for independent Europe, 174

Ghana: author's inappropriate advice in, 187 n. 3 (Ch. 2); conventional planning in, 99

Griffith-Jones, Stephany: on socialist financial policies, 120, 190 n. 1 (Ch. 8)

Guesswork: in national income estimates, 23, 186 n. 9 (Introduction)

Haile Selassie, Emperor: repression under, 7

Harberger, Arnold: and neo-classical internationalism, 50

Harrod-Domar model: in conventional planning, 100; and internationalism, 50; and neo-classical doctrine, 43; and System of National Accounts (SNA), 134, 135

Healey, Denis: and British financial policy, 127

Health care: in development strategy, 104; as input to production, 100; and life expectancy, 5

History: national, and education, 105

Hong Kong: economic performance of, 2

Household: economy of, 38

Housing: in national income estimates, 22

Human rights: *See* Political repression

Hungary: economic liberalism in, 191 n. 2 (Ch. 10)

Ideologies: East-West convergence of, 178; common roots of, 172; imported, and social inequality, 114; and international crisis, 47; lack empirical basis, 9; and statistical methods, 132-5; taxonomy of, 12, 46, 47, 48-50, 187 n. 2 (Ch. 2)

Illegal activity: ignored, in national accounting, 23, 131

IMF, 61, 94; and Jamaica, 126; and neo-classical internationalism, 32, 51; and neo-colonial system, 153; and Portugal, 65; resisted, in Chile, 124; role of, misconceived, 127-8

Immigration: colonial, 51; and nationalist development strategy, 106-7. *See also* Migration

Imperialism, Marxist concept of: and nationalism, 47

Import dependence: of advanced capitalist countries, 84, 85-7; of China, 88; for Latin America, 53; of petroleum-exporting countries, 87-8; and room to manoeuvre, 61; of Soviet Union, 84-5

Import substitution: justified, 52, 79

Imports: statistical treatment of, 24, 137-8

Income, comparison of: international, 25-6; inter-temporal, 41

Income distribution: in European Community, 168; change in, 41; and imports, 103; and national income estimates, 25; in regional blocs, 183-4. *See also* Distribution

Incomes policy: and emigration, 107

Incremental capital-output ratios: in conventional planning, 100; contradict neo-classical doctrine, 43, 187 n. 4 (Ch. 1)

Independent development: and cultural identity, 72-6; and economic efficiency, 90; and ethnic separatism, 74; European strategy for, 165-71, 173-4, 177-8; and financial policy, 119-20; and international crisis, 90; and military capacity, 102; as planning objective, 100; for small countries, 13; Third World, and European Community, 182. *See also* Development strategy

India: and British retreat from Empire, 15; national accounting data in, 186 n. 10 (Introduction); nationalism in, 151

Indonesia: 'Berkeley mafia' in, 70; retaliates against British protectionism, 164

Industrial policy: in European development strategy, 170

Industrialization: and neo-colonial system, 15; and geographical location, 65; in neo-classical doctrine, 42; and oil import dependence, 109-10; and population size, 68; in Prebisch doctrine, 52; Latin American, 53; technology imports in, 81

Inequality, social: and conventional development policies, 113-14; and cultural dependence, 71; and economic growth estimates, 4, 19; in European Community, 167-70;

and internationalism, 10–11; and Keynesian national accounting, 136; and military capacity, 103; and nationalism, 49; and political repression, 7; in regional blocs, 183–4; in socialist countries, 7, 121; in Third World, 4–5; and three-world classification, 146

Inflation: in Chile, 125; in colonial system, restrained, 149; international, 1; and internationalist aid programmes, 146–7; in Latin America, 53, 126; neo-classical view of, 44–5; not target of monetarism, 158; and populist financial policies, 124; under socialist governments, 120, 121, 122

Informal sector: statistical treatment of, 23, 139

Input–output analysis: in development strategy, 116; role of, misconceived, 124; by social accounting matrix, 190 n. 4 (Ch. 7)

International institutions: Brandt Report on, 157; and room to manoeuvre, 94; and statistical policy, 131, 132–3

Integration, international: for continental Europe, 178–9; in neo-classical doctrine, 42, 47; and neo-colonial system, 12, 16

Integration, social: and statistical policy, 138–9

International Monetary Fund: *See* IMF

International system: crisis of, 1–8; European Community in, 172–3, 183; and ideological change, 50, 92; post-war liberalism in, 32; and regional blocs, 183–5; three-world division of, 143

Internationalism: East/West leaders, 37; and superpower domination, 12, 18; and neo-classical models, 50–1; no guide to population policy, 108; and political Left, 47; and social inequality, 144; sustains neo-colonial system, 16, 145, 158; of Third World élites, 10–11

Investment: in conventional planning, 100; in European development strategy, 167; neo-classical criteria for, 59; in neo-classical development theory, 43–4; statistical

treatment of, 22, 140; in System of National Accounts, 136

Investment, external: European, cost of, 154; in European Community, 17; in neo-colonial system, 152

Iran: impact of neo-classical ideologies in, 42

Iraq: social deprivation in, 5, 186 n. 3 (Introduction)

Ireland, Northern: and cultural separatism, 74; and European integration, 171

Islam: revival of, 51

ITT: plots against Allende (Chile), 62

Jamaica, 12; financial indiscipline in, 126

Japan: challenges colonial system, 151; cultural autonomy of, 72; development time-scale in, 101; East Asian regional role of, 192 n. 4 (Ch. 12); and neo-colonial system, 154, 155; room to manoeuvre of, limited, 86–7; strategic planning in, 97; and technological transfer, 81; trade balance of, 191–2 n. 3 (Ch. 1)

Jolly, Richard: influenced author, ix

Kahn, Hermann: in neo-classical tradition, 42

Kaldor, Nicholas: and national accounting, 134

Kalecki, Michael: influenced author, xi

Kaser, Michael: on concept of 'productive', 20

Keynes, John Maynard: and System of National Accounts, 134

Keynesian economics: author misapplies, in Ghana, 187 n. 2 (Ch. 3); in Brandt Report, 157; and planning, 98; historical context of, 32; and neo-classical internationalism, 50; as neo-classical model, 31; and statistical policy, 135

Kissinger, Henry: and Chile, 1970–3, 62

Korea, South: economic performance of, 2; egalitarian tendency in, 5

Kuwait: room to manoeuvre of, limited, 87; migrants in, 72–3

Kuznets, Simon: national income concept of, 20; as scientist, 43

Labour: mobility of, and national accounting, 136

Labour Party (Britain): author advises Bevanite MPs of, 190 n. 4 (Ch. 8); and British overseas role, 163-4; economic policy under 1974-9, 126-7; nationalism in, 49; national protectionist programme of, criticized, 163-5; post-war government of, 15

Language: and cultural dependence, 73, 75; and nationalist development strategy, 106; neo-classical doctrines ignore, 44

Latin America: internationalism resisted in, 51-2; neo-classical influence in, 51; as regional bloc, 184

Leadership, political, 50, 189 n. 2 (Section C); and armed forces, 102; in Cuba, 64; and development staff work, 115; and formation of European regional bloc, 168, 174-5; and neo-classical models, 37; and official statistics, 130-1; and patriotism, 96-7; and room to manoeuvre, 13, 91-9; in small countries, 116

Left-wing movements: and financial discipline, 128-9

Lesotho: dependence of, 75

Liberalism: and Brandt Report, 155; and Chicago school, 33; and class interests, 48; European, and neo-colonial system, 144

Life expectancy: rising, since 1945, 5; as social indicator, 138

List, Freidrich: influences Presbisch, 52; mercantilism of, 52

Literacy: in development statistics, 138

Location, geographical: and cultural dependence, 74-5; and military security, 102; and room to manoeuvre, 12, 65

Malaysia: distributional policy in, 99

Malta: room to manoeuvre of, limited, 93

Malthus, Robert: and neo-classical internationalism, 37, 57; doctrine of, inappropriate, 68

Manley, Michael (Jamaica): and financial indiscipline, 126

Manufactures, exports of: by newly-industrializing countries, 2; and wage costs, 103

Marx, Karl: Eurocentric, 38; view of history, 41; and nationalism, 187 n. 1 (Ch. 2)

Marxism: affinity with capitalist economics, 9, 38; appeal of, 34-6; author's approach to, 29-30; on concept of 'productive', 20; and nationalism, 30, 49; as neo-classical doctrine, 33-45; relativism of, 34, 39; in South Africa, 49; Soviet, and internationalism, 48

Material Product System: *See* National accounting, material product system of

McElhone, Frank: on British overseas role, 163-4

Meade, James: and System of National Accounts, 134

Means, Russell (Sioux 'indian'): on Marxism and European culture, 38-9

Mexico: Cambridge economists in, 188 n. 6 (Ch. 2); economic performance of, 2; migration from, 65

Middle East: *See* West Asia

Migration: and cultural dependence, 72-3; effects of, 65-6, 107; and European Community enlargement, 169; into petroleum-exporting countries, 87. *See also* Immigration

Military capacity: colonial system based on, 149; and decline of neo-colonial system, 155; dependency school ignores, 57; egalitarian policies enhance, 103; for European bloc, 177-8; and geographical area, 67; and independent development, 57, 101-3; and population growth, 106; and technological dependence, 82

Military expenditure: and imports, 102; and independent development, 57

Military governments: and repression, 6-7; aid to, 156-7

Military intervention: in Chile (1973), 62-3; and financial indiscipline, 120, 123, 125-6; foreign, reduced threat of, 93; and nationalist development strategy, 56, 102;

and structuralist reform, 54. *See also* Armed forces

Military planning: and development strategy, compared, 114-15

Military security: in development strategy, 13-14, 95; and domestic political mobilization, 190 n. 1 (Ch. 6); and European integration, 176, 177

Mineral resources: and dependence, 80; supply of, 94

Minorities, ethnic: *See* Ethnic differentiation; ethnic separatism

Mintoff, Dom: and role of political leadership, 93

Modernization: destructive effects of, 12; and East/West leaderships, 37; in neo-classical doctrine, 42

Monetarism: in Britain, 15; in Chile, 125; as defence of neo-colonial system, 158; in East and West, 44-5; in socialist regimes, 121

Monetary policy: in European development strategy, 166-7

Monnet, Jean, 167

Mortality: and development strategy, 106-7; trend, in developing countries, 5

Mugabe, Robert: and Zimbabwean external relations, 160

Multinational corporations: *See* TNCs

Myrdal, Gunnar: on aid, 163

Narcotics: official statistics ignore, 131

National accounting: Eurocentricity in, 44; Keynesian, 14, 32; and statistical policy, 133-7. *See also* National income estimates

National accounting, material product system of: and planning problems, 20; origins of, 19, 20

National income: neo-classical concept of, 33, 40

National income estimates: agricultural investment in, 22; education in, 43-4; empirically and conceptually criticized, 19-25, 27; guesswork in, 23, 186 n. 9 (Introduction); inadequate for strategic planning, 96; industrial investment in, 22; and inequality, 13; Kuznets' system of, 20; not central, in statistical policy, 137; and social differentiation, 19; in estimating elasticities, 21. *See also* Economic growth; National accounting; Statistical policy

Nationalism: in the Americas, 148; Anglo-Saxon cultural tradition rejects, 10; benefits of, 12; in colonial empires, 151; encompasses Left-Right spectrum, 49; extended, and European Community, 17, 18, 165, 171-3; great power hostility to, 12; and Marxism, 30, 46-7, 187 n. 1 (Ch. 2); mass appeal of, 11; and neo-classical doctrine, 9, 30; and neo-colonial system, 15; and political Right, 47; regional pattern of, 165; and taxonomy of ideologies, 45-50; and war, 17-18

Nationalization: in Latin America, 54

NATO: and European integration, 177; limits German room to manoeuvre, 86

Neo-classical doctrine, 31-45; and academic conservatism, 45; and British economic crisis, 163; capital emphasized in, 44; cultural and political effects of, 42; dissent from, 36; economism of, 57; embraces capitalist economics and Marxism, 39-45; ethnocentricity of, 39; Harrod-Domar model exemplifies, 43; and nationalism, 9, 30, 46; positivism of, 42-3; Prebisch challenges, 52; and source of capital, 59; and superpowers' external policy, 35; and System of National Accounts, 135

Neo-colonial system, 14-15, 16, 152; and colonialism, 153; cost of intervention under, 182; costs of clinging to, 161, 185; disintegrating, 162; European development supersedes, 180; and European interests 16, 182; European internal, 169; harmful to Third World, 181

Netherlands: national accounting in, 134

New Economic Policy (Soviet Union): financial conservatism of, 121

New International Economic Order: moral emptiness of, 146

Newly-industrializing countries: aid to, criticized, 155-6; economic performance of, 2; import penetration

Newly-industrializing countries (*cont.*):
by, 158; political repression in, 7;
social inequality in, 5

NICs: *See* Newly-industrializing
countries

Nigeria: fails to diversify exports, 109;
oil revenues of, 3, 88; low nutritional levels in, 5, 186 n. 2 (Introduction); wages policy in, 112

N'Krumah, Kwame: on planning, 99;
author's naïve Keynesian advice to,
187 n. 3 (Ch. 3)

Norway: and European integration,
178

Nott, John: on commercial retaliation,
164

Nuclear arms, 18

Nuclear power: and East/West leaderships, 37

Obote, Milton, 15

OECD: in neo-colonial system, 153

Oil: and food constraint, 80; and
global resource constraint, 77; price
of, and strategic planning, 118;
price of prospective, 78; Soviet
exports of, declining, 159; supply
of, and room to manoeuvre, 77–8,
83–90

Oil, imports of: and conventional
growth pattern, 109–10; and
European deflation, 155; and income distribution, 103; and major
companies' control, 77–8

Okita, Saburo: plans for Japanese reconstruction, 97

Olivier, Borg (Malta): as political
leader, 93

OPEC: financial role of, 93; and
oil price rise, 8; and oil supply,
78; as target of monetarism, 158.
See also Petroleum Exporting
Countries

Organization of African Unity: not
regional representative, 184

Organization of American States: not
regional representative, 184

Patents: and technological dependence,
83 n.

Paternalism: and areas of study, 14; in
colonial system, 150; European alternative to, 181–2; internationalism

as, 16; in neo-colonial system,
152–3

Patriotism: education to promote, 105;
and national independence, 71; and
political leadership, 94

Peace, international: and European integration, 147, 176–8; and international equity, 18; in neo-classical
doctrine, 42; and regional blocs,
17–18, 147, 185

Peasant movements: and nationalism,
48

Petroleum-exporting countries: economic performance of, 2–3; fail to
diversify production, 109; limited
room to manoeuvre of, 87–8;
migration into, 72–3; oil revenues
of, 3, 109; regional interests of,
184; social inequality in, 5. *See
also* OPEC

Philippines: economic performance of,
2

Planning, conventional, 13, 98–101;
and government coordination, 112;
ignores military capacity, 101;
and international economic crisis,
108; redundancy of, 94–5, 98–9;
urban and regional, 99–100

Planning staff: conventional role of,
111–13; political resistance to, 113;
as general staff, 14; and nationalist
development strategy, 95, 97

Poland: dependence of, 88–9; economic crisis in, 160; political repression in, 8; and Soviet military
insecurity, 85; view of West in, 35

Political repression: in Chile, 125;
European intervention to oppose,
182–3; economic costs of, 7–8; and
internationalist aid policy, 156–7;
by socialist governments, 8, 121,
122, 123; in Third World, 6–8,
182–3; and three-world classification, 146; weakens policy-making
process, 157

Population: and economic development, 67, 106–7; growth of, case
for promoting, 57, 68–9, 95;
growth of, internationalist leaders
fear, 37; and military capacity, 57,
67, 87; and nationalist development strategy, 13, 95, 106–8; and
room to manoeuvre, 12, 67–8;

structure of, and European regional integration, 177

Populist governments: and financial indiscipline, 123-4

Portugal: dependence of, 64-5, 88; financial indiscipline in, 126; foreign exchange crisis in, 64

Poverty: and Chicago school, 33; in conventional planning, 98

Powell, Enoch: and British nationalism, 49

Prebisch, Raul: influenced author, xi; misinterpreted, in Chile, 124; and nationalism, 30, 52; official Western view of, 52

Prescott, Latin American studies by, 38

Production, non-marketed: in national income estimates, 23-4, 186 n. 8 (Introduction)

Professional groups: and external dependence, 60-1; salaries of, externally determined, 71

Progress: assumed, in neo-classical economics, 9; concept of, 39, 41-2

Progressive Federal Party (South Africa): opposes nationalism, 49

Protectionism: and European integration, 17, 165-6; of Labour Party (Britain), 163-5; in Latin America, 52, 53; now inevitable, 167

Puerto Rico: dependence of, 75

Puritanism: in neo-classical doctrine, 43

Quantitative analysis: in Chicago-school economics, 45; and development strategy, 116; in US culture, 172

Race: and neo-classical ideology, 37; and three-world classification, 143

Regional blocs: core–periphery relationship in, 183-4; and ethnic differentiation, 73; Europe as one among, 176-83; and international peace, 17-18, 147, 185; possible emergence of, 183-5; succeeding neo-colonial system, 17

Regional policy: and development statistics, 139-40; and European Community enlargement, 169

Religion: and East/West leaderships,

37; and nationalist development strategy, 106; neo-classical doctrines ignore, 44

Rent: in national income estimates, 22

Resource limits, 1, 12, 77; and monetarist policies, 158; neo-classical doctrine ignores, 42; and technology, 80-1

Resources, natural: and formation of European bloc, 170, 177; and dependency school, 57; and geographical area, 67; neo-classical doctrines ignore, 44

Ricardo, David: and neo-classical doctrine, 38

Robinson, Joan: influenced author, xi; on algebra and pedagogy, 45

Romania: joins IMF, 92

Room to manoeuvre, 55-8, 91; for Chile, 61--3; for China, 88; and class interests, 61; vs comparative advantage, 78-9; and country size, 67-9; for Cuba, 63-4, 88-9; and culture, 69-76; for East Germany, 86; and education, 104-6; and food supplies, 78-80, 83-90; and health care, 104; for Japan, 86-7; and migration, 66; and new pattern of ideologies, 92; and oil supplies, 77-8, 83-90; for petroleum-exporting countries, 87-8; for Poland, 88-9; and population, 67-9; for Portugal, 64-5, 88; for Soviet Union, 84-5; and technology imports, 80-90; and tourism, 66; for United States, 84-5, 154; for West Germany, 85-6. *See also* Dependence; Development Strategy; Independent development

Rottenberg, Simon: and neo-classical internationalism, 50

Royal Navy: maintained colonial system, 149; and protectionist strategy for Britain, 163

Salaries: and migration, 65

Saudi Arabia: social deprivation in, 5, 186 n. 3 (Introduction)

Savings: in neo-classical doctrine, 43

Science: and neo-classical doctrine, 42-3; social, and internationalist orthodoxy, 144-5

Seers, Dudley: advises Left (Bevanite)

Seers, Dudley (*cont.*):
Labour MPs, 190 n. 4 (Ch. 8);
changes view of nationalism, 9–12;
concerned with nationalism, viii;
gives naïve Keynesian advice, in
Ghana, 187 n. 3 (Ch. 2); on meaning of development, 187 n. 3 (Ch.
1); operational roles influence;
personal background influences, xi;
rejects environmentalism, 9; rejects
internationalism, 9; small-country
experience of, x; social accounting
matrix of, 190 n. 4 (Ch. 7); view of
Raul Prebisch, 52
Self-reliance: *See* Independent development
Separatism, ethnic: and ideological
pluralism, 49; in Soviet Union, 180
Shah of Iran: costs of repression by, 7
Singapore: economic performance of,
2
Sistema Economico Latino-Americano:
as regional organization, 185
SITC: *See* Standard International
Trade Classification
Size, country: and need for regional
blocs, 183; and room to manoeuvre,
67–9
Small countries: use of development
strategy in, 115–16
Smith, Adam: on concept of 'productive', 20; and neo-classical
doctrine, 38; not Eurocentric, 38;
view of history, 41
SNA: *See* System of National Accounts
Social Democratic Party (West Germany); Mediterranean 'Marshall
Plan' of, 192 n. 8 (Ch. 11)
Social indicators: and nationalist
development strategy, 138–9
Socialism: European, and neo-colonial
system, 144
Socialist countries: converge ideo-
logically with capitalist countries,
36, 145; corruption in, 7; financial
policy in, 128; ideology and class
in, 34; influence in Third World,
159; political repression in, 8, 121,
122, 123; social inequality in, 7;
and three-world classification, 143–
4; warfare between, 47. *See also*
Europe, Eastern
Socialist governments: and external

financial constraints, 127; and financial indiscipline, 119–20
Somoza family (Nicaragua): costs of
repression under, 7
South Atlantic War (1982): and British
decline, 163; and British dependence on USA, 155; and nationalism, 165
South Africa: nationalism opposed in,
49; coal/oil conversion in, 77;
dominant over Lesotho, 75; European support for, 181, 192 n. 3
(Ch. 12)
Soviet Union: agriculture in, 8, 84; and
continental European integration,
177–80; East German dependence
on, 86; financial policy in, 121–2;
import dependence of, 8, 78, 84–5;
inherits Tsarist empire, 150; international power of, limited, 85, 127,
147, 159–60; Marxism in, 33–4,
35; national accounting in, 20;
room to manoeuvre of, limited,
84–5; support for Cuba, 63, 64,
189 n. 7 (Ch. 5); nationalism in, 47;
and Western aid, 153. *See also*
National accounting, material
product system of
Standard International Trade Classification: inadequate, 137–8
Statistical data: omit key international
transactions, 133; and political
perceptions, 130; lags in, 133;
social issues not covered by, 5–6;
and strategic planning, 14; unreliable, 135–6
Statistical policy, 130–41; and anthropometric data, 138; external influences on, 131; ideological roots
of, 132–5; on institutional factors
in development, 137; and national
accounting, 133–7; and nationalist
development strategy, 96, 137–40;
on non-marketed production, 139;
political influences on, 6; professional influences on, 132, 140; and
public accountability, 141; on
TNCs, 139; and use of non-
professional staff, 141. *See also*
National income estimates
Stone, Richard: and System of National
Accounts, 134
Streeten, Paul: influenced author, xi

Structuralism: evolution of, 53; influenced author, xi; policies implied by, 54

Studenski: on concept of 'productive', 20

Subsistence: in national income estimates, 140

Suez: Anglo-French assault on, 93

Sunkel, Osvaldo: influenced author, xi

Superpowers: Europe as battlefield for, 176, 177; and regional blocs, 17-18

Sweden: and European integration, 178; paternalism in aid from, 16

System of National Accounts (SNA): assumptions underlying, 135-7; empirical weakness of, 23-4; and Harrod-Domar model, 134, 135; ideological nature of, 133-5; and neo-classical economics, 135

Taiwan: economic performance of, 2; egalitarian tendency in, 5

Technology: in neo-classical ideology, 37, 42

Technology, imports of; aggravate inequality, 181; and energy imports, 109-10; and foreign investment, 81-2; and room to manoeuvre, 57, 80-90; selectivity in, 81-2

Technological capacity: and colonial system, 148, 149; constraints on British policy, 14, 15; and independent development, 12, 90; and neo-colonial system, 162; and purchase of patents, 83 n.

Technological dependence, 3, 82; of Kuwait, 87; measurement of, 83 n.; and military capacity, 82

Terms of trade: in Prebisch doctrine, 52; little secular change in, 188 n. 5 (Ch. 2)

Thailand: room to manoeuvre of, 88

Theory: archaic, influence of, 31-2; neo-classical, not testable, 33; orthodox, need to relinquish, 9, 31

Thinking, conventional: need to question, xii

Three-world classification: and internationalism, 143-5; international trends undermine, 145-6

Time budgets: and unemployment data, 139

Time horizons: in development strategy, 116; in planning, 101

Time series: in national income estimates, 24

TNCs: adapt to socialist policies, 37; constrain trade pattern, 60, 82; and consumption pattern, 3; and East-West European integration, 178; in independent European bloc, 166, 181; and local social interests, 60; political and economic leverage of, 3, 59-60; in small-country industrialization, 68; statistical treatment of, 139; and technological dependence, 81-2; and three-world classification, 144. *See also* Foreign investment

Tourism: affects room to manoeuvre, 66; cultural impact of, 70

Trade: British, and protectionism, 164; in colonial system, 148; intra-regional, by developing countries, 184; preferences, and neo-colonial system, 16; in primary products, with Europe, 166; and TNCs, 60, 82

Trade liberalization: cost of, to Western European economies, 154-5; and neo-colonial system, 152

Trade unions: and external dependence, 60; and income distribution, 103

Trans-national corporations: *See* TNCs

Transportation: cost of, and dependence, 65

Travel, international: and cultural dependence, 70

Turkey: benefits from migration, 65; economic performance of, 2; and European Community, 176

Uncertainty: conventional planning ignores, 99

Unemployment: British, and Labour financial policy, 127; in conventional planning, 98; Cuban, and financial policy, 123; and decline of neo-colonial system, 162; global, rise in, 1; and monetarist policies, 158; Soviet, and financial policy, 121; and statistical policy, 134, 135, 138-9; and trade liberalization, 155

United Nations: and System of National Accounts, 135; and neo-colonial system, 153

United States: challenges old colonial system, 150, 151; and continental European integration, 177-8; and Cuban revolution, 63, 64; differences with Europe, 172; dominates Puerto Rico, 75; ideology in external policy of, 35; in Latin America, 54; loses international hegemony, 154, 162; military constraints on, 85; moralism of, 172; national accounting develops in, 134; neo-classical ideology in, 33; and neo-colonial system, 152; room to manoeuvre of, limited, 84, 89; and overthrow of Allende (Chile), 62; view of Prebisch in, 52

Universities: and national culture, 106

Urbanization: in neo-classical doctrine, 42

Venezuela: fails to diversify exports, 109

Vietnam: impact of US defeat in, 93; Soviet role in, limited, 159

Wages: and protectionist programme, in Britain, 164-5

Warren, Bill: Marxism interpreted by, 29-30

Warsaw Pact: continental European integration supersedes, 177

West Asia: traditional nationalism in, 51

Working class: and external dependence, 60; metropolitan, benefits from colonialism, 149

World Bank: capitalist powers dominate, 153

World War I: colonial rivalries induce, 150

World War II: and decline of colonialism, 151

Women: in unemployment data, 139

Young, Andrew: and US attitude to Jamaica, 126

Youth culture: East/West leaders reject, 37